THE REAL THING

An Exhortation for
the Authentic Christian Life

---

by
W. E. Smith

WWW.LIVINGWALK.COM
Grove City, OH 43123

2010

LIVINGWALK BOOKS

THE REAL THING

An Exhortation
for the
Authentic Christian Life

LIVINGWALK BOOKS

Grove City Ohio 43123
www.livingwalk.com

ISBN: 1-450-54243-3 | 978-1-450-54243-2

Electronic Version: An electronic version of this book is available at no charge online at www.livingwalk.com.

Additional Copies: Additional copies of this book can be ordered at *www.livingwalk.com* and other online book sellers.

Contents

Preface

My name is W.E. Smith, and I offer this series of messages to my fellow brothers and sisters in Christ with the sincerest humility and hope of blessing. To be sure, I never started out with a book such as this in mind, but merely to share some of the mighty things the Spirit of God has been revealing in recent years, as I started to behold the Lord Jesus Christ in a new way, in all of His preeminent glory.

Although I have technically considered myself a Christian for most of my adult life, it was only a number of years ago that something really started to happen inside me, as I started to yearn for the authentic Christian life portrayed in the Scriptures.

> *"Father, please show me your beloved Son, in all of His fullness and beauty and sufficiency."*

– was perhaps the prayer that truly changed everything in my Christian walk. The contents of this book are what I believe was the Lord's response to this simple request. In addition to the Word of God, the Lord was ever gracious during this time to introduce me to a number of seemingly forgotten teachers of old - *Andrew Murray, George Mueller, T. Austin-Sparks, G.H. Pember, Robert Govett, Watchman Nee, A.W. Tozer* and *Hudson Taylor,* among others. Ever gradually and wonderfully, the light started to shine in my spirit, and to reveal what this thing called the Christian life was really all about. Each day brought some new and brighter revelation of the Lord Jesus Christ, as the Spirit took me on a whirlwind tour of both the Old and New Testaments.

As this personal *awakening* began, I felt somehow compelled to share what the Holy Spirit was conveying to me, so, with much prayer and trepidation, I started an online journal called *LivingWalk*. This name arose rather spontaneously from an earnest desire to pursue a more dynamic, moment-by-moment relationship with my Lord and God; where I could actually hear Him and walk with Him, and bring glory to Him as His grace permitted.

I suppose what I ultimately discovered over much time and travail, was that when the God of heaven and earth reveals Himself to one fully (in His Beloved Son and Holy Spirit), every man-inspired religious enterprise shows itself for what it is – artificial and empty. To have the Lord Jesus Christ in all His fullness, and to grow daily and vicariously in Him, is to have it all; everything you truly need – *joy, peace, power, direction, wisdom, enlightenment*, and perhaps most of all, *a hunger for more of Him*. To hunger and thirst for righteousness is to hunger and thirst for Him, for He is the "*righteousness of God*". (2 Corinthians 5:21).

To know what is in the Father's vast heart pertaining to summing all things up in His Son; to abandon our own plans and to join in His plans and purposes; to see what He sees and to desire only what He desires; to breathe life only on His terms, in all of its fullness in the spirit; to be restored to the place where only the Lord sits on the throne of our heart; to live and walk in Him constantly and to have every aspect of our lives fully surrendered to His will – this is truly the end of the Christian life. To seek anything less is to shortchange our Heavenly Father's love, and to confound His great purpose in sending His Son into the world.

I have titled this compilation, *The Real Thing: An Exhortation for the Authentic Christian Life* for a couple of reasons. First, because there are, in my view, far too many false or lesser things out there representing the true Christian experience. And secondly, because this series of messages represents an expression of the gift that I have been granted by the Lord for the edification of His Body, that of *exhortation (see Introduction: The Gift of Exhortation)*.

It may be helpful to the reader to be aware that the messages presented here were not originally conceived to be shared in book form, and although some effort has been made to arrange chapters by theme or topic, each message (chapter) very much stands alone in terms of its message and content. It may also serve the reader to know that this is not primarily a book of teachings or theology, with structured points on Christian doctrine. Like the epistles of the New Testament, it is offered for believers that they might enter more fully into the practical truths of what it is assumed they already know. In this sense these words represent *meat* not *milk*. As the title of the book suggests, the major theme addressed herein is the authentic expression of the life of Jesus Christ in one who has surrendered himself wholly to Him as a *living sacrifice*; the *real thing* in other words.

Dear Christian, if you are discouraged by men so readily replacing the "*mystery of godliness*" with humanly derived substitutes; if your spirit is thirsty for God and Christ alone; if you want your walk with Jesus Christ to be alive, dynamic, vibrant, intimate and truly heart-changing, then I offer these messages humbly in the hope that you may be blessed by what is presented here in the spirit.

In compiling these messages, it is the author's sincere hope and prayer that the reader will be encouraged, challenged and exhorted, such as the Spirit would permit. Any shortcomings in these messages, in terms of Scriptural accuracy, interpretation or completeness is fully the weakness of the author, for which he humbly solicits the reader's grace and kindness.

Finally, we thank our ever-gracious Lord and God in advance if this little book should, even in some small way, bring spiritual edification to His people. If indeed you have been spiritually blessed by these words, we would ask that you let us know, and that you might pass this book along freely to your friends, family and fellow saints. Additional copies of this book, as well as similar messages can also be found at our online address: *www.livingwalk.com*.

Your servant in Christ Jesus,

W. E. Smith

WWW.LIVINGWALK.COM

Introduction: The Gift of Exhortation

The Lord willing, I would like to introduce this book by sharing a short message on the spiritual gift of *exhortation* to be exercised on behalf of His saints. This, like so many areas in Scripture, has been too little understood and exercised among the Church of Christ. By His grace we will dig deeper into such matters, here a *little and there a little*, to see what the Spirit has to say.

Before we begin, I would like to interject some foundational thoughts from T. Austin-Sparks on the meaning and purpose of all spiritual service –

> *Now, my point is this, that when it comes to the heavenly order of the Church, all ministries, all appointments, all positions, all relationships exist solely for the increase of Christ. That is the thing which governs all. No one has any position or ministry which is merely official. What is position in the Church from the heavenly standpoint? What is ministry in the Church from the heavenly standpoint? What is the significance that attaches to all the relationships of the Lord's people? They are all, by Divine intention, for the increase of Christ. I suppose that we will accept that, so far as the special ministries are concerned. Yet that might need examination. Such as exercise those special ministries are not there to give addresses or to preach sermons. In the heavenly order, there is no ministration of any kind which does not mean a ministration of Christ to the increase of Christ, so that the Church becomes more fully Christ in expression, and any ministry that does not,*

> *or that cannot, lead to that is not in the heavenly order. (from, The Law of the Spirit of Life in Christ Jesus)*

To *exhort* (*parakaleo* in the Greek) means to *call near, to invite, to urge strongly, to beseech or implore others to action, to make a forceful appeal for some kind of immediate response*. The word *exhortation* is actually derived from the same Greek term translated *comforter, helper* and *counselor* in the 16th chapter of John's gospel. And a careful study of the Word will reveal that exhortation is indeed the basis for many of the epistles delivered to the saints in the New Testament, and that it is a spiritual gift in its own right.

Consider Romans 12 and 1 Corinthians 14 –

> *Therefore I urge you, brethren, by the mercies of God, to present your bodies a living and holy sacrifice, acceptable to God, which is your spiritual service of worship. And do not be conformed to this world, but be transformed by the renewing of your mind, so that you may prove what the will of God is, that which is good and acceptable and perfect. For through the grace given to me I say to everyone among you not to think more highly of himself than he ought to think; but to think so as to have sound judgment, as God has allotted to each a measure of faith. For just as we have many members in one body and all the members do not have the same function, so we, who are many, are one body in Christ, and individually members one of another. Since we have gifts that differ according to the grace given to us, each of us is to exercise them accordingly: if prophecy, according to the proportion of his faith; if service, in his serving; or he who teaches, in his teaching; or he who exhorts, in his exhortation; he who gives, with liberality; he who leads, with diligence; he who shows mercy, with cheerfulness. (Rom. 12:1-8)*

> *Pursue love, yet desire earnestly spiritual gifts, but especially that you may prophesy. For one who speaks in a tongue does not speak to men but to God; for no one understands, but in his spirit he speaks mysteries.*

> *But one who prophesies speaks to men for edification and exhortation and consolation. One who speaks in a tongue edifies himself; but one who prophesies edifies the church. Now I wish that you all spoke in tongues, but even more that you would prophesy; and greater is one who prophesies than one who speaks in tongues, unless he interprets, so that the church may receive edifying. (1 Cor. 14:1-5)*

Here we discover that each member of the body is to exercise gifts according to the "*grace given to us*" and "*according to the proportion of our faith*". The very health and spiritual vitality of the Body is dependent on this apparently. To some it is given to prophecy, to others to serve, to teach, to lead, to give, to show mercy, and to still others, to *exhort*. All of these various gifts are granted and empowered by the grace of God for the edification or building up of the body, and each member is to exercise such gifts based on the "*proportion of his faith*".

What does this mean – "*proportion of his faith*"? Well, not only is each member granted a differing gift, but not all are given the same degree of faith (in the exercise of that gift), as the Lord conveyed in the parable of the talents (Matt. 24) and minas (Luke 19). To each servant is given a certain portion to invest (or exercise for the profit of the Master Builder) while He is away. When He returns, there will be an accounting (at the Judgment Seat) of each servant's faithfulness in transacting His Master's business with whatever portion he was given.

Now in a very substantial sense, His business involves the establishing and development of His Church ("*I will build My Church*") in preparation to reign with Him in His Kingdom, and each member of the body is to invest the talents given to him by exercising gifts for the building up (edification) of the body. It is vital in God's plan that each son brought into His household by the grace and provision of the Lord, fully matures in the life of God such that he might enter into all that the Master has planned for him.

In other words brethren, Paul is laying down the practical application of what our Lord suggested previously in these parables to

His own. And to certain individuals, the talent or gift given, is that of *exhortation.* Let us therefore consider this further, as the Spirit permits.

Before we do, let us back up a bit and consider what Romans 12 tells us about the exercise of all such spiritual gifts –

> *Let love be without hypocrisy. Abhor what is evil; cling to what is good. Be devoted to one another in brotherly love; give preference to one another in honor; not lagging behind in diligence, fervent in spirit, serving the Lord; rejoicing in hope, persevering in tribulation, devoted to prayer. (Rom. 12:9-12)*

Here then, we are given the over-arching and under-girding principles by which all gifts are to be expressed as intended by the One who grants them –

- *Sincere service, without hypocrisy* (singular in intent and heart; not seeking honors or promotion in the church by the exercise of the gift; see Luke 14:10)

- *A commitment to what is good* (regardless of the cost in terms of acceptance or popularity; because character and integrity always look to God's approval and not to that of men)

- *Brotherly love and devotion* (to pour oneself out for the Body, as did the Lord, placing the needs of others ahead of our own; see John 15:12)

- *Fervency of spirit* (only harm and self-glory can result if the flesh and not the Spirit is the source of anything in the church)

- *Serving the Lord* (because all of us will be judged according to our faithfulness at His Coming; see Romans 14:10)

- *Rejoicing in hope* (because the edification or preparation of the Bride leads to the future hope of glory; reigning with Christ as His consort Queen in the Kingdom of God)

- *Persevering in tribulation* (because not all will welcome or appreciate the authentic exercise of these spiritual gifts in the church)

- *Devotion to prayer* (because the faithful steward is most humbly aware that he must be about his Master's business, and both the provision and the results must come from Him alone)

Brethren, for 2,000 years now there has been much activity conducted in the church of Jesus Christ, much of which has been well intended and carefully managed. Great human talent and planning has been directed at any number of great goals in churches and groups all over this world. Seemingly, every mode and method of *doing church* has been devised, tried and tested. And yet, to those with true spiritual insight, they have all failed miserably, because Christians, by and large, have forgotten that it is the Lord alone who (as the Master Builder) will build His church, and the Holy Spirit who will make the Bride ready, and not men.

And He will build His church by equipping and empowering each member of His Body to actively fulfill select responsibilities and functions, for the preparation and edification of the whole. And as we shall see, the gift of exhorting the brethren, as with all of the gifts, is absolutely essential if the Bride is to be ready at the Bridegroom's return.

Let us continue in this brief study by considering what the Scriptures reveal regarding this ministry and gift of exhortation, as inspired and directed by the Holy Spirit.

> *Finally then, brethren, we urge and exhort in the Lord Jesus that you should abound more and more, just as you received from us how you ought to walk and to please God; for you know what commandments we gave you through the Lord Jesus. For this is the will of God, your sanctification: that you should abstain from sexual immorality; that each of you should know how to possess his own vessel in sanctification and honor, not in passion of lust, like the Gentiles who do not know God; that no one should take advantage of and defraud his brother in this matter, because the Lord is the avenger of all such, as we also forewarned you and testified. For God did not call us to uncleanness, but in holiness. Therefore he who rejects this does not reject*

man, but God, who has also given us His Holy Spirit. (1 Thess. 4: 1-8)

Here we see brethren, that exhortation, strictly speaking, is not the same as teaching, although it is an earnest pleading for those being exhorted to walk according to the manner laid down previously in the teaching; to enter in and possess the fullness of that promised in the teaching, in other words. There is always a need it seems, while we are in the flesh and the world, to be exhorted to continually and actively appropriate the blessings and promises of God by faith, as expressed by His Word (both the Living Word and the Scriptures which contain that Living Word).

In verse 2 above, we see that the Apostle Paul had earlier given the injunctions related to how they should walk in this newness of life. And here he was merely exhorting them to continue walking in them, to live the life, to press onward into the very fullness and holiness of the Lord Jesus Christ. For the Christian faith, this is nothing less than a *living walk* originating in, and empowered by the Living Word that came down from heaven. It is not enough to merely receive some teaching about what this life means or represents, but we are urged to actually enter into this abiding life, to apprehend (through teaching) and appropriate it (by faith) in all of its fullness and spiritual reality.

Because we so readily seem to forget this essential fact, and allow our testimony to become little more than hollow religious experience, the Holy Spirit is constantly reminding us of what "*newness of life*" actually means; that it is an existence apprehended and appropriated by faithful obedience to every word breathed by God. This, when all else is said and done, is the aim of all spirit-breathed exhortation – to appeal to, and encourage believers to appropriate all that the Lord Jesus Christ has wrought for them, and promised in His Word. It is, therefore, not a gift for the faint of heart, or those who so readily shun controversy or opposition. For with such a gift, comes also a God-given courage and boldness to direct His truth and light to wherever He chooses.

Notice, for example, how frequently in his epistles Paul is urging and beseeching, exhorting and encouraging his readers to do more, to go further, to run faster, to grip tighter, to labor more intently, to focus more narrowly on what it is out ahead, to be careful, to exercise wisdom, to be adequately equipped, to fight the good fight of faith, to move on towards maturity (and the list goes on).

> *And we urge you, brethren, to recognize those who labor among you, and are over you in the Lord and admonish you, and to esteem them very highly in love for their work's sake. Be at peace among yourselves. Now we exhort you, brethren, warn those who are unruly, comfort the fainthearted, uphold the weak, be patient with all. See that no one renders evil for evil to anyone, but always pursue what is good both for yourselves and for all. Rejoice always, pray without ceasing, in everything give thanks; for this is the will of God in Christ Jesus for you. Do not quench the Spirit. Do not despise prophecies. Test all things; hold fast what is good. Abstain from every form of evil. (1 Thess. 5: 5-22)*

> *For even when we were with you, we commanded you this: If anyone will not work, neither shall he eat. For we hear that there are some who walk among you in a disorderly manner, not working at all, but are busybodies. Now those who are such we command and exhort through our Lord Jesus Christ that they work in quietness and eat their own bread. But as for you, brethren, do not grow weary in doing good. And if anyone does not obey our word in this epistle, note that person and do not keep company with him, that he may be ashamed. Yet do not count him as an enemy, but admonish him as a brother. (2 Thess. 3:10-15)*

Again, there is an obvious correlation between teaching on the one hand, and exhortation on the other. They are often mentioned together in Scripture, and it would be a rare teacher indeed who would never exhort his students to apply that being taught. And yet in Romans 12:8, we see the gift of exhortation identified as a distinct function of the body, quite apart from that of teaching. This being so, it is well worth our time to dig deeper to comprehend how the gift of exhortation is to be expressed and directed by the Holy Spirit.

Notice in the verse mentioned above that Paul is exhorting the brethren in Thessalonica "*through our Lord Jesus Christ*". The very basis of his appeal is through, or by the authority of the Master. Now to exhort through the Lord Jesus Christ suggests that the exhortation (whatever it happens to be) flows from the Master Himself, and His intuitive understanding of the condition of the Body. It is (and must only be) His perfect perspective from which the exhortation to change, or continue, or to do anything must come. And so if any of His servants are to exercise the gift of exhortation for the edification of the Body in the sense laid down in Scripture, then it can never be derived from their own opinion or judgment of what is needed. What we see simply doesn't matter, and in another sense, we are not even permitted to judge another man's servant (Rom. 14:4). Only He who searches the heart can know the true condition of any individual or company of believers at any moment in time.

> *I charge you therefore before God and the Lord Jesus Christ, who will judge the living and the dead at His appearing and His kingdom: Preach the word! Be ready in season and out of season. Convince, rebuke, exhort, with all longsuffering and teaching. For the time will come when they will not endure sound doctrine, but according to their own desires, because they have itching ears, they will heap up for themselves teachers; and they will turn their ears away from the truth, and be turned aside to fables. But you be watchful in all things, endure afflictions, do the work of an evangelist, fulfill your ministry. (2 Tim. 4:2-5)*

Those exercising the spiritual gift of exhortation are to do so with "*all longsuffering and teaching*" (or patience and instruction). The sense here is that exhorting the brethren into the deeper things of Christ is not a '*one time, fix all*' proposition, but a continuing calling, requiring patient devotion and love toward those being exhorted, especially as we draw nearer to His coming for His own. A helpful illustration might be that of a devoted and loving parent training children. Any parent knows that it is not enough to merely teach your child something important once and for all; but there is a perpetual need to patiently exhort them in the required behavior or pattern. Patience, therefore, is not an option for the fruitful exhorter of the brethren. Note the depth of such patience and longsuffering in the Apostle Paul, throughout all of his letters to the saints as an example. And lest we think this is a quality or disposition found naturally in the human heart, it is most definitely not. Galatians 5 reminds us that patience and longsuffering are fruits of the Holy Spirit, just as exhortation is a gift of the same Spirit.

We also observe above that the imperative for spiritual exhortation flows out of the times and seasons, as lying in the foreknowledge of our Lord and Master. Indeed, the great falling away, or apostasy of the last days, as revealed in the Scriptures, may well be upon us brethren, and yet there will always be a remnant who hunger and thirst for the authentic life of God and His righteousness, regardless of the many who have chosen the broad way that leads to emptiness and rejection at His Coming.

There must also be a willingness, on the part of exhorters, to "*endure hardship*" in the exercise of their gift. Now there will always be those in the church, perhaps the many, who will not suffer to be exhorted to change their ways, or forsake the path of men for the path of God. For them the deeper things of Christ, and the fullness of His Life mean little, for to them church is about affirming all that they are already, and for tickling their ears with sugary reinforcement. To them (like the official teachers and religious leaders of Jesus' day), he who exhorts is most decidedly unwelcome, and to be silenced at all costs. This is why, brethren, our churches are too often filled with syrupy, man-affirming believers, who are blind and ignorant of the *faith once delivered*. This is also the reason the word of exhortation has, for the most part, moved beyond the walls, as the days before our Lord's Appearing are short.

In addition to teaching, the gift of *exhortation* is intimately aligned with that of *prophecy*. Note again 1 Corinthians 14 –

> *Pursue love, yet desire earnestly spiritual gifts, but especially that you may prophesy. For one who speaks in a tongue does not speak to men but to God; for no one understands, but in his spirit he speaks mysteries. But one who prophesies speaks to men for edification*

> *and exhortation and consolation. One who speaks in a tongue edifies himself; but one who prophesies edifies the church. Now I wish that you all spoke in tongues, but even more that you would prophesy; and greater is one who prophesies than one who speaks in tongues, unless he interprets, so that the church may receive edifying. (1 Cor.14:1-5)*

The New Testament endowment of prophecy (Gk – "*propheteuo*", meaning *to speak under divine inspiration*), suggests edification, exhortation and consolation to the companions of Christ. Similar to prophets of old, such as Jeremiah and Isaiah, who constantly urged the people of Israel to return to the Lord, to love Him above all else, and to put away the false gods and idols in their midst, the one who exhorts the brethren does so out of an insufferable love for His people, and a heartfelt desire to see them realize all the blessings that the Lord has wrought for them.

And here is another point regarding exhortation – that it is intentionally directed at the heart and not so much the mind, as is teaching. It is an appeal to heavenly ideals such as love and steadfastness; to a return to a manner of life and living as it was ordained by the Creator to be. It urges fellow saints onward to maturity and the putting away of "*childish things*" (1 Corinthians 13:11; 14:20). But lest you be mistaken, it is not about the development of theologians, but of saints and servants who are fruitful and profitable to their master. For this reason it invariably involves an appeal to repentance and continuing endurance. It pierces forcefully through every example of falseness and shadow to reveal what is authentic, sincere and substantial. Purity of the faith once delivered, and bringing our spiritual minds into alignment with the Lord's ways and wisdom, is always where true spiritual exhortation leads.

He who exhorts stands not for himself, nor his group or denomination, but for the Lord Himself. He defends and represents God's position, perspective and point of view regarding the condition being addressed. Consider if you will the entire message given by Elihu (Job 32-37) to Job and his friends, as perhaps the greatest Old Testament example of exhortation to be found. Although a young man, who rightly deferred to his elders, once Elihu started speaking, what came forth was the full force, inspiration and authority of the Holy Spirit; even to the point of commanding his listeners to be silent while he spoke (see 1 Cor. 14 for a New Testament example of this principle).

If we care to look closely brethren, we will see that much of the New Testament is exhorting us (and warning us of the consequences of not doing so) to press tenaciously onward toward our inheritance in the sabbath rest of God; the "*Kingdom of our Lord and of His Christ*" (see Rev. 11:15, and note that this will ultimately be fulfilled in the "age to come", the last 1,000 years called the millennium and the Lord's Day). This passage in Hebrews is one of many examples –

> *Beware, brethren, lest there be in any of you an evil heart of unbelief in departing from the living God; but exhort one another daily, while it is called "Today," lest any of you be hardened through the deceitfulness of sin. For we have become partakers of Christ if we hold the beginning of our confidence steadfast to the end, while it is said:*
>
> *"TODAY IF YOU HEAR HIS VOICE, DO NOT HARDEN YOUR HEARTS, AS WHEN THEY PROVOKED ME."*
>
> *For who provoked Him when they had heard? Indeed, did not all those who came out of Egypt led by Moses? And with whom was He angry for forty years? Was it not with those who sinned, whose bodies fell in the wilderness? And to whom did He swear that they would not enter His rest, but to those who were disobedient? So we see that they were not able to enter because of unbelief. (Heb. 3:12-19)*

Throughout this and other epistles, Christian disciples are exhorted to learn from the mistakes made by the children of Israel, and to remain steadfast until the coming of the Lord. And although all are encouraged to exhort one another daily in the Spirit, there is the sense in Scripture that certain individuals are granted this particular gift for the edification of the body. Yet perhaps more important than the source of the exhortation, is the response of the people when it is presented. Let's note some additional passages here in Hebrews –

> *And you have forgotten the exhortation which speaks to you as to sons:*
>
> *"My son, do not despise the chastening of the LORD, Nor be discouraged when you are rebuked by Him;*
>
> *For whom the LORD loves He chastens, And scourges every son whom He receives.*
>
> *If you endure chastening, God deals with you as with sons; for what son is there whom a father does not chasten? But if you are without chastening, of which all have become partakers, then you are illegitimate and not sons. Furthermore, we have had human fathers who corrected us, and we paid them respect. Shall we not much more readily be in subjection to the Father of spirits and live? For they indeed for a few days chastened us as seemed best to them, but He for our profit, that we may be partakers of His holiness. Now no chastening seems to be joyful for the present, but painful; nevertheless, afterward it yields the peaceable fruit of righteousness to those who have been trained by it. (Heb. 12:5-11)*
>
> *And I appeal to you, brethren, bear with the word of exhortation, for I have written to you in few words. (Heb. 13:22)*

Lest we take too lightly the words given by the exhortation of our Lord through His servants, here we see that the consequences of neglecting or despising the word of exhortation are severe. In fact, we have the example of Israel ever before us in the testimony of God's Word to see where their hardness of heart and stubborn disobedience led them. Similarly, if the church dismisses or ignores genuine God-breathed exhortation, then the result over time will be nothing short of apostasy, a falling away from the faith once delivered; from the Lord Himself. This, sadly, has been the story of the Christian testimony since that first generation when "*wolves*" and *false shepherds* first slipped into the sheepfold and the Lord's shepherds failed to protect (by exhortation among other things) the sheep. This is serious business, little ones, and the times are short! Will we in fact heed the exhortation of the Lord, through those imbued with His Spirit of exhortation, or will despise it, seeking rather to have our ears tickled with feathery words of "all is well"?

If indeed we are sons of the kingdom and of the day (Matt. 13:38; 1 Thess. 5:5) and children of light (Eph. 5:8), then chastening and correction is absolutely necessary for us to mature in the faith, that we might be partakers of His holiness, and to be able to stand at the coming judgment of the saints. Exhortation by its very nature makes us uncomfortable and unsettled to be sure; it forces us to evaluate whether we are truly living for the Lord, abiding in Him and not in this world. It gives weight and substance to the teaching we have received related to what we are as new creations, and sons of the kingdom. It reveals that which is hidden or false, as a spotlight pierces into the darkness and exposes it as such. For this must surely be true, if indeed we are to be *children of the day*, who are not afraid to have all things in our hearts revealed and laid bare.

Yet again, the one who exhorts is not merely standing loftily in judgment over his brethren, but he is enabled through the Spirit to see that which the Lord sees, first (always this must be first) in himself, and then in the body at large. His zeal is singularly for the Lord's glory, and for the manifest well-being of the brethren. He is constantly aware that it is salt that preserves and not sugar, and that it is light that exposes things for what they truly are and not the darkness.

In this light, let us revisit the final words of Joshua to the children of Israel just prior to his death –

> *And the LORD your God will expel them from before you and drive them out of your sight. So you shall possess their land, as the LORD your God promised you. Therefore be very courageous to keep and to do all that is written in the Book of the Law of Moses, lest you turn aside from it to the right hand or to the left, and lest*

> *you go among these nations, these who remain among you. You shall not make mention of the name of their gods, nor cause anyone to swear by them; you shall not serve them nor bow down to them, but you shall hold fast to the LORD your God, as you have done to this day...*
>
> *"Behold, this day I am going the way of all the earth. And you know in all your hearts and in all your souls that not one thing has failed of all the good things which the LORD your God spoke concerning you. All have come to pass for you; not one word of them has failed. Therefore it shall come to pass, that as all the good things have come upon you which the LORD your God promised you, so the LORD will bring upon you all harmful things, until He has destroyed you from this good land which the LORD your God has given you. When you have transgressed the covenant of the LORD your God, which He commanded you, and have gone and served other gods, and bowed down to them, then the anger of the LORD will burn against you, and you shall perish quickly from the good land which He has given you." (Josh. 23:516)*

This brethren is as good an example of God-breathed exhortation as can be found anywhere in the Word. Notice that Joshua's appeal is to what they already knew (in all their hearts and souls), to what they have seen (that the Lord is faithful; that not one word of His had failed them), and to "*hold fast*" to the Lord their God, that they might ultimately possess all of the land He had sworn to them as an inheritance.

Well, we too, dear brethren, have an inheritance set out ahead of us, and it is nothing less than entrance into our Lord's Heavenly Kingdom, to rule and reign over this earth with Him for a thousand years. Yet in this wilderness journey, from faith to faith, from children needing milk, to mature saints sustained by meat, we have so very much to learn, so very much to let go of and so very much to apprehend. And the spiritual gift of exhortation is a most essential condition of our training and development as children of God.

Tragically, as we read in the Book of Judges following this appeal from Joshua, the children of Israel proved just how pitifully they took his words to heart. They did in fact perish quickly from the good land, rather than go on to possess all of it with the Lord's fullest blessing and purpose (to be a light to the gentiles). Indeed, they always seemed to react with hostility to the Lord's prophets and messengers, who meant them only that which is good. Ultimately, they rejected and then crucified the One sent from heaven, the One greater than Moses, whose heartfelt words of exhortation and truth fell always on uncircumcised ears (Acts 7:51) and stony hearts.

It is fitting here also to add to Joshua's final words, what well might be some of the final words of Peter (at his approaching death), and the similarity of the message is rather striking –

> *Now for this very reason also, applying all diligence, in your faith supply moral excellence, and in your moral excellence, knowledge, and in your knowledge, self-control, and in your self-control, perseverance, and in your perseverance, godliness, and in your godliness, brotherly kindness, and in your brotherly kindness, love. For if these qualities are yours and are increasing, they render you neither useless nor unfruitful in the true knowledge of our Lord Jesus Christ. For he who lacks these qualities is blind or short-sighted, having forgotten his purification from his former sins. Therefore, brethren, be all the more diligent to make certain about His calling and choosing you; for as long as you practice these things, you will never stumble; for in this way the entrance into the eternal kingdom of our Lord and Savior Jesus Christ will be abundantly supplied to you.*
>
> *Therefore, I will always be ready to remind you of these things, even though you already know them, and have been established in the truth which is present with you. I consider it right, as long as I am in this earthly dwelling, to stir you up by way of reminder, knowing that the laying aside of my earthly dwelling is imminent, as also our Lord Jesus Christ has made clear to me.*

> *And I will also be diligent that at any time after my departure you will be able to call these things to mind.* (2 Pet. 1:10-15)

Yes, beloved saints, as long as we too are in this tent, we need to be constantly reminded of essential and important things, to be "*stirred up*", that we will "*be neither barren nor unfruitful in the knowledge of our Lord Jesus Christ*", and ready to present ourselves to Him at His Coming. God-sent, Spirit-breathed exhortation, if it is heeded and taken to heart, keeps us from stumbling; it keeps us established in the present truth, and advancing in the faith, such that an "*entrance will be supplied to you abundantly into the everlasting kingdom of our Lord and Savior Jesus Christ.*"

And so to conclude, dear brethren, do not despise this gift, whether you are the one to whom it has been granted, or those who are being exhorted. It is one of those most precious gifts given to the church, ministered under the watchful care of the Holy Spirit, our Helper and Comforter, who will lead us into all things in Christ Jesus our Lord.

We offer these words by way of introduction, as the messages which follow are messages of spirit-breathed exhortation and reminder. They are a call to seek the very best things the Lord has for us, to go deeper, to put off all that which is merely distraction at best and deception at worst.

Our most simple prayer is that these words would be received in the spirit in which they are being offered to the Lord's people, and that we would be watchful, mature and ready when He comes for His own. In Jesus' name, we pray. Amen.

The Real Thing

Watchman Nee asked one of the most searching questions ever uttered by man, when he asked – "*What is the Normal Christian Life*"?

Well, what is it my brethren, this thing called the Christian life? What does it look like, and would you recognize it if it stood square out in front of you? I ask again, what does the real Christian life look like? Is it the life being lived out by most western Christians in the world today? Is it expressed in the pursuit of life, liberty and happiness perhaps? Is it embodied in patriotism, nationalism or good civic virtues? Is it a *religious* thing? Is it the manifest life being lived out by you and I?

What does a real Christian live for? What is the passion and pursuit of his heart? What is his first and last thought at the beginning and end of each day? What is his place and purpose in this world, in the short life he lives on this earth? What is the preoccupation and focus of his inner life? What lights his eyes, and informs his spirit, and compels him from moment to moment in this life?

What are his expectations and ideals? What is the living dynamic that enables and energizes him? What is his first love? Do you know my friends; I mean really know, as only the inner piercing of the Holy Spirit can allow you to know? Do you ever even contemplate such questions?

Be careful now. There are many counterfeits and shadows. There are countless notions and assumptions about what real Christianity is and is not. Indeed, every sect and division in the faith each has their own institutional and theological answers to all these essential questions; a creed, a statement, a formalized and inviolable doctrinal affirmation. Often they are printed on a card and handed out to new converts as the beginning and the end. Consider these stabbing words from T. Austin-Sparks –

> *'The Christian Faith' embraced as a religion, a philosophy, or as a system of truth, a moral or ethical doctrine, may carry the temporary stimulus of a great ideal; but this will not result in the regeneration of the life, or the new birth of the spirit. There are multitudes of such 'Christians' in the world today, but their spiritual effectiveness is nil. (from, What is Man?)*

Yet we are not asking your church or your pastor, but you personally. Do you know? If you met a real Christian on the street tomorrow would you know it? What would give them away? Good works or a kind heart perhaps? Selfless charity? Manifest piety or devotion to the cause of Christ?

We say we are Christians; all well and good. Yet are we really living the essential and authentic Christian life? Is the Living Christ being formed in us? I am not asking if you are a Christian, no not that at all, please don't misunderstand. For that is far easier to determine. Many have said *the prayer* and claimed the blood, then maybe gone forward to some altar in the presence of the saints; perhaps even been immersed in the baptism and death of the old man. Yet this new birth, this cataclysmic beginning, may or may not have any bearing on how one lives and walks afterward. It is a sad reality brethren, and one that grieves the Father terribly, that so many who have received the fullness of eternal life in His Son, at so great a cost to Himself, have failed to walk in this life.

> *My children, with whom I am again in labor until Christ is formed in you – (Gal. 4:18)*

> *For this reason also, since the day we heard of it, we have not ceased to pray for you and to ask that you may be filled with the knowledge of His will in all spiritual wisdom and understanding, so that you will walk in a manner worthy of the Lord, to please Him in all respects, bearing fruit in every good work and increasing in the knowledge of God; strengthened with all power, according to His glorious might, for the attaining of all steadfastness and patience; joyously giving thanks to the Father, who has qualified us to share in*

the inheritance of the saints in Light. For He rescued us from the domain of darkness, and transferred us to the kingdom of His beloved Son, in whom we have redemption, the forgiveness of sins.

He is the image of the invisible God, the firstborn of all creation. For by Him all things were created, both in the heavens and on earth, visible and invisible, whether thrones or dominions or rulers or authorities—all things have been created through Him and for Him. He is before all things, and in Him all things hold together. He is also head of the body, the church; and He is the beginning, the firstborn from the dead, so that He Himself will come to have first place in everything. For it was the Father's good pleasure for all the fullness to dwell in Him, and through Him to reconcile all things to Himself, having made peace through the blood of His cross; through Him, I say, whether things on earth or things in heaven.

And although you were formerly alienated and hostile in mind, engaged in evil deeds, yet He has now reconciled you in His fleshly body through death, in order to present you before Him holy and blameless and beyond reproach— if indeed you continue in the faith firmly established and steadfast, and not moved away from the hope of the gospel that you have heard, which was proclaimed in all creation under heaven, and of which I, Paul, was made a minister...

Of this church I was made a minister according to the stewardship from God bestowed on me for your benefit, so that I might fully carry out the preaching of the word of God, that is, the mystery which has been hidden from the past ages and generations, but has now been manifested to His saints, to whom God willed to make known what is the riches of the glory of this mystery among the Gentiles, which is Christ in you, the hope of glory. We proclaim Him, admonishing every man and teaching every man with all wisdom, so that we may present every man complete in Christ. (Col. 1:9-23; 25-28)

> *Therefore as you have received Christ Jesus the Lord, so walk in Him, having been firmly rooted and now being built up in Him and established in your faith, just as you were instructed, and overflowing with gratitude. (Col. 2:6-7)*

Oh dear ones, is He being formed in us? Are we walking in Him every moment of every day? Are we being made complete in Him such that He might fill all of the Creation with Himself? Are we walking in a manner worthy of our Lord, in other words?

Or does each day just bring with it more of ourselves? More of the old man? More of the old creation? More of our opinions? More of our best efforts and failures? More of our soul? More of our carnal appetites? More of us seeking a future in this ephemeral and perishing world? More religious idols that we allow to supplant Him, and eclipse Him, and shun Him in the inner sanctuary of our hearts? Oh dear ones, this must not be so, for He willingly and graciously poured out all of His life and His love for us, that we might take it up, and walk in it, and grow in it, and become something else; something new; something heavenly and mysterious, that even the angels rub their eyes to glimpse more perfectly.

> *For this reason I bow my knees before the Father, from whom every family in heaven and on earth derives its name, that He would grant you, according to the riches of His glory, to be strengthened with power through His Spirit in the inner man, so that Christ may dwell in your hearts through faith; and that you, being rooted and grounded in love, may be able to comprehend with all the saints what is the breadth and length and height and depth, and to know the love of Christ which surpasses knowledge, that you may be filled up to all the fullness of God. (Eph. 3:14-19)*

"*Filled up to all the fullness of God.*" Oh dear saints, does this sound anything like our Father in Heaven is trying to improve you or make you a better man; with all that you are still intact, alive and well? No and never! Rather He is intent on filling you with all the fullness of His perfect and beloved Son! Oh that you might see this with spiritual eyes, and that it might shatter everything that religion and self-help and humanism has wrought over 6,000 years! No, the first lie is still the only lie. You shall not be as God. Only God shall be as God. And only God; only His Son being formed in you shall bring a smile to the face of the Father and satisfaction to His heart.

And so – Is He being increased in us or are we?

"He must increase, but I must decrease. (John 3:30)

Oh my brethren, my heart yearns that you would see this once and for all as did John the Baptist, and put aside all and anything that confounds this wonderful and mysterious purpose. Oh that you would stop being so impressed and so compromised with religious things and religious men and religious buildings and religious formalities, and that you might see with eyes wide open in the spirit what the Father wants us to see – the beauty and the majesty, and the glory, and the absolute and universe-filling perfection that is Christ Jesus, the Son of God, the King of Kings, the Light of All the Universe! He, my friends, and He alone, is the *Real Thing*. In point of fact, *He is the only thing*! And His mystic Body, what Paul reveals in his letter to the Ephesians, is what we are in the process of becoming, individually joined to Him one to one another, onward to the fullness of Christ Jesus!

> *And He gave some as apostles, and some as prophets, and some as evangelists, and some as pastors and teachers, for the equipping of the saints for the work of service, to the building up of the body of Christ; until we all attain to the unity of the faith, and of the knowledge of the Son of God, to a mature man, to the measure of the stature which belongs to the fullness of Christ. As a result, we are no longer to be children, tossed here and there by waves and carried about by every wind of doctrine, by the trickery of men, by craftiness in deceitful scheming; but speaking the truth in love, we are to grow up in all aspects into Him who is the head, even Christ, from whom the whole body, being fitted and held together by what every joint supplies, according to the proper working of each individual part, causes the growth of the body for the building up of itself in love.*
>
> *So this I say, and affirm together with the Lord, that you walk no longer just as the Gentiles also walk, in the futility of their mind, being darkened in their understanding, excluded from the life of God because of*

> *the ignorance that is in them, because of the hardness of their heart; and they, having become callous, have given themselves over to sensuality for the practice of every kind of impurity with greediness. But you did not learn Christ in this way, if indeed you have heard Him and have been taught in Him, just as truth is in Jesus, that, in reference to your former manner of life, you lay aside the old self, which is being corrupted in accordance with the lusts of deceit, and that you be renewed in the spirit of your mind, and put on the new self, which in the likeness of God has been created in righteousness and holiness of the truth. (Eph. 4:11-24)*

Dear saints and children of the day, so many in this hour, at the end of this age, are so easily deceiving you and distracting you and diverting you from the Real Thing, from He who is our beginning and end, our very life and reason for life. Oh how this grieves me terribly and brings the Holy Spirit's tears to my eyes and my heart. So many idols set up to perpetuate man on this earth; all dressed up in his Sunday best, keeping rules and rituals, day after day and year after year, on and on and on.

Gracious Father, forgive us Lord, every single one of us, for falling prey to every lesser thing, every earth-bound, man-inspired thing. Oh Lord, grant us just such a heart to love Thee Father, and to allow all that it takes for Your Beloved Son to be formed in us, such that His fullness might fill everything in every way. Oh Lord, there are many out there still pretending and still patronizing groups and following men and cardboard creeds, who have utterly no idea at all what the real Christian life is all about. Even worse, Lord, so many are using the name of Your precious Son as a means of worldly gain and enrichment. Oh gracious Lord, I pray not for such wolves but for Your precious sheep, for whom the blood of the Lamb was spilled. I pray You will save those just as You called Noah out of the world, and Lot out of Sodom, and Israel out from Egypt prior to Your terrible wrath being poured down. Oh Lord, turn our hearts to Thee, and open our eyes that we might see such wonderful things. Save us Father, please save us in Your great mercy and longsuffering! In Jesus' glorious name, we pray. Amen.

Jesus As God

Unlike the original twelve, and many other early disciples, the Apostle Paul never actually experienced the man Jesus. All that he knew, from that blinding first encounter on the road to Damascus to the end of his life, was Jesus as God, the locus and fulfillment of "all things" in Colossians 1 –

> *He is the image of the invisible God, the firstborn of all creation. For by Him all things were created, both in the heavens and on earth, visible and invisible, whether thrones or dominions or rulers or authorities—all things have been created through Him and for Him. He is before all things, and in Him all things hold together. He is also head of the body, the church; and He is the beginning, the firstborn from the dead, so that He Himself will come to have first place in everything. (Col. 1: 15-18)*

Whereas the original twelve ate and drank with Jesus of Nazareth in daily personal contact here on earth, Paul's revelation and consideration of Him was as one seated at the right hand of God –

> *...in the heavenly places, far above all rule and authority and power and dominion, and every name that is named, not only in this age but also in the one to come. (Eph. 1:19-20)*

> *And He put all things in subjection under His feet, and gave Him as head over all things to the church, which is His body, the fullness of Him who fills all in all. (Eph. 1:22-23)*

For Paul, to truly see and affirm Jesus Christ, was to behold the "*all in all*" for whom and through whom all things in the past, present and future must come to fulfillment and fruition. What the original disciples were permitted by the Spirit to glimpse on the mount of transfiguration, and what the apostle John beheld on the island of Patmos, Paul was afforded the language and theology to express.

For Paul, everything existed such that the Heavenly Father might honor and bless His beloved Son; that He might exalt Him above all else that would be exalted and magnified. Through the New Testament we discover that it is primarily through the ministry and testimony of Paul that Jesus is revealed and presented as God.

My brethren, there is a vast and immeasurable difference between a man that does god-like things and one who is in fact God. There is an incalculable gulf between one who is true and one who is Truth; one who is righteous, and one who is Righteousness; one who is loving, and one who is Love; one who is wise, and one who is Wisdom; one who is living and one who is Life! Maybe let that stir around in your spirit a bit before reading further.

Many of the prophets of the Old Testament, such as Moses and Elijah, performed god-like acts, controlling nature and manipulating the material world in one sense or another. In fact, until His resurrection, nothing that Jesus did in terms of miracles outmatched anything seen before. Elijah revived the widow's son as surely as Jesus raised Lazarus, and Elisha multiplied bread as readily as our Lord multiplied the loaves and fishes.

Indeed, there is much evidence that the disciples struggled mightily with this question of whether the one they were following was merely a man doing god-like things or very God Himself. "*Who are you*?" – was not just something the religious leaders of the day wrestled with, but also Peter and James and John and all of those in His immediate company. Was He a prophet? Indeed was He "the prophet", the one spoken of by Moses? Or something more? The Lord Himself relieved them of this burden when He declared, in no uncertain terms, that He was in fact the Son of God. In declaring this, He was clearly and unmistakably asserting His divinity, His godhood. Recall that many walked away from Him over this very issue. And indeed, this is still the only issue that truly matters for any of us – who we believe that He is.

For Paul, from the moment the Lord met him on that Damascus Road, the issue was settled. Interestingly enough, he was blinded to all material reality for a time, that he might come to see the One whom he persecuted elevated in ultimate glory at the right hand of the Father in heaven. This is where He resides today my friends. Yes, He obviously came and experienced life as a human being on this earth, but it is important now to recognize and consider Him as God, above all things, shining in ultimate glory.

Is this then how we consider and relate to Him? Like Paul, is He the "*all in all*" in our own lives and experience? Is our admiration and adoration of Him essentially limited to Jesus the man; or do we see Him raised up, drawing all things unto Himself as only God can do? Which Jesus do we find most compelling – a saintly man with god-like abilities, a sagacious teacher perhaps, or the very Son of God for whom all creation was intended?

The Apostle Paul sees a preeminently heavenly Jesus, in all of His former and even His more endowed glory (by virtue of the incarnation, cross and resurrection as the firstborn of men into the household of God). Although they are one and the same, there is night and day between the carpenter Jesus who walked this earth and the Jesus portrayed throughout the Book of Hebrews and Revelation.

> *God, after He spoke long ago to the fathers in the prophets in many portions and in many ways, in these last days has spoken to us in His Son, whom He appointed heir of all things, through whom also He made the world. And He is the radiance of His glory and the exact representation of His nature, and upholds all things by the word of His power. When He had made purification of sins, He sat down at the right hand of the Majesty on high, having become as much better than the angels, as He has inherited a more excellent name than they. (Heb. 1:1-4)*

Now I know that there is some debate on this, but I personally have no trouble believing that these words are the words of Paul, for in style and substance they reflect his message perfectly – Jesus as the heavenly fulfillment of all things. He continues in verse 5, and as you read along, notice how everything bows and falls before the ultimate fulfillment found in the Son: the ministry of angels and patriarchs and priests, even human prophets; all swallowed up and eclipsed by He who Paul calls the "*all in all*". Now many scholars will admit that the English language is not very precise when it comes to expressing ultimacy or quintessence. Yet in the "*all in all*" we come as close as we can to that which is the most or the ultimate. Jesus, in the end, is the very most that the Father had to give. He is the author and finisher of our salvation, the beginning and the end, the supreme One in whom all life and reality and purpose converges and turns. It is His glory which shines brighter than any other, for He too is God.

His face is the face of God. His hands extend the touch of God upon our lives. His love shares the very heart of God. His light represents the wisdom and truth that is God. His very words uphold and sustain life as only God can. Every living cell in this universe pulses with vitality because He ordains and sustains it. Without and apart from Him, there would be no created reality as we know it, for He made it and holds it all together in Himself. There is no other way around it, my friends – the Christ whom we serve and love and worship – **He is God!**

And if there be any call on this Christian path; be it an evangelical call, a prophetic call, or a call to repentance and sanctification; then truly it can only flow from the inescapable reality of the ultimate divinity of the Lord Jesus Christ!

Now we can certainly acknowledge, without reducing anything we have said above, that it can be useful to consider the humanity of Jesus, for indeed He was all man as well as being all god. Yet the recorded example of the perfect man does no more to help us in practical terms than the Book of Proverbs help us to be wise. What really counts is the power to attain; the life within; and then even our Lord told His followers that it was better that He went away (to return to His pre-incarnate glory), for only then would His presence and power be unlimited and unconstrained by His humanity.

Certainly there was an earthly Jesus, but consider also how frequently the Apostle Paul uses the terms heaven and heavenly throughout his writings. Clearly here is where he thinks our emphasis and attention should be. It is here in the heavenlies where the Father is reconciling all things to Himself, in and through His Son. Here is the final stage, where the final acts of creation's history are played out in the Book of Revelation. Here is the true home of the church, and the hope of all who would follow the Firstborn into the household of God.

Dear brethren, can we ever emphasize this too strongly? Whereas so many secondary things (*doctrines, methods, programs, themes, etc.)* grow old and worn, can we ever be reminded too much of what our Lord truly is and represents as the Beginning and End, in the eternal present of God? So many other things, lesser things, seem to be so important today, when He is really all that matters, and has ever mattered. Why haven't we learned the lesson of so many generations and movements that every vain attempt to add to the "ALL" that He represents can only lead to idolatry and delusion? Why does He never seem to be enough for some folks, when He is more than enough for the Father?

Oh Most High and Holy Father – We thank You dear Lord, for giving the very most You had to give in the form of Your Beloved Son. We thank You Lord Jesus that You are the Father's all, the utmost and ultimate provision; the supreme sum of all things! That we need nothing more. May You increase our faith and assurance that all things are possible for those who love You. In Jesus' high and heavenly name, we pray. Amen.

Code Words for Christ

My dear friends, as usual, I feel totally and utterly inadequate and ill-equipped to express anything even close to what He is. My puny words cannot fully contain Him. My thoughts, however high, fail to ascend anywhere near the height in which He dwells in all His ascendant glory. It is like trying to describe light or truth or peace with mere words and language. You can't really, you can only come to possess them, and know that you have them. Yet, something within compels me to try. Oh that I would see Him in anything but form and shadow, as He truly is. That I would come to know Him – the awesome and absolute life known as the Christ.

> *Therefore having such a hope, we use great boldness in our speech, and are not like Moses, who used to put a veil over his face so that the sons of Israel would not look intently at the end of what was fading away. But their minds were hardened; for until this very day at the reading of the old covenant the same veil remains unlifted, because it is removed in Christ. But to this day whenever Moses is read, a veil lies over their heart; but whenever a person turns to the Lord, the veil is taken away. (2 Cor. 3:12-16)*

He is the essential theme and focus of the Scriptures, is He not? Is He not there *in the beginning* and in that final *amen*? Does His glory and promise not shine on all pages in between? As we approach the Word of God is it anything less than He we are searching for? If so, then we will surely not see Him there, for He is the All and Everything in time past, present and future. He is the meaning we must seek throughout. Only in Him is the veil of the Scripture lifted so that the Lord's message can unfold. He is the One, my brethren, and this bears repeating in this hour when it seems we have taken our eyes off of Him and His preeminence in the perfect plan and purpose of God.

He alone is that great Mystery, Truth, Wisdom, Life and Light of the World as recorded in our Holy Bible. He alone is our ultimate objective, and only in Him does every good thing flow down from the Father in Heaven in all fullness and life. Only when we as Christians really comprehend this spiritually, will all of the wondrous glories of the Scriptures be unveiled to us.

Consider the literally hundreds of shadows, types, names and titles, figures and ideals recorded throughout the Bible – in both Old and New Testaments – that in some way or another point to or are affirmed in Him. As disciples, we understand (or should anyway) on a practical level how all divine promises and ideals are realized in Him, and in the newness of life that He represents for us. Yet in much of our Christian teaching and practice today, we hold this rather loosely don't we. And the result far too often is that these ideals, once removed from the root and ground of Christ, become little more than abstractions and empty sermons.

Fellow saints, I would like to suggest something that may be a little controversial to some, but shouldn't be. It is this – that when we come to our Bible and discover such mysterious and perfect concepts such as *Life, Light, Truth, Wisdom, Righteousness, Grace, Peace, Joy, Holiness, Victory, Freedom, Strength,* and *Godliness*, we can quite easily view these as synonymous with the person of Jesus Christ. Indeed, it is entirely helpful to do so, both in terms of our fruitfulness in study and application. These words, as they are presented throughout the pages of Scripture, are practically "code words" for Christ. He, as the "*fullness of God*", embodies the superlative perfection they contain.

Like these words, He is the ultimate; there is nothing higher, or deeper, or more complete. Just as you cannot add anything to life or truth to get something more or greater, you cannot add to Him. For us, He is the very most we can hope for, or realize as new spiritual creatures. And when we approach the Scriptures seeking Him there, it is quite natural and even appropriate to see Him in all of these many aspects of ultimate reality.

Did He not declare that He is the Way, the Truth and the Life? And also is He not love, for the Scriptures affirm that God is love. As we gain Christ, do we not also acquire all of the many aspects of His perfect nature, including grace, truth, righteousness, wisdom, peace, holiness, godliness and the like. He is the entirety of fullness and completeness – anything less is empty and incomplete. As we are equipped in Him, in all of the power and freedom of this new spiritual reality, are we not clothed in His attributes?

For example, when He says that blessed are they that hunger and thirst for righteousness, is this not essentially the same as saying we are to be spiritually hungry for Him? Is He not the living bread that came down from heaven and the life-giving water from the rock?

When the Book of Proverbs enjoins us to "*get wisdom and understanding*", does this not translate for the Christian that we are to pursue Christ, and as a result, His wisdom and understanding will be accessible to us?

> *Where is the wise man? Where is the scribe? Where is the debater of this age? Has not God made foolish the wisdom of the world? For since in the wisdom of God the world through its wisdom did not come to know God, God was well-pleased through the foolishness of the message preached to save those who believe. For indeed Jews ask for signs and Greeks search for wisdom; but we preach Christ crucified, to Jews a stumbling block and to Gentiles foolishness, but to those who are the called, both Jews and Greeks, Christ the power of God and the wisdom of God. (1 Cor. 1: 20-24)*

Go ahead and try it, my friends. Replace every instance of the word *wisdom* in Proverbs with the name of Jesus Christ, and see if this doesn't blow this book wide open with meaning and relevance. And in Deuteronomy 30, where the choice between life and death is presented to the nation of Israel, we Christians can comprehend this as a decision for or against Christ, for He is Life and there can be no possibility of blessing apart from Him.

In Colossians 3:12-15, substitute "*tender mercies, kindness, humility, meekness, longsuffering, love and the peace of God*", with "*the Lord Jesus Christ*", and see if it does not instantly put it all into the right perspective. Nor is there holiness, godliness, righteousness, victory, liberty, glory or light other than that flowing out of Him into the redeemed soul of the new man.

You, dear Christian, who presume to have these things apart from the exchanged life in Him, I say with all the frankness of personal experience, as one who has *been there and done that,* that you will be sorely disappointed. Although to others it may seem you are far along the path, you are not. For He alone is the way! Not merely to point the way there, but to carry us within Himself all the way home to the Father's heart.

When we fall on our knees before the Holy Father and pray for strength or power or freedom or victory, are we in fact not merely asking for more of the life of Jesus Christ pulsing in our soul and spirit. Is He not the Tree of Life we so desperately require, and the heavenly ladder that ascends into the heart of the Father? And are not all of these, in ultimate fulfillment, the Lord Jesus Christ?

He is the ideal man, the perfectly wise One who always does the Father's will, and fulfills His good pleasure and intent. We cannot hope to be equipped with wisdom or any other perfect thing, unless we are filled with all the fullness of God. These too, are code words for Christ, for He alone is the very fullness of god in all perfection and light.

As students of the Bible, we tend to toss these high words around as if we actually know what they represent, as if they actually mean anything apart from Him. The truth is, they do not, and when we stumble down this path we fall into that same godless humanism spawned in Eden and fulfilled at the height of Babel; the satanic notion that man can fulfill his creative purpose if only he knows where to look, and applies himself perfectly to the task.

We seem to have put the cart before the horse in so much of our teaching today, whereby we teach young converts that if they live pure lives, resist sin and temptation, keep their hands clean, etc, then Christ will seem closer and more real to them. Nonsense! It is only when Christ gets inside of us that this purity or any other high thing is even possible. Until this happens, nothing happens!

What is it you want, my brother – power, strength, victory, peace, knowledge? Well I tell you here and now that these are all code words for Christ! Get Him, and all the rest will follow and flow, and watch and see how the old man begins to be undone from the inside, as His regenerative life and spirit begins to clear out the cobwebs of 6,000 years of man's rebellion and death.

Oh Father in Heaven, help us to see Your Beloved Son on each and every page of Your Holy Bible. Keep us, Oh Lord, from the lie that there is anything good in us apart from Him. Help His glory and life to shine forth in our study as we search the Scriptures, and realize deep down in the heart how much we need Him. Help us to grasp this life-changing truth that until He enters our hearts and assumes the throne of our lives, we are no better or different than Adam. Equip us, dear Father, with His most perfect nature, with all the fullness of God found solely in Him, that we may finally and ultimately be all that we were created to be, for Your Glory and Honor. In His wondrous name, we pray. Amen.

Jesus Christ, the Great Superlative

He is the image of the invisible God, the firstborn of all creation. For by Him all things were created, both in the heavens and on earth, visible and invisible, whether thrones or dominions or rulers or authorities—all things have been created through Him and for Him. He is before all things, and in Him all things hold together. He is also head of the body, the church; and He is the beginning, the firstborn from the dead, so that He Himself will come to have first place in everything. For it was the Father's good pleasure for all the fullness to dwell in Him, and through Him to reconcile all things to Himself, having made peace through the blood of His cross; through Him, I say, whether things on earth or things in heaven. (Col. 1:15-20)

Superlative*: of the highest kind, quality, or order; surpassing all else or others; supreme. (Dictionary.com)*

While reading Paul's letter to the Colossians I was practically paralyzed by a sense of the unspeakable wonder of this being known as Jesus Christ. Language itself flounders and very nearly fails as this skillful communicator begins to consider the Living and Eternal Word, the One who reconciles all the world to God the Father through Himself.

Clearly, He who is our Lord and Life is the Great Superlative of history. And brethren, it should also be clear to us that all of the Father's eternal purposes are bound up in His Son, Jesus Christ. All that the Father is doing, in terms of restoring all that has fallen, whether it be in the realm of the angels, the physical world, or the inner human condition, involves His Son. If we could only grasp this, and be granted an enlarged vision of His central place in all history and destiny. Oh Lord, let it be so!

Speaking on the "*All Things in Christ*", T. Austin-Sparks, has left us the following words -

> *To begin with, it is supremely important that we should recognize that there is one basic and all-governing factor with God, which is a supreme matter for our knowledge, and that is the inclusiveness and exclusiveness of His Son, Jesus Christ.*
>
> *Everything intended and required for the realization of Divine purpose and intention is in, and with, Christ, not only as a deposit, but all is Christ. That is the inclusiveness of Christ.*
>
> *Then, on the other hand, nothing but what is of Christ is accepted or permitted by God in the final issue. That is the exclusiveness of Christ. However God may seem in His patience and long-suffering, in His grace and mercy, to be bearing with much, even in us His people, which is not of Christ; however much He seems for the time being to allow, it is of supreme importance that we settle it once for all that God is not really allowing it. He may extend to us His forbearance, His long-suffering, but He is not in any way accepting what is not of Christ. He has initially said that it is dead to Him, and He is progressively working death in that realm. So that in the final issue, not one fragment anywhere that is not of Christ will be allowed. Christ excludes everything that is not of Himself. That is God's ruling of the matter. (from, The Stewardship of the Mystery, Vol 1. – All Things in Christ)*

Which is really just another way of saying that He alone is the Beginning and End of All Things! That all from the Father is contained in His Son and nothing else! That Jesus Christ is the Center of Everything in God's Eternal Purpose! Oh how we have reduced

Him, my brethren. How we have repackaged Him to all the world as so much less than what He is. How small and shallow are our conceptions of Him, in whom *"all the fullness should dwell"*.

Does He then, in the realm of your heart and life and being surpass all things? Does the supremacy, the exceeding excellence of the Lord Jesus command your utmost attention and devotion and praise? Or is He merely some great *teacher* or *prophet* or *guru*? Do you merely follow him (or attempt to anyway), or do you live every single moment of your life in and through Him? Deep and wide is the difference between the two dear saints – Deep and wide indeed!

Here, again, is Austin-Sparks -

> *This passing, this breakdown, this confusion, this deadlock is all because the course of things is in His hands, and He is holding it all unto Himself. He is King! He is Lord! It is a tremendous thing to recognize that the very course of the nations, the very history of this world, is held in the hands of the Lord Jesus unto His own destined end. God has for ever set His Son as the only One to be full, complete, and final Lord of His universe, King of kings and Lord of lords, with a beneficent sway and reign over all the earth. Peace and prosperity is locked up with the Lord Jesus, and He holds the destiny of nations unto that. Men may attempt it of themselves, and they may go a long way to usurp His place, but the end is foreseen, foreshown. He must come whose right it is, and of His Kingdom there shall be no end. It has commenced in heaven; it is already vested in Him and held in His hands. That is how we must read history. That is how we must read our daily papers. That is how we shall be saved from the evil depression and despair that would creep into our hearts as we mark the state of things in this world. All is being held by Him to a certain end. The meaning is that nothing can take the place of the Lord Jesus. (from, The Stewardship of the Mystery, Vol 1. – All Things in Christ)*

All things belong to Him, whether the creation acknowledges it or not. He alone will be exalted in God's eternal plans and purposes, with or without the cooperation or consent of the world. He alone is our *hope of glory.* He alone defines and enables this mystery of godliness, whereby a created and corrupted human being is indwelt by the life and glory of God Himself.

He is the one who disarms the adversary and accuser of the saints by reducing all of his accusations to dust. He alone fulfills all divine requirements and obligations. He is the eternal substance represented by all shadows and forms and symbols since the dawn of that first day.

> *For you have died and your life is hidden with Christ in God. (Col. 3:3)*

Take a few moments, my friends, and just stop and consider the immensity of this statement. Amazing! Truly Amazing! Here it is, my brethren, in a nutshell, the mystery and the power of the Christian life. Christianity is not *a way of life* (as so often it is portrayed), but rather it is *a life*; the very life of the Lord Jesus Christ. He is the living principle; the divine agent of holiness that makes the mystery of godliness in fallen man possible. He is the heaveanly *Vine* and we are the *branches*!

He did not come to show us the way home to the Father; He is the Way. He did not come with some new truth about the Godhead; He is that Truth! He did not come to show us a better way of life; He is that Life! He is not merely some divine dispenser of heavenly gifts; He is that Gift!

Clearly we see many ways and truths and lives in the church today; but do we see and touch and taste the living Christ?

This is no empty mysticism either, my friends. I dare say that if we have not come to fully believe and experience the living Christ inside us, then I must ask just what is Christianity anyway? What can it be without He Himself joined to us in vital union, and expressing His divine and holy life through us? This thing called sanctification (the saving of the soul) is an inside job, as only it can be.

He is our life now. He sustains us in this life that He might present us holy and blameless to the Father in the next.

> *Blessed be the God and Father of our Lord Jesus Christ, who has blessed us with every spiritual blessing in the heavenly places in Christ, just as He chose us in Him before the foundation of the world, that we would be holy and blameless before Him. In love He predestined us to adoption as sons through Jesus Christ to Himself, according to the kind intention of His will, to the praise of the glory of His grace, which He freely bestowed on us in the Beloved. (Eph. 1:3-6)*

Does your life consist in Him my brother? Does mine? Oh how I wish I could affirm that with supreme confidence. Although others on this earth see the old familiar us, what are they seeing really? Is it a life hidden in Him? How much of the old self has truly died? Or is it merely the same old man in religious garb, looking and sounding pious, but still the same deep down?

Have we really died, my brethren? Really? To the world and the self and to lust of every created thing? To power and prestige? To the sound of others praising our name? To the lure of riches and unredeemed pleasure? To all of the worldly things that we never should have been unequally yoked to in the first place?

Are our lives truly hidden in Him, or are we just pretending? If so, then let us forsake it all, and surrender. Let us stop pretending, for His alone is the light of living and pure reality, in whom there is no darkness. He alone is the Father's beloved Son –

> *I will proclaim the decree of the Lord: He said to me, "You are my Son; today I have become your Father." (Psa. 2:7)*

> *"This is My beloved Son, with whom I am well-pleased; listen to Him!" (Matt. 17:5)*

Do you see this brethren, for this is tremendous! All that the Father is doing is bound up entirely in His beloved Son. He is, as Watchman Nee puts it, the "*Sum of All Spiritual Things*". To see this, as only the Holy Spirit can reveal, is so absolutely vital to our advancing in the faith; in this newness of life. To see the Living Christ as He really is, in all of His scope and supremacy, changes everything. Notice what Austin-Sparks conveys regarding the importance of this spiritual sight, and that the object seen must be the Lord Jesus in all of His glorious and exclusive splendor –

> *The purpose of God from eternity is concerning His Son - the place that His Son holds in the very universe according to God's mind; the tremendous comprehensiveness of Christ; the tremendous implications of the very being and existence of Christ; the tremendous consequences that are bound up with Jesus Christ. They did not see it all at once, but they began to see the Lord Jesus. They began to see that this was not just a man among men, not just the man of Galilee. No, He is infinitely greater than that, overwhelming. This mighty impact of a meaning about Jesus Christ is too big to hold, so great that you cannot grasp it. It is overwhelming and devastating. They began to see that; that was their vision. Out of that vision everything else came. Look at them and hear them, recognize what a new and great Christ they have found, what a significant Christ He is, how everything is bound up with Him. All destiny is centered in Him; He is the only consequence. (from, Prophetic Ministry)*

Oh that He alone would be our Everything! Our Destiny! Our Beginning and End! Oh that we might truly see Him, saints, in all of His Fullness; as the Great Superlative in God's Eternal Plans and Purposes! Oh Lord, let it be so for everyone reading these words at this very moment!

In Jesus' Holy and Glorious name, we pray. Amen.

Do We Modern Christians Fear the Lord?

It is easy, is it not, to affirm our love for our precious Lord and God. But can we go so far as to say that we actually fear Him, and that we tremble at His Word? Put another way – does not keeping His every word and instruction fill us with a sense of dread and foreboding? And does it at all bother us in the spirit that we dishonor Him so? What has happened to the fear of God among us dear brethren? Have we listened to the lie that says the fear of the Lord is of the old, yet love is of the new? As the Spirit permits, let us look into this a little closer by the light of His Word.

It is sad, perhaps even tragic, to observe the church of the present hour, wantonly departing from the sacred truths of Scripture; so ready to embrace the foolishness of the world in the name of Christ. It is doubly sad to watch the redeemed Body of Christ being deluded by methods and philosophies that are incapable of producing the fruit of holiness and faithfulness in the lives of God's people. Yet, despite this, the *self-esteeming* church, the *psycho-analyzing* church, the *method-driven, program-developing* church is running headlong after diverse and unsanctified opinions regarding the subject of motivation. "*Love, and love alone, must motivate us to follow Christ*" is the message of the day heard from many a pulpit and seminar tape. "*Fear is from the devil and is the opposite of faith; nothing done from the motivation of fear is emotionally healthy*", goes the modern message on this subject. Sadly, many are listening with their ears wide open and their Bibles closed.

By emphasizing love (or other psycho-social forces such as friendship, for example) as the singular motivating influence on our obedient response to the Lord, while at the same time effectively ignoring what the Bible calls the "Fear of God", the modern church has done a great disservice to new disciples and the Word of God. Clearly, the Bible teaches that we are to obey God out of love for Him and a desire to be formed in His likeness. But it also teaches that we are to approach God from the perspective of created beings in the presence of the Awesome and Terrible One who holds our very existence between His fingers.

To fear God, and Him alone – this is the plain and consistent imperative of both the Old and New Testaments. What the patriarchs, prophets and apostles all had in common was this, that they feared the Lord. All wisdom, knowledge and edifying counsel has its source and beginning in the one kind of fear that is sanctioned and promoted in the Scriptures. It is not a negative, irrational and debilitating fear, as all others are, but rather a positive and empowering fear that impacts the heart, mind and the spirit in man. It is the only reasonable and honest response of the creature in the presence of the Creator. It implies, by necessity, a posture of deference and servitude to a higher and perfect being.

Consider the clear and emphatic words of the Savior, when He said –

> *"Do not fear those who kill the body but are unable to kill the soul; but rather fear Him who is able to destroy both soul and body in hell." (Matt. 10:28)*

And the Apostle Peter –

> *Honor all people, love the brotherhood, fear God, honor the king. (1 Pet. 2:17)*

Consider the fruits of walking in the fear of the Lord, as described in Acts 9 –

> *So the church throughout all Judea and Galilee and Samaria enjoyed peace, being built up; and going on in the fear of the Lord and in the comfort of the Holy Spirit, it continued to increase. (Acts 9:31)*

Oh little ones, to walk in the fear of the Lord does not result in psychological ill-health, but peace, edification and fruitfulness. To act from a healthy and informed fear of God is to operate from a genuinely positive and God-ordained motivation. Yet the modern preacher-turned-therapist, having chosen to borrow from humanist psychology rather than the Bible, has banished all fear as unhealthy, negative, immobilizing, and threatening to one's self-image. Better to convince the believer that he is loved, and loved unconditionally, that he is a friend to Jesus, and that God accepts Him for what he is. Our Lord does indeed accept the newborn babe for what he is when born, but then He fully expects (and empowers us) to walk in His ways (actually in His Life to be more precise), to please the Holy Father and to present a true and righteous testimony of the Master and His Kingdom in this world. I dare say by His abiding grace this is impossible apart from the fear of the Lord abiding within the child of God.

The Fear of God Defined

Note: The Greek root for *fear* in the Scripture passages above is *phobo* (from which we get out English word, *phobia*) and means:

> *a) to fear, be afraid of; b) reverence; c) to be struck with fear, to be seized with alarm; d) to fear to do something for fear of harm; e) venerate, to treat with deference or reverential obedience; f) terror, dread.*

When the Bible speaks of the fear of God (or the fear of the Lord) it truly means fear; a genuine fear, not simply *respect* or *fear lite* as some commentators have wrongly emphasized. Fear certainly embodies the notion of respect, but it goes much deeper. Webster's Dictionary hits it right on the head in defining fear as –

> *"profound reverence and awe, esp. toward God" and "an unpleasant often strong emotion caused by anticipation or awareness of danger".*

Does this not effectively describe the responses of most human beings in the Bible as they came into the awesome presence of the Most High?

Consider Job's posture after being questioned by Jehovah –

> *Then Job answered the Lord: "I am unworthy—how can I reply to you? I put my hand over my mouth. I spoke once, but I have no answer—twice, but I will say no more." (Job 40:3-5)*
>
> *Therefore I despise myself and repent in dust and ashes." (Job 42:6)*

And Isaiah, who lost himself in beholding the Lord –

> *Then I said, "Woe is me, for I am ruined! Because I am a man of unclean lips, And I live among a people of unclean lips; For my eyes have seen the King, the LORD of hosts." (Isa. 6:5)*

And the disciples on the Mount of Transfiguration –

> *While he was still speaking, a bright cloud overshadowed them, and behold, a voice out of the cloud said, "This is My beloved Son, with whom I am well-pleased; listen to Him!" When the disciples heard this, they fell face down to the ground and were terrified. (Matt. 17:5-6)*

The Lord Himself asks –

> *Do you not fear Me?' declares the LORD. 'Do you not tremble in My presence? For I have placed the sand as a boundary for the sea, An eternal decree, so it cannot cross over it. Though the waves toss, yet they cannot prevail; Though they roar, yet they cannot cross over it. (Jer. 5:22)*

The compelling message of the Bible is that true peace can only result when we fear God and nothing else. How is this possible? If we fear the Lord, we have nothing to fear from the created realm, over which He alone is sovereign. The understanding and God-fearing Christian appreciates that all there is to fear, be it death, loss, pain, etc, abide under the sovereign control of the Lord of Hosts. A true feeling of security, then, comes from a healthy, inspired fear of God that inevitably produces obedience, respect, trust, reverence and deference. Only God can satisfy the real need of the human heart for purification and holiness. The God-fearing man never fails to remember this.

> *Since we have these promises, dear friends, let us purify ourselves from everything that contaminates body and spirit, perfecting holiness out of reverence (or fear; author's note) for God. (2 Cor. 7:1)*

As we dig deeper into the Scriptures brethren, we discover that holiness and the fear of the Lord are beautifully and wondrously aligned. Consider further what the Proverbs tell us of the fear of God –

> *But he who listens to me shall live securely, And will be at ease from the dread of evil." (Prov. 1:33)*

> *The fear of the LORD is to hate evil; Pride and arrogance and the evil way. (Prov. 8:13)*

> *The fear of the LORD is the beginning of wisdom, And the knowledge of the Holy One is understanding. (Prov. 9:10)*

Why is this? Because God alone is the fountain-head of wisdom, understanding, knowledge, meaning, truth, and moral purpose. We fear God because only He assumes the place of the uncreated One. He alone is sovereign and all powerful, able to create and destroy by divine decree, able to subdue or promote that which He has made for His glory. Life and death, blessing and cursing; these are in His hands and no other.

"Their Fear Toward Me is Taught by the Commandment of Men"

But isn't it true today brethren, that in the church there is a tendency to recreate and redefine God in our own image; to have more of a benign, man-sized God (Isaiah 29:13)? We skip gleefully over the many Bible passages that speak of the fearsome, holy wrath of God, yet in so doing we misrepresent His loving-kindness and tender mercies. Again, as with so much in the modern gospel to all people, there is only partial truth, which is no truth at all, but a cleverly disguised prescription for confusion and deprivation.

Few, if any, churches in America would invite *Robert Govett* or *G.H. Pember* (let alone the apostles Peter or Paul) to preach from their pulpits, were they alive today. And it would be hard to imagine *T. Austin-Sparks* or *Watchman Nee* being regular guests on Christian talk radio with their emphasis on the whole salvation of man – *spirit, soul and body*, and selective entrance into the Lord's Kingdom.

Is it not true brethren, that we have fabricated a uniquely kinder and friendlier deity, because that is what we modern believers feel comfortable with (it seems that comfort is more important today than accountability or truth); this is the gospel that appeals to those in search of emotional healing and personal well-being. Oh dear little ones, indeed He is a healer, a mender of emotional wounds, a friend and brother to us. Yes, indeed fellow saints, He is all these things and more, but He is also the awesome and terrible God who loathes evil and will not, under any circumstances, allow sin to pollute His universe.

Should we not duly fear Jesus Christ, who said –

> *"Every plant which My heavenly Father did not plant shall be uprooted." (Matt. 15:13)*

And reckon with other Scriptures that teach –

> *Sheol and Abaddon lie open before the LORD, How much more the hearts of men! (Prov. 15:11)*
>
> *God is a righteous judge, And a God who has indignation every day. If a man does not repent, He will sharpen His sword. He has bent His bow and made it ready. (Psa. 7:11-12)*
>
> *The fear of the LORD is the beginning of knowledge; Fools despise wisdom and instruction. (Prov. 1:7)*
>
> *"Then they will call to me but I will not answer; they will look for me but will not find me. Since they hated*

> *knowledge and did not choose to fear the Lord, since they would not accept my advice and spurned my rebuke, they will eat the fruit of their ways and be filled with the fruit of their schemes. For the waywardness of the simple will kill them, and the complacency of fools will destroy them; but whoever listens to me will live in safety and be at ease, without fear of harm." (Prov. 1:28-33)*

And –

> *How much severer punishment do you think he will deserve who has trampled under foot the Son of God, and has regarded as unclean the blood of the covenant by which he was sanctified, and has insulted the Spirit of grace? For we know Him who said, "VENGEANCE IS MINE, I WILL REPAY." And again, "THE LORD WILL JUDGE HIS PEOPLE." It is a terrifying thing to fall into the hands of the living God. (Heb. 10:29-31)*

Should we not tremble before the God who pronounced destruction and woe on the religious hypocrites who led people into judgment with their dead and deceptive teachings and example. Should we not rather fear the Lord who said to them in Matthew 23:33 –

> *"You serpents, you brood of vipers, how will you escape the sentence of hell?"*

But Does Not Love Cast Out All Fear?

The fear of God compels us to know, understand, and depend upon the will of the Lord, as represented in Holy Scripture and empowered by the indwelling Spirit. But, says the modern proof-text Christian, does not love cast out all fear? Does not the Bible teach that –

> *There is no fear in love. But perfect love drives out fear, because fear has to do with punishment. The one who fears is not made perfect in love. (1 John 4:18)*

True, very true, yet to fear God, unlike the fear of anything that is created, is healthy and good for us. He alone must be the object of our fear (Revelation 15:3-4). The fear of God stands distinct from all other fears, whether they be real or imagined. In this matter and as a necessary principle, we must allow the ever-teaching Spirit of Truth to place Scripture alongside Scripture to gain the whole counsel of the Lord. The same David who wrote –

> *The LORD is my light and my salvation; Whom shall I fear? The LORD is the defense of my life; Whom shall I dread? (Psa. 27:1)*

also wrote –

> *The fear of the LORD is clean, enduring forever; The judgments of the LORD are true; they are righteous altogether. (Psa. 19:9)*
>
> *Who is the man who fears the LORD? He will instruct him in the way he should choose. (Psa. 25:12)*
>
> *The secret of the LORD is for those who fear Him, And He will make them know His covenant. (Psa. 25:14)*

The man who fears the Lord waits upon Him in a posture of humility, dependence, deference, submission, obedience, trust, respect, and awe. When the Lord speaks, he listens. When He commands, he obeys. When He promises, he trusts Him. When He chastens, he learns. When He teaches, he esteems it as absolute truth. And when He appears in His Awesome Glory, he falls on his face as though dead (see John in the Revelation of our Lord).

Oh how I wish this would describe yours truly even on my best days brethren. Oh how we need to pray always for one another that this would be so for all His little ones. Oh Lord, save us from ourselves in Your Beloved and Holy Son!

When the Bible says that perfect love casts out fear it is referring to all creaturely fears that are unhealthy and unfounded. There is no incompatibility between our love for God and our fear of Him (Deuteronomy 10:12). It is the fear of the Lord that compels us to take sin as seriously as God does. It is the fear of the Lord that compels us to worship Him in spirit and in truth (John 4:24), by inspiring a reverential attitude towards His attributes.

> *But as for me, by Your abundant lovingkindness I will enter Your house, At Your holy temple I will bow in reverence for You. (Psa. 5:7)*

To Truly Know God as He is, is to Fear and Revere Him

It seems evident that the main reason we modern Christians do not fear the Lord as we should, is because we do not truly know Him as He is. With all the emphasis these days on worshipping in the spirit, experiencing God, and true spirituality, there is a disturbing lack of hard, spiritual teaching on the attributes of God. Just recently, I found myself listening again to a series of sermons given by A.W. Tozer (circa 1956-1958) on this subject, and I found myself grieving the absence of such powerful instruction in the church today. Dear saints, to know Him requires that we see Him as He is; and only His Spirit can lead us deeper into His very being. To see the Lord Jesus Christ in all of His unsurpassed holiness and glory and righteousness and truth, is to see the Eternal and Most High Father who sits over the circle of the earth. Oh that we would be blinded to everything and everyone else that we would truly behold Him, and see with the eyes of the Spirit that we are as nothing, and less than nothing.

Perhaps more young (and old, for that matter) Christians would take God more seriously if they discovered what He is like, that He is in fact *holy, omnipotent, omnipresent, omniscient, all-wise, creative, preeminent, infinite, eternal, perfect, loving, merciful, judgmental, exclusive, a god of justice, immense*, and so on. Perhaps we all would fear Him more if we were more consistently reminded of the degree to which our God is unlike us. Instead, the preachers of the day would bring Him down from His throne as did the serpent in the garden. They would suffer the temptation to present the Most High in man-like terms, so that we might relate to Him easier. They would forget that the man Jesus came to lead us up to the Father, not the other way around. They would devise a theology that is man-centered and humanistic rather than God-centered, God-sourced and God-glorifying.

Oh Lord, please forgive us, for how we have strayed so terribly.

There is Fear in the Gospel as Well as Love

Oh that we would realize and learn dear saints, that both the love of God and the fear of God flow together to lead us into the very heart of our God!

The hope of the gospel message does not remove fear entirely, as psychology does, or seek to rationalize it away, but it consists in having the appropriate fear object. Christ's teaching in Matthew 10 on the fear of God in no way conflicts with other passages that emphasize our love relationship with Himself and the Father. We can love God deeply and spiritually, while also recognizing our utter dependence on Him; our absolute hopelessness apart from His salvation and grace. We can praise Him for His loving-kindness and tender-mercies, while also acknowledging His fearful power and preeminence; that indeed our very destiny lies in the hollow of His hand.

If we fear God most truly, we should necessarily fear everything else less. Reverence for the Lord includes an acknowledgement of the power of God and a sober recognition of the consequences of trying to violate His ordained will. Reverence for the Lord is a healthy recognition of our creature-hood. Man is dependent upon one greater and more glorious than himself, and it is the very foundation of wisdom to recognize this fact. From the fear of God proceeds a unique outlook on life that influences every thought, action, and intention. When we fear God we take Him into account as He is, and what He thinks about a particular subject is the baseline upon which all opinion and conduct is measured. To acknowledge and exalt God's exclusive attributes, to recognize that He alone inhabits a place above all else, is to fear Him as the Bible commands. No man can ever be the same after coming to an awareness of the preeminent and perfect nature of God.

Conclusion

> *The conclusion, when all has been heard, is: fear God and keep His commandments, because this applies to every person. For God will bring every act to judgment, everything which is hidden, whether it is good or evil. (Ecc. 12:13-14)*

Only those who heed every word and command given by Our Lord Jesus Christ will share with Him in His Holy Kingdom coming soon to this earth. Let us therefore return to a balanced teaching and understanding of this matter among His people. Let us teach from the whole Bible and not just the parts that appease our fickle human sensitivities. Let us bring new converts to the true God and the real Jesus Christ, without neglecting the tougher aspects of His sovereignty, character and judgment. Let us forfeit the counsel of the ungodly and return to instruction in doctrine and righteousness (2 Timothy 3:16) from the Holy Scriptures.

In Jesus' precious and mighty name, we pray that this would be so. Amen.

Religion or Relationship

Now we are aware of the dictionary definition of the term *religion*. What we are referring to below is any system of belief and practice that has no inspiration or foundation in the Word of God, and effectively denies the living presence and power of God in the complete salvation (*spirit, soul and body*) of man.

Now the religious urge is immensely powerful in man, and the devil knows it. He knew it and acted upon it in the garden with the very first lie. He is masterful at using humanly-derived religion, trappings and traditions to keep us from the presence of the Living God. With subtle deception, he secretly sets about his work of replacing the expression of spiritual life with machinery, true things with shadows, divine power and wisdom with human effort, intellect and initiative, and an intimate fellowship with the Lord God, with what amounts to a man-mediated hierarchy.

From where I stand, my friends, this is largely what this thing called Christianity has become, and I am not at all limiting this reference to Romanism either. It seems everywhere you turn, more and more believers are adopting practices, expectations and opinions that indicate that they love their religion more than they love the Living God.

Dear brethren, this saddens me tremendously. For it is this very religion, and all of its machinery, that is blinding us to our need for an intimate and life-filling encounter with a redeeming God. Religion, by its very nature, puts its trust in man, and not God, so it is, in essence, the perfect realization of the pagan, humanistic trend sweeping the world and the church.

Yet, it is insidious because it is, at its core, LIFELESS and POWERLESS!

No mere religion can turn a devil into a disciple, or a rebel into a beloved son. No empty orthodoxy can turn a sinner into a saint, or hope in any way, shape or form to rescue the sin-ravaged soul of man, and restore him to his place in the garden of God.

Only Jesus Christ, abiding within each of us, can do this! Why then do we persist in undermining and sidelining His redemptive and restorative work on the cross at every turn. Why are we believers so readily titillated by the latest trick, trend or technique that seeks to supplement or replace the divinely ordained process of sanctification? Why is the Helper and Comforter, Teacher and Shepherd, the One who came down from heaven to dwell among us, and die for us, seemingly never enough?

Did not the Jew's religion blind them to the love of God as revealed in their Messiah? Consider the harshness of our Lord's language as He condemned them in the most extreme terms for obscuring the true God with their oral traditions and practices. If we called any individual or group a "*brood of vipers*" or "*serpents*" today we would be promptly condemned as divisive and critical. Yet, it was their religion, you see, and ours today, that establishes the framework for exalting men in the place of the Most High.

> *"... but I know you, that you do not have the love of God in yourselves." (John 5:42)*

And do we?

All of their religion had taught them absolutely nothing about God; that He in fact loved them dearly, and standing right before them, with His arms stretched out, ready to embrace them, was proof of that love.

Our Lord, when He left this earth, did not leave us with any system or methodology, or *religion*. He left us with the Holy Spirit that enables and empowers us from within to relate to Himself and the Father on a divine and intimate level. Neither did He leave us with a song book or memory verse, but newness of life and the animating power of Himself as the Living Vine. Indeed, He alone was the Way home to the Father. He was the Truth about God and man and how the two could be reconciled, once and for all. Without Him, we can do nothing. This was true 2,000 years ago and it is still true today.

> *"I am the vine, you are the branches; he who abides in Me and I in him, he bears much fruit, for apart from Me you can do nothing." (John 15:5)*

It is most interesting that James in the New Testament defines "*pure and undefiled religion*" as loving service, and not faithful adherence to creeds and tradition, or the smells and bells of church buildings, or any vain form of liturgical reality. It is the love of Christ and the Father spilling out into the streets, and into our homes, and into the broken lives of the most vulnerable among us.

The Bible is clear here, my friends, so please don't consider me too harsh in this assessment.

Religion, as it has become, by its very nature constrains, binds, obligates and obscures the expression of divine reality and life. It distances one from the ultimate object of worship. It esteems external observance and conformity over what is really at the heart of a man. Despite its bold claims, it directs our faith away from God, and towards created things, especially human beings and the objects of their adornment. Religion thrives solely on human energy, human ideas, human disciplines and soulish human sentiment. It is essentially man-sized, and not god-sized, reaching into the highest heavens. It is primarily of the flesh and not of the spirit, so it is incapable of entering into spiritual realities.

It defies the *mystery of godliness* and the abandoned life at the heart of Paul's gospel. It fosters a righteousness that cannot adequately withstand the rigors of life, the temptations of the flesh and the world, nor the assaults of the adversary. It is loud and brash, and promises so much, yet delivers so little. By necessity, it must borrow from the world, because it holds no innate power or vitality of its own. Inevitably it leaves one confused and empty, and even more estranged from their God; the very opposite of what it claimed to be able to do. Because it is a deception and a mighty one at that, it can be said to represent the enemy's greatest work. It knows nothing of the living context of restored fellowship offered by our Savior. It is deaf and dumb before the Living Word, accompanied by the Author Himself, as He fulfills its meaning by fleshing it out in our daily lives.

Religion may inspire you; in this there is no doubt. It may sweep you aloft in a rapturous chorus of praise and sentiment. It may appeal to a part of your soul (*sentiment, intellect and emotion*) that wants to be appealed to. It is happy to meet your consumer needs and desires, and to satisfy the senses. It may make it look like you are venturing forth into the holiest of all, with fine linen and brass and glimmering light. But, my friends, it will never, ever change you, or save you from this hopeless body of death. It will not because fundamentally, it cannot.

> *Wretched man that I am! Who will set me free from the body of this death? Thanks be to God through Jesus Christ our Lord! (Rom. 7:24-25)*

Only the Shepherd of your soul can do that. Only Life can ultimately deal with death and the power it holds over a sin-cursed creation.

> *Now I say this, brethren, that flesh and blood cannot inherit the kingdom of God; nor does the perishable inherit the imperishable. Behold, I tell you a mystery; we will not all sleep, but we will all be changed, in a moment, in the twinkling of an eye, at the last trumpet; for the trumpet will sound, and the dead will be raised imperishable, and we will be changed. For this perishable must put on the imperishable, and this mortal must put on immortality. But when this perishable will have put on the imperishable, and this mortal will have put on immortality, then will come about the saying that is written, "DEATH IS SWALLOWED UP in victory. "O DEATH, WHERE IS YOUR VICTORY? O DEATH, WHERE IS YOUR STING?" The sting of death is sin, and the power of sin is the law; but thanks be to God, who gives us the victory through our Lord Jesus Christ. (1 Cor. 15:50-57)*

Oh Lord, we thank You that You alone are that Life, and that victory, and we pray that You might lead us further and deeper by the Spirit into You as our Life in this world. Oh Lord, let it be so, in Jesus' name. Amen.

Christianity – An Inside Job

If you are like me, then perhaps you have wondered at a practical level how this thing called Christianity actually works. I am not so much referring here to the high theology of it, but rather, how does it genuinely transform us from selfish, earth-bound, soulish slaves of sin and self, to loving and obedient children of God, with eternity written on our hearts?

Many Scriptures in the Bible suggest that our dark hearts, blackened by an inherited nature and a lifetime of sin and self-will, can supernaturally, by the indwelling life of Jesus Christ, be transformed and restored to the image of our Maker. Here are some examples –

> *And do not be conformed to this world, but be transformed by the renewing of your mind, so that you may prove what the will of God is, that which is good and acceptable and perfect. (Rom. 12:2)*

> *Therefore we do not lose heart, but though our outer man is decaying, yet our inner man is being renewed day by day. (2 Cor. 4:16)*

> *And although you were formerly alienated and hostile in mind, engaged in evil deeds, yet He has now reconciled you in His fleshly body through death, in order to present you before Him holy and blameless and beyond reproach—if indeed you continue in the faith firmly established and steadfast, and not moved away from the hope of the gospel...the mystery which has been hidden from the past ages and generations, but has now been manifested to His saints, to whom God willed to make known what is the riches of the glory of this mystery*

> *among the Gentiles, which is Christ in you, the hope of glory. (Col. 1:21-27)*

Clearly the Scriptures indicate throughout that this renewing or transforming work is an inside job; that God (the Holy Spirit) actually takes up residence within us to deal with the problem at its very core. This makes sense. If the real problem resides within us, deep in the hidden chambers of our heart and mind at the source of all thought, desire and will, how then can any external effort or solution have any real or lasting impact?

It is what we are on the inside that ultimately defines us and makes us what we are. All of our behaviors, habits, instincts, words and patterns (what the Scriptures refer to as "*strongholds*") merely flow from what we already are deep down. Any religion or humanly derived system attempting to address the human condition, that does not go deeper than how a man acts on the surface of life, is ultimately destined to fail.

The Bible teaches that the salvation of man, in all its fullness, constitutes the saving of the human spirit (*the new birth in the Spirit*), the human soul (*walking in the spirit, and growing by spiritual milk and meat*), then finally the human body (*at the resurrection, when the physical takes on a new and glorified body*). And although theologians have many lofty names for what is happening here – justification, sanctification, glorification, etc. – what is essentially going on is that the Savior is settings things back in order from the inside out, such that the *spirit* directs the *soul* and the soul directs the physical *body* in fulfilling the will of God.

When our Lord commands us to come to Him, and follow Him, He is not offering us a remedy or technique for suppressing our carnal, God-defying condition. He is offering us a new, wholly restored nature, "rooted and built up in Him" (Colossians 2:7). We are to become a new person in Christ, with an entirely new and effective source of life and inspiration.

As pure and simple Christians, we are aware how this process occurs over time as we learn to present our lives in loving submission to the Source of all life. The renewing of our hearts and minds is the only way we will ever truly be changed, my friends, and for this we must be released from the old self. There is no short cut or superficial remedy to what truly ails us.

As the Lord draws us deeper into Himself, it becomes increasingly clear that no hidden area of our lives can be left undisturbed; not the deep, dark pride of life, not the seemingly indomitable power of self, not our deluded faith in created things, nor the lusts of the flesh and the world that reduce us to dumb puppets of passion.

Such strongholds will not surrender without a fight. They will rear up, and stubbornly resist any attempt to undermine their control over our lives. They must ultimately be shaken loose, sometimes painfully and violently, by the indwelling and transforming Spirit. Many have likened this process to a kind of internal surgery, whereby Our Lord, with loving precision and the sharp blade of His Word, cuts out the cancerous elements residing within our heart.

Our Lord is not as interested in changing our conduct as He is with what exists far beneath the surface at root level; the very elements that define us, that which we grip so tightly; those powers and forces that we so unconsciously serve. Here is where haughty idols reign over us with iron-clad control, where the self sits proudly and stubbornly enthroned, shaking its little pink fists at God. Like an active volcano, once the eruption occurs and dragon's breath and liquid flame start spewing forth to the surface, it is too late. Deep down, hidden beneath our outer shell, is the hellish cauldron where all is determined and set in motion.

It is here, my friends, where modern-day psychology and *small 'c' christianity* completely miss the mark. With all of their step-by-step methods and behavior modification techniques, all they can do is target how we live and what they can see on the surface, not the inner regions of the heart where *spirit touches bone.*

The preacher who is constantly encouraging us to study more, pray more and be more honest or more kind needs to question whether anything is truly happening beneath the surface. My experience is that those who are truly being changed from the inside by the transforming power of God's Spirit – being restored to the image of their Creator, to love Him and conform to all that He is – don't need to be nagged to do what increasingly comes naturally to them. This is very much like telling an apple tree to bear apples and not peaches.

My friends, let us learn to simply trust the One who made us, who knows what we are and how we are wired, to effectively solve the problem of man's condition at its source. Be wary of any attempts to get you to first act differently as a means to changing what you are. This message, prevalent in much of the psycho-heresy being preached from our pulpits, has it all backwards, as I trust you can see.

And, dear friends, it can never work. What you will be led into is heart-numbing legalism and mere conformity to men and groups and systems.

THIS IS NOT, AND CAN NEVER BE, THE AUTHENTIC CHRISTIANITY OF THE BIBLE – that restores and transforms a man from the inside out, in preparation for an eternity with an eternal and holy God. As our Lord draw us near unto Himself, and changes us from within, what we will experience will be far richer than any religious gymnastics or compelled morality; for our inward man will be renewed moment-by-moment, and day by day.

As He gradually releases us from long-held idolatries and dependencies, He wants us to grab on ever more tightly to Him, to trust Him to replace every unredeemed and harmful habit, security blanket, coping mechanism, attitude, opinion and sin that keeps us pinned down and failing in this broken world. No vile and godless element within us will remain untouched as He brings the full force of His Spirit, Word and Love to bear in releasing us to true victory and life. In closing, we will recall the words of David, in Psalm 51 –

> *Wash me thoroughly from my iniquity*
> *And cleanse me from my sin...*
> *Purify me with hyssop, and I shall be clean;*
> *Wash me, and I shall be whiter than snow...*
> *Create in me a clean heart, O God,*
> *And renew a steadfast spirit within me. (Psa. 51:1-10)*

You Are Not Your Own

Or do you not know that your body is a temple of the Holy Spirit who is in you, whom you have from God, and that you are not your own? For you have been bought with a price: therefore glorify God in your body. (1 Cor. 6:19-20)

Therefore I urge you, brethren, by the mercies of God, to present your bodies a living and holy sacrifice, acceptable to God, which is your spiritual service of worship. (Rom. 12:1)

For not one of us lives for himself, and not one dies for himself; for if we live, we live for the Lord, or if we die, we die for the Lord; therefore whether we live or die, we are the Lord's. (Rom. 14:7-8)

"I have been crucified with Christ; and it is no longer I who live, but Christ lives in me; and the life which I now live in the flesh I live by faith in the Son of God, who loved me and gave Himself up for me." (Gal. 2:20)

My friends and brethren, the Christian life is very much the *exchanged* life. Whether we comprehend it completely or not, we have voluntarily forfeited our right to exist that He, the Lord Jesus Christ, might live in us. By accepting the immense and eternal benefit of the cross we have also affirmed the obligation to lay down our lives for Him and His brethren. If we have duly submitted to the blessed Lordship of Jesus Christ, then we no longer hold any right to govern our lives as we choose. We are, in fact, not our own. The title to our lives has been rendered unto the Son of God. Maybe allow that to settle into your spirit a little bit before reading further.

For as we begin to discover in this life of faith, Christianity is very much about laying one thing down in order to take up something else. Recall how Jesus lovingly invited us to take up His yoke, which was easy and light, in exchange for a heavy burden which is impossible to bear. By giving His all for Adam's fallen offspring, we can now surrender all of Adam's sin-wrought burden to Him.

Meaty theology for sure, but what practical impact would this newfound reality have on us once we really got hold of it at the spirit level? What difference would it make in our lives? In our testimony? In our homes, jobs, activities, conversations, thoughts and motives?

In order for us to be filled with Him, with inherent newness of life, we must first be emptied; emptied of self, the world and the flesh, pride, stubborn self-will; in short anything that is less than He, and all that He represents.

This is powerful stuff, my brethren. Despite what many will tell you, Christianity has absolutely nothing to do with improving the human life (which is nothing short of *humanism*), and everything to do with the appropriation of a new and heavenly life.

Just as our Lord willingly and graciously laid His life down for the Father, we must surely lay down ours for Him. And just as He put off His grave clothes and walked out of that festering tomb, alive in all the fullness of the Spirit Life, so must we. And this new and better life, lived above and apart from the desperate tumult of the carnal world, is lived in Him and through Him and for Him, only that it might magnify Him.

Our life, as the truth of Scripture most powerfully confirms, now belongs completely to Him. He purchased it at a tremendous price, with His very blood. Not that we would become mere chattels or slaves, but redeemed children in the heavenly household of God. Only here can we once and forever realize our truest potential as defined by the Maker – to enjoy God and His Family long into eternity.

Yet, as we all know, getting there is the tricky part, isn't it? It is so much easier to slaughter and sacrifice some dumb beast on a physical alter at a single point in time, than to lay down our lives in constant and living sacrifice. It is in the giving up, the emptying, this reduction, that we stumble and fail, and are prevented from apprehending all the blessings and wonders that the Lord extends to us.

What is it today that we are still holding back from Him, my brethren? What aspect of our lives are we still stubbornly clinging to as *our own*, or off limits and untouchable?

Each of us will have a different response to this question, but the result is the same. Our Lord can never be satisfied with only fragments of our lives, or an incomplete sacrifice. In order to restore and bless us fully, we must surrender fully all things to Him who loves us and promises us so much in His Son. The exchange must be complete, all for all, without exception.

I have spent today considering over and over again that "*my life is not my own, my life is not my own*". Yet, on the surface it appears that it still very much belongs to me; that I am still very much the lord of my life and king of my castle. Oh, if only I would release it all to Him, right here and now.

What is it then that holds us back; that prevents us from living completely in and through and for Him? Perhaps the answer is found in the verse above, where Paul writes that "*the life which I now live in the flesh I live by faith in the Son of God, who loved me and gave Himself for me.*"

It is by faith you see, that we are able to apprehend His life, and by love that we in turn lay ours down. We must trust Him completely in order to surrender to Him completely, and our love for Him must be unrivalled and uncompromising. Once again, it all seems to come down to this thing called love, and all that makes it real – t*rust, hope, gentleness, meekness, humility, and honesty.*

Why is this so hard for us, my brethren, when Jesus assured us that His yoke was so easy and light? What is so wrong with us that we just can't seem to let go of ourselves and our precious little control? It still gives us something doesn't it? It still meets some raw need in us?

Perhaps what we have to realize is that all of the needs inside us, if indeed the Creator placed them there, can be met only by Him, not any created thing existing in the world, ourselves or other people.

So where does this bring us, my friends? If this is true, then what does it mean? What are the implications? It all sounds pretty serious, doesn't it?

"Last Chance to Turn Back"

Some years back, I was at an amusement park with my family. On one of the scary rides, there were a series of exits that you could take if you really didn't want to go through with it. "*Last Chance to Turn Back*" was the message on the final sign.

As the pressing reality of the Christian life draws us ever deeper into God's presence, it will increasingly demand more of us in the way of trust, commitment, consecration, courage and love. As our Lord strips us down to bare facts, and we are asked to surrender the many things we hold dear – our precious time and money, our status, rights and claims in the world, our blind devotion to things and pleasure, our relentless fears, and the many sordid idols that keep us rooted in this life – what we will discover is that all that we have left is Him. He is the only One standing there in the place where we once stood.

This is what we signed on for brethren. I am sorry if something less than this or something easier than this was promised you by another. This is the real deal, and must surely cause each of us to consider whether we truly want to advance further into His life or retreat back into our own.

Yet how can we turn back now after having tasted of the glorious life? We must advance, and grow, for this is why we exist now. He is all we have? Once begun, is there really any turning back for the surrendered child of God? Once we have tasted the living bread from heaven, can there truly be any other?

> *So Jesus said to the twelve, "You do not want to go away also, do you?" Simon Peter answered Him, "Lord,*

> *to whom shall we go? You have words of eternal life."*
> *(John 6:67-68)*

We must never be afraid, my friends, at the prospect of losing it all. We must never listen to all the voices that keep trying to convince us that it just doesn't make any sense, that we have to protect ourselves and hold tightly to all the many aspects of our lives that have shaped and manipulated us since birth.

And don't be troubled when that old familiar self starts to change before your eyes, when a new and strange consciousness begins to inhabit your heart and mind. Just trust Him my friends, and believe with all that He gives you that He loves you, and will never leave you nor forsake you.

Do not think for one second that He doesn't know or appreciate how hard this is for you. Certainly He does, and this is why throughout all the Word of God we find His loving promise that He will uphold us; that He will carry us onward to victory and peace; that in the end we will receive such great and precious promises. The price is very high indeed. Yet the reward, the inheritance of the saints, is priceless.

Let us tackle this question from another angle if we might – is our life as a newfound Christian, claimed by the Most High in His Son, really our own? Are we free to come and go as we please, to hold and release things as we will, to live as lord of all that we believe to be ours? Are there any claims upon us that supersede what we consider our freedom and independence? Are we truly the master of our choices and circumstances, or is there another, whose thoughts and intents toward us take precedent?

It seems all so very un-American or un-western doesn't it – this idea that we may not be free to come and go as we please; that our rights and liberties as earthly or national citizens are somehow limited?

Yet, my brethren, when we surrendered ourselves to Him absolutely (assuming of course that this is what we did), what did we think it could mean? What were the practical consequences? Let us revisit the words of the Apostle Paul to the Corinthians –

> *Or do you not know that your body is a temple of the Holy Spirit who is in you, whom you have from God, and that you are not your own? For you have been bought with a price: therefore glorify God in your body. (1 Cor. 6:19-20)*

"*Not your own*" – now, now brother, calm down. Don't start getting too radical or extreme. The Scriptures don't really mean that in its fullest extent. It's language, you know, religious hyperbole or some such thing.

Oh really? My reading of this, and I believe I have the Spirit's authority here, is that if indeed God has claimed us as His dwelling place, then the deed and title to our lives henceforth belongs to Him.

Not yourself!

Not your family!

Not your husband or wife!

Not your nation or government!

Not your church group or denomination!

But to Him! And His claim on us is absolute, unconditional and non-negotiable. And if we feel compelled to squirm out from under this, then I fear that perhaps we might not truly comprehend or accept what sonship and discipleship are all about.

> *Therefore I urge you, brethren, by the mercies of God, to present your bodies a living and holy sacrifice, acceptable to God, which is your spiritual service of worship. (Rom. 12:1)*

A "*living and holy sacrifice.*" Not some dead beast slung upon a bloody altar, but alive and breathing, thinking and choosing, and walking this way or that; with nothing spared or held back, with nothing claimed as untouchable, the whole thing relinquished without condition or limit, offered freely and willfully to He who is singularly worthy of such a claim.

Dear brethren – our God has really been hammering home this concept to me lately – that I must lay it all down before Him, as a lamb perfectly trusting the shepherd; that I need to let it all go; this world and all of my inborn ways of responding to it, its hopes and ambitions, its empty promises, everything without exception or excuse; even all of the many aspects of my personality and identity that have served or supported me for so long, at least on a worldly level.

I must confess to all of you here that this is more than a little frightening. So much easier it is to come out of the world and abandon our love for it, or our pride in it, than to allow ourselves to be so nakedly exposed, to trust something outside of ourselves so utterly. Here is where our faith requires something profoundly real and raw. Here are all of those difficult Scriptures that we modern Christians are so quick to powder over or ignore.

You must realize that I have always attempted in so many ways, to plan and control my life down to the last detail. Yet, now He is saying that this deeply ingrained control has to give way to absolute trust in Him. I must relinquish it all; even all of it that helps life to make sense to me, that helps me cope in a world under the thumb of the devil and the carnal whims of man.

From the earliest age I learned, rather painfully, that men and the institutions of the world are not to be trusted; not strangers nor even those who were my own blood. Probably before I even realized what I was doing at a conscious level, I had resigned to take my life into my own hands, to become my own guardian, provider, master and protector. Only then (so I assumed at some psychological or instinctive level) would I stand a better chance of not being hurt or disappointed. And for many years this has hardened into a muscle that is flexed constantly and as naturally as breathing in and breathing out. It runs hard and deep into everything I do and think and it is actually almost impossible to imagine myself without these coping and defense mechanisms; these controlling instincts that preserve and protect me from the world and everything in it.

It's a subtle form of idolatry really, and yet it is so easy and almost natural for me to justify. It protects me (or at least promises to), gives me confidence (when really deep down I am a small little man in my own eyes), it projects me into the world such that the world even rewards it. We become what many would consider successful. Yet, it too, like every other vain thing, must be seen for what it is and surrendered to Him. Trusting in Him when we have no control, such as a child does (they have no choice), will keep us from reducing His place on the throne of our lives.

Slowly, gradually, painfully, all that I have tried to bring under my sphere of influence and control over these many years is being released. And it must be so, for only then can the real Lord and Master be presented and advanced. Better that I step back into the shadows and He is revealed. He, not I, is worthy of the world's attention. He is the one deemed as worthy by the Father.

Dear saints, while out walking the other night, I heard His voice just as crystal clear in my spirit as anything, and He asked me; "*Do you trust Me my son?*" I replied that He knows all things, and that I didn't feel worthy to give an answer. But I wanted to trust Him, and to know that I could. You see, we cannot trust Him as we should and still be in control over our little empire down here, whatever it is. I have somehow made *being in control* so intrinsically part of my life that it has become a reflex. It offers me something, something I need to sustain myself in this world. It is a lie and a dangerous one at that.

My sense is that this is typically the last frontier of the self that we hold back from Him. Again, it may be relatively easy to give up our first love of people, family, things or our pride of life. Yet, self-will and self-governance do not fall so readily. They are bound into the very fabric of our being and our personhood; they form our reality and experience; they rise up almost on their own, and usually with all of the best intentions. They may have served us admirably for years, and yet if these last bastions of the self-life are not surrendered to Him, as is everything else, then His claim on us can never be complete; we will have not left all to follow our Lord as the *Shepherd of our Souls.*

He must know that we love Him and trust Him completely; that left with nothing to cling to or depend on, we will brave this evil world until His purposes in us are realized. Oh, dear saints, don't think for one second that this is just another religious exercise to be attended to, for it is so much more than that. And to even associate it with such is to admit that His Lordship has not penetrated that deeply into our heart and lives.

This is not that at all, but an often bewildering journey into darkness and uncertainty. If being in control has become something of a god to you, then He will most certainly ask you to give it up. The very ground beneath your feet will start to tremble and shake. All that you have trusted in when life gets hard, and circumstance and people press in on you will be out of reach. All you will have is Him, and His loving assurances. He will be all you have because you must come to the place where you realize that He is all you need.

My friends, if this sounds more than a little like the self dying, then there is a reason for that. For this is precisely what it means to die unto ourselves that the Lord Jesus Christ may be duly formed in us; that all we are will be assimilated and redeemed by His life and essence. Just as our Lord fell backwards into the arms of the Heavenly Father on the way to Calvary and the cross, we too must come to trust Him perfectly, as all that we are is exposed, stripped away, and consecrated to the Lord of All Life. He invariably must bring us through the fire of sanctification, that all of our tricks, and strategies for preserving and advancing ourselves in the world may be burned away. They are merely phantoms anyway!

Do you trust Him perfectly – He whose love for you exceeds that of any other you know or trust? Will you present yourself to Him as a total living sacrifice with nothing held back? Will you submit to what must be in order for Christ to be fully formed in you, and His life manifested fully? Will you say to Him – "*Lord I want You to take all of me or none at all*" – and trust Him perfectly through whatever darkness, disorientation and uncertainty that will be necessary to bring this about?

My friends, we are complete in Him, as the Scripture reminds us, and His power and provision is more than capable of dealing with these hidden idols of the self that are so inherently rooted in all that we are. There is no good thing in us that He needs to retain in order that the Life of God may be created in us. He will perform a new thing, a heavenly thing, and there is no need for Him to resort to any of the ways or wisdom of man to do this. In fact, He more often than not confounds these in order that we might know that His ways are so much higher than our ways. Real and radical change (a transfer of trust and lordship from the self to the Lord Jesus Christ in the Father's will) at the level we are talking about here can never be the result of human self-discipline, will power or any related psychological tricks.

Please know that I am not writing these words as someone who has crossed over the Jordan already, but as someone who is knee-deep and presently going through some very awkward and mortifying experiences. Deep down where spirit touches bone, I am learning rather painfully that He is all I have and need, and that trusting Him is not optional or supplemental to the Christian life, but rather the very essence of it. He will hold us up, and catch us when we fall, and carry us through – this is beyond question. All that remains is for us to embrace this, and to let our Lord do what only He can do –

> *...and to know this love that surpasses knowledge—that you may be filled to the measure of all the fullness of God. Now to him who is able to do immeasurably more than all we ask or imagine, according to his power that is at work within us – (Eph. 3:19-20)*

Oh Gracious and Faithful Father in Heaven – We ask that in forming Your Son in us none of our idols will be spared, including the many aspects of the self-life that we have come to depend on to provide for and protect us in this world. We pray that You will take all of us or none at all, and that You will bring us lovingly to the place of trust and total reliance on You. Help us, dear Father, to fall blindly into Your care as did Your Precious Son on the way to the cross.

In Jesus' glorious name, we pray. Amen.

Religion and the Thirsty Soul

I love how David poetically equates his dependence on God with physical sustenance in Psalm 63 –

> *O God, You are my God; I shall seek You earnestly;*
> *My soul thirsts for You, my flesh yearns for You,*
> *In a dry and weary land where there is no water.*
> *(Psa. 63:1)*

And again how another thirsty soul offers this same imagery in Psalm 42 –

> *As the deer pants for the water brooks, So my soul pants for You, O God. My soul thirsts for God, for the living God. (Psa. 42:1-2)*

Here were individuals who, at the deepest level of spiritual awareness, yearned for more than what this created realm could offer. Here also, we see human language being pushed to its very limit as it feebly attempts to capture the intimate condition of a soul longing after its creator. Here is the language of expressive human need, of yearning, of a heart crying out desperately to survive in a dry and barren land.

Our Lord also employed this transcendent language when He spoke to the Samaritan woman at the well –

> *There came a woman of Samaria to draw water. Jesus said to her, "Give Me a drink." For His disciples had gone away into the city to buy food. Therefore the Samaritan woman said to Him, "How is it that You, being a Jew, ask me for a drink since I am a Samaritan*

woman?" (For Jews have no dealings with Samaritans.) Jesus answered and said to her, "If you knew the gift of God, and who it is who says to you, 'Give Me a drink,' you would have asked Him, and He would have given you living water."

She said to Him, "Sir, You have nothing to draw with and the well is deep; where then do You get that living water? "You are not greater than our father Jacob, are You, who gave us the well, and drank of it himself and his sons and his cattle?"

Jesus answered and said to her, "Everyone who drinks of this water will thirst again; but whoever drinks of the water that I will give him shall never thirst; but the water that I will give him will become in him a well of water springing up to eternal life." (John 4:7-14)

Clearly brethren, the text-book descriptions found in our earth-bound religion and formalized Christian faith fail miserably when trying to capture the vocabulary of this inner thirst. It penetrates far deeper and wider than any derived scholarship, tradition, program or method-driven ministry, or the quaint booklets presented to new converts each Sunday.

Those among the *fellowship of the thirsty soul* crave so much more, you see. And perhaps more importantly, they are acutely aware of the natural incapacity of religion (as it has come to be) or any other created thing to satisfy this mysterious, inner thirst.

My dear friend, if you are tired and burned out in your service to our Lord, then perhaps this is what you are experiencing.

I must confess to you that I, for one, am tired of thirsting over and over again, only to be left even more parched and barren than the time before. This is not what this new life was ever intended to be, nor should it ever be acknowledged as the normal Christian experience. We were created, after all, by Him, and for Him, in order that we might live and grow in Him. And the first lie uttered in the garden is still, to this day, negating this fundamental reality for most inhabitants of the earth (and sadly, many twice-born Christians).

Clearly, the thirsty soul, panting after the Source of all life, will be content with nothing less than the abiding presence and spirit of the Living God. Anything less is mere sugar water, and immediately recognizable for what it is. Like soda pop, it may snap and fizz for a moment, but it will never satisfy that deep spiritual thirst, which represents the absence of God at the center of our inner life.

The real and living water, offering real sustenance and vitality does not flow from this earth, or out of our temples and creeds and man-made fountains; it flows from He who made us, and seeks to stamp His image on our spirit, that we may love Him and enjoy Him forever without end.

The reaction of the woman at the well to Jesus' invitation of living water was –

> *"Sir, give me this water, so I will not be thirsty nor come all the way here to draw." (John 4:15)*

And that is my prayer here and now for all of us panting after God, that no longer will we come to the world's well, whatever it happens to be, hoping to be satisfied, but ever walking away unfilled.

> *"Blessed are those who hunger and thirst for righteousness, for they shall be satisfied." (Matt. 5:6)*
>
> *Jesus said to them, "I am the bread of life; he who comes to Me will not hunger, and he who believes in Me will never thirst." (John 6:35)*
>
> *"They will hunger no longer, nor thirst anymore; nor will the sun beat down on them, nor any heat; for the Lamb in the center of the throne will be their shepherd, and will guide them to springs of the water of life; and God will wipe every tear from their eyes." (Rev. 7:16-17)*

May Our Heavenly Father satisfy your hunger and thirst for righteousness and for His Son.

The Reconciling Wisdom and Purpose of God

> *For it was the Father's good pleasure for all the fullness to dwell in Him, and through Him to reconcile all things to Himself, having made peace through the blood of His cross; through Him, I say, whether things on earth or things in heaven. (Col. 1:19-20)*

> *And He put all things in subjection under His feet, and gave Him as head over all things to the church, which is His body, the fullness of Him who fills all in all. (Eph. 1:22-23)*

Dear saints, I dare say the Lord has been revealing some mighty things to us lately, and the last few days in particular have been quite extraordinary. Almost out of nowhere and so unexpectedly, He launched me on a whirlwind tour through the Scriptures revealing aspects of various matters that on the surface did not appear connected in any way: the usurping of man's dominion on the earth by the deceiver, the rebellion and conflict in the heavenly places, the division of Ephraim (and the northern tribes of Israel) from his brothers. Fascinating, I thought, but what is the point Lord; what are You trying to show me?

My brethren – when we are called to the Father through the Son, into Himself and His Kingdom, we are called to a particular wisdom and understanding that defies and usurps all that we know and have known as defiant creatures on this earth. It is a wisdom and a way set in stark contrast to the manner of life being wrought by the current condition as we comprehend it. And more than this we are called to a demonstration of God's wisdom so perfectly executed and expressed in His Son, who, as the Bible teaches, is the fullness of all things in God. This wisdom serves to fulfill the great work of God in this age; which is nothing less than the complete and perfect reconciliation of all things to Himself in and through His Beloved Son, the Lord Jesus Christ.

The amazing and seldom expressed truth is that, as His redeemed body, the church in its collective calling has been called to share actively in God's reconciling work through His Son, and to demonstrate this wisdom throughout His creation. The highest ends of this wisdom as we will see, are familiar themes running through all the pages of the Bible, from beginning to end – *peace, unity, reconciliation, redemption, and restoration.*

I believe the Lord, in taking me through His Word, back to the origins of things and into the depths and height of His active realm (both seen and unseen), peering into the dark councils of the heavenly places where fallen beings assume an unnatural dominion over the earth – has moved me to consider the extent to which the scope of His reconciling wisdom and purpose is so much grander and more expansive than anything I had before realized.

> *"How large and how god-sized is your understanding of the awesome and universal magnitude of My reconciling purpose? How big is your Christ?"*

– such were the hard and piercing questions put to me by that still small voice.

And I ask the same of you here: Have you fully and completely, deep down in the very fiber of your understanding and life, comprehended the awesome enormity of His redemptive and reconciling purpose and ministry? I ask this because the church in all of its presentation of the gospel over the last 2,000 years has done an admirable job of conveying the limited, self-serving aspect of personal reconciliation of the individual – in presenting Christ as personal savior. Yet, we need to consider that there is so much more, that God's purpose reaches higher and farther and deeper, having to do with all of the unfinished business, all of the loose ends of God's creative history, the "*all things*" that have been set against Him and His original creative intent.

If our Lord is reduced down merely to the level of personal savior, to saving you or me or anyone else; if this is all that is being offered to those alienated from the life of God – in glossy little booklets, and "*Jesus is your friend*" tracts, then I dare say that we have reduced and deflated the message entirely. The gospel is good news primarily because it reaches to the "*all things*", beyond mere individuals or nations or even realms. By failing to see this, we have not yet glimpsed into the ultimate mystery as the Apostle Paul had, that which caused him to place so much impassioned and spirit swooning emphasis on being *in Christ*, that in Him, through blood and suffering and death and sacrifice – in the demonstration of a such an altogether different wisdom – the Father was reconciling *all things* opposed to Him and His purpose.

He is so much more than my personal savior, and the gospel is so much more than my personal *get out of hell free card*. His life and death and resurrection were about so much more than me or you or even all that we see on this earth. Unless and until we come to fathom this, He will never be magnanimously increased in our life and witness as our Heavenly Father desires and as He must be. Our testimony may bring a tear to the eye, but it will never have any real power or authority against the dark powers amassed against God and His Kingdom. As long as we are focused on personal, denominational or even global well-being or revival, we will remain short-sighted and earth-bound in our perspective. We are called to a high, holy and heavenly calling in contributing to, and sharing in our Lord's reconciling work, not only on this earth for man, but as a witness to those who occupy the heavenly places – to angels both fallen and true, as we shall see.

We would do well here, in the interest of emphasis to repeat the proposition that the Christian gospel, as presented, has rightly conveyed the truth that we, as sin-alienated individuals have been reconciled to God the Father through His Son who, through His righteous sacrifice, has become our peace. But the Scriptures unveil so much more, and by entering into this truth and allowing it to take hold of us, and broaden our understanding, the full extent and scope and glory of God's creative and reconciling wisdom will bring Him and His Son even more honor. Yes, the gospel begins with the reconciliation of the individual, but heaven forbid it should end there! If this is all it is to us, then I dare say we may not understand it perfectly.

The Present State of Things

> *For it was the Father's good pleasure for all the fullness to dwell in Him, and through Him to reconcile all things to Himself, having made peace through the blood of His cross; through Him, I say, whether things on earth or things in heaven. And although you were formerly alienated and hostile in mind, engaged in evil deeds, yet He has now reconciled you in His fleshly body through death, in order to present you before Him holy and blameless and beyond reproach— if indeed you continue in the faith firmly established and steadfast, and not moved away from the hope of the gospel that you have heard, which was proclaimed in all creation under heaven, and of which I, Paul, was made a minister. (Col. 1:19-23)*

So what in fact are the *all things* that are set against God, both in heaven and earth? We don't have to look too hard, or think too deeply to become aware that hostility and conflict characterize this present creative reality from end to end and top to bottom. Seemingly all creation is in a state of antagonism and anarchy; in active and persistent opposition to the Creator's original design and intent. On the minutest of levels, this was conveyed to me the other day, when, sitting on my porch (trying to read the Bible) I was literally attacked by a relentless swarm of little black bugs. As I was already by this time deep into this subject, it occurred to me that, yes even this imbalance in nature must be included in this universal reconciliation. All that we see around us and all that we have ever known – man against God, man against himself (the disorder of spirit, soul and body), man against nature, nature against itself, nation against nation, the nations against God and His covenant people, predator versus prey, angels against angels, angels against God, kingdom against kingdom, the spiritual realm against the natural, brother against brother, Jew against Gentile, Ephraim against Judah, father against son, son against father, heaven against earth – all in a swirling and seemingly hopeless state of disorder and alienated from the creative life and wisdom of He who made it all.

My brethren, the Bible from Genesis on speaks of an enmity against God by His creation in many forms, and from many sources, both natural on the earth, and supernatural, in what the Scriptures call the heavenly places. Now this is not heaven itself, where God the Father dwells, but rather an unseen realm inhabited by spiritual forces that exist beyond the scope and comprehension of natural things. It is here where principalities and powers – spiritual beings of various ranks and agencies – influence the natural world (men, nations, institutions, etc.) and function in open hostility to the Creator's purposes and design. A fellow brother has expressed this quite clearly –

> *"Clearly "the heavenly places" is a phrase that refers – not to heaven itself, conceived as the abode of bliss to which the faithful go – but rather, as the whole realm of the unseen, inhabited by all those spiritual forces that exist beyond the realm of things seen – and behind them. In that realm, great forces are at work, forces that have an order and an organization of their own. Those spiritual agencies, too, like us men on earth, have rebelled against God: at least some of them have – so that the upper realms also have become disordered by the entry into them of sin and of evil.*
>
> *The rift sin has produced extends both higher and deeper than the merely human level of creation. The whole universe as God created it exhibits a gigantic rift that runs through its whole fabric! The powers of the upper world are in conflict – in conflict among themselves, in conflict with God. And their conflict is not separate from our earthly conflicts. In some way, their conflict with God bears on our conflict with God. There is an interplay between the two, so they react on each other. What happens on earth can have a profound effect on what happens in the heavenly places; what happens in the heavenly places can have a profound*

> *effect on what happens on earth." (P.T. Harrison, The Heavenly Places)*

Indeed, the Scriptures convey vividly the sense that all created things are at cross purposes with He that made them for Himself. Both heaven and earth testify to the fact that there is no order, peace or agreement between them and the God of creation. We read of angels, such extraordinary beings, rebelling against God and one another; of their unnatural rule on this earth, setting them against God's will and purposes in creating humankind. We read of open hostility in the heavenly places, defiance and conflict at the very highest levels. We read of a covenant people, born of promise and under great signs and wonder, reduced to bare-fisted rebellion and defiance against the One who formed them and loved them. From whatever angle you look, and however you choose to define it, sin – in all of its varied aspects and expressions – has fouled God's universe and aligned it against Him. Not just your personal sin or mine (as grievous as that is), but a general and universal state of sinfulness, enmity and rebellion that encompasses and includes much of the created realm and its inhabitants.

God's Ultimate Solution

And so what is God's ultimate solution? Indeed we know the answer to that, for Paul in his epistle to the Colossians tells us. And in telling us he allows us to glimpse the divine *foolishness* that is at the very heart of the Christian gospel and witness. We have said elsewhere, and it is worth repeating, that the great work of God in this age is the reconciliation of all things in His Son, or "*in Christ*" as Paul would say. Our God is the preeminent peacemaker, and as a peacemaking God He has chosen to restore peace to His creation by the blood of a pure and spotless lamb – His righteous and beloved Son. Whatever enmity exists; whatever "*middle wall of separation*" stands before God and His creation; however far off we or any created thing might be; God the Father's peace and restoration is to be transacted solely in His Son.

And yes and hallelujah, this peace has been brought near to us also, as Paul affirms –

> *And not only this, but we also exult in God through our Lord Jesus Christ, through whom we have now received the reconciliation. (Rom. 5:11)*

We have indeed been personally reconciled to the Father through the death of His Son on the cross. This is where the Scriptures indicate that this peacemaking and reconciling God begins His ministry of reconciliation, of restoring all things to their original creative intent, according to His manifold wisdom and purpose. This is important and vital, for it is through this community of called out ones, gathered to Himself from out of the nations in this age, that He will actively continue to restore and perpetuate peace and reconciliation throughout all of His creation. Amen!

A point should be made here (for the Lord really impressed his upon me in a powerful way), and it is this –

THE CREATOR GOD DOES NOT LOWER HIMSELF TO THE LEVEL OF HIS CREATION – TO ITS WISDOM – TO RESTORE AND RECONCILE IT TO HIMSELF.

> *"For My thoughts are not your thoughts, Nor are your ways My ways," declares the LORD.*
>
> *"For as the heavens are higher than the earth, So are My ways higher than your ways, And My thoughts than your thoughts. (Isa. 55:8-9)*

He enacts it in His own way, according to His thoughts and purposes, which are so much higher and transcendent than anything our soulish intelligence can fathom or attain. It is, in fact, a spiritual wisdom that is indeed foolishness to anything less than what He is, for it reflects the very essence of His nature as an all-wise, loving, sacrificing and peacemaking Personality.

We understand therefore, that this work of reconciling all things to Himself through His Son is a work of peace, carrying a supreme cost. Only death and the shedding of blood can begin to restore peace to the created realm. This is the manner in which He has purposed it, and this is how it will be enacted. Here again, we begin to glimpse deeper aspects of this divine wisdom, that it has much to do with rejection, suffering, death and resurrection. The demonstration of this wisdom in Christ and His Church represents God's final and ultimate response to all things set against Him (and each other) in the created order. For example:

- Adam will be reconciled within himself (spirit, soul and body) and with His maker
- Ephraim will be reconciled to His brothers and then they to God and their land
- The angels will be reconciled to God and their rightful place in relation to man and the earth, although at great loss
- The nations will be reconciled to Israel and to God – they will be restored to their rightful boundaries and borders as intended by the God of the nations
- Heaven and earth will be reconciled as even God Himself comes down to dwell with His Creation
- The natural realm will restored to peace, harmony and balance, as a place of great blessing and bounty

The Church Called to Participate in this Reconciliation

Now, we have hinted at the idea that the Church, as the Lord's redeemed Body, is to be involved in His reconciling life and ministry. In this aspect, we turn to a seldom mentioned yet astounding revelation by Paul to the Ephesians –

> *To me, the very least of all saints, this grace was given, to preach to the Gentiles the unfathomable riches of Christ, and to bring to light what is the administration of the mystery which for ages has been hidden in God who created all things; so that the manifold wisdom of God might now be made known through the church to the rulers and the authorities in the heavenly places. This was in accordance with the eternal purpose which He carried out in Christ Jesus our Lord, in*

> *whom we have boldness and confident access through faith in Him. Therefore I ask you not to lose heart at my tribulations on your behalf, for they are your glory. (Eph. 3:8-13)*

My brethren, for some time now I have been personally grieved in the spirit by the fact that the church, as it has come to be, has become almost completely oblivious to its awesome and eternal calling and destiny. Now did you catch what this is telling us here – that the church, composed of reconciled creatures like you and me, has been called to make known, or demonstrate the "*manifold wisdom of God*" to the "*authorities in the heavenly places*" and that this whole thing is part of God eternal purpose which He accomplished in Christ Jesus our Lord. We who were made a little lower than the angels and were assigned dominion over the earth by God, are to convey in some manner God's wisdom to them through our lives and testimony. May our God be glorified as He communicates His wisdom and counsel throughout His universe, by and through whomever He wills. Oh the richness and depth of our calling as His saints and His children!

My spiritual sense is that Satan and his dark host will one day see that they jumped the gun in assuming arrogantly that the dominion over the earth was there to usurp, that they were somehow more worthy and qualified; that God's wisdom in setting something so much less than them will be vindicated when they see us raised to all glory and power in His Son. This too reflects God's wisdom and His ways, that are all to often scorned by the proud and lofty heart, wherever it resides.

My friends – we also demonstrate this wisdom to the lost in this world by expressing the very nature of His Son in all lowliness and meekness, in a self-sacrificing love that lays itself down for another, in purity of heart and purpose, in a hunger and thirst for righteousness, in seeking to live at peace and agreement with our God and Father and Creator. All outside of us on this earth, even nature itself and all of the elements even, are estranged and alienated from the life of God, subject to cursedness and pending judgment. Our very lives and witness represent the supreme hope of the gospel, which is that all things will be reconciled to God, that peace will finally and ultimate prevail, and all will be brought near to He who is reconciling all things to Himself.

All around us, and mounting up in this hour, is estrangement and division, war and conflict, bitterness and pride; people devouring one another without a second thought, without remorse, everyone vying for their own place, property and position – usurpers all of them – stealing and opposing the very purposes of the God who made them. The earth and all creation groans, my brethren, and longs for reconciliation and peace. Ruling spirits behind the nations and their leaders are defying God's authority over the peoples and nations. In their ravenous and murderous pride they defy God's wisdom by not accepting that the human race has been given dominion over the earth, and in seeking his annihilation.

> *Therefore, we are ambassadors for Christ, as though God were making an appeal through us; we beg you on behalf of Christ, be reconciled to God. (2 Cor. 5:20)*

Having been reconciled by the precious blood of the Lamb, we are to faithfully assume our place as representatives of His reconciling kingdom; a kingdom that in all its many aspects will reflect the peaceable wisdom of God. As such, we are to be living, breathing demonstrations of God's reconciling wisdom and purpose, not only to men, but to the unseen powers in the heavenly places. Angels are watching His wisdom as it unfolds and manifests itself in our very calling and sanctification, in our becoming a little higher than them in some regard. Now again, this is a wisdom springing forth from His very character and nature as He defers humbly to His creation – it is the face of peace, purity and sincerity, truth, faith, trust, gentleness, mercy, service, grace, light, and love. It is summed up in all of the Master's blessings in Matthew 5 and fleshed out in His earthly example.

This too, my friends, is what is represented by the glorious kingdom of God. Not only will this wisdom characterize His kingdom, it will also reflect the means to which we arrive; it is the very pathway of our citizenship through the Son and His cross. Although for now it suffers violence by those who consider it all foolishness and refuse to be reconciled – those who reject His offer of peace by way of His Son – ultimately it will prevail, for our Lord cannot fail, and perfect are His ways. All death will be swallowed up in life, and all things that will be reconciled will be.

Dear saints – consider all of this when reflecting on what our Lord, this lowly carpenter's son, carried in His spirit as every step took Him closer to the weight of the cross. Consider the enormity of this ministry the next time you contemplate the Lamb's words – "*It is finished*". The "it" here is profoundly more than the scope of your own personal salvation or well being, though in these we can certainly rejoice and be forever thankful. Consider the cross as so much more than our own personal gateway to glory. Consider that when all is fulfilled, all things will be brought near to the throne of the Most High, if not in peace and reconciliation, then for judgment.

Oh how precious and unfathomable is the Lord's reconciling wisdom and purpose. Oh that we would be as little children in demonstrating the majesty of this calling and purpose to all creation. Oh that this wisdom would be a pearl of great price and a treasure in our hearts, worthy of all we have to give. Oh that the church would walk in living demonstration of the manifold wisdom of God, as manifest in His Son of glory. Oh that we would agree with Him in all aspects of life and living, fully at peace with Him in the Lord; that we would appropriate this heavenly wisdom as our very own, that it would shine forth in our testimony of the one who paid the ultimate price as the Peace of God!

Oh Holy Father – Most High God of all Glory – grab hold of us Father, that we might see the awesome splendor of Your ways and wisdom; that all things will be reconciled and restored; that we have been called at such a price to forever be Your children, to have Your love and peace shining on us without end. We pray for Your people, that through the indwelling and impressing Lord Jesus, we may exhibit and demonstrate Your manifold wisdom to all powers and peoples. We pray that ultimate peace will come to Your universe, dear God, on Your terms alone, and by Your means, and for Your glory. In the name of the Prince of Peace, we pray. Amen.

Knowing Our God

To know Christ is the beginning of everything! To know what it truly means to be in Christ is everything!

To know Christ as savior is the beginning! To know Him as our resurrection and life is the reason for the beginning!

Recently, dear saints, I have found myself wading into the very tangled thick of things in the first chapters of Jeremiah, where the Lord, in no uncertain terms, indicts His people, Israel, on a number of fronts. But one thing in particular really jumped out at me; that despite all of their history with their God; despite all of His magnanimous revelation; and despite His munificent blessing and grace towards them, they still, at the end of it all, did not "*know Him*".

> *The priests did not say, 'Where is the LORD?' And those who handle the law did not know Me; The rulers also transgressed against Me, And the prophets prophesied by Baal And walked after things that did not profit. (Jer. 2:8)*
>
> *"For My people are foolish, They know Me not; They are stupid children And have no understanding. They are shrewd to do evil, But to do good they do not know." (Jer. 4:22)*
>
> *The prophets prophesy falsely, And the priests rule on their own authority; And My people love it so! But what will you do at the end of it? (Jer. 5:31)*

Amazing this, that the very people, priests and prophets who were called to know Him, and to singularly represent Him to the nations of the earth, did not; and they actually exalted in this. Apart from His original intent for them and the patient showering of much divine favor on them, they had by some strange means derived a life and religion completely divorced from the blessing, guidance and governance of their God.

Well folks, that was them, but what about us; what about you and me? Do we genuinely know the Lord, and are we actually aware that knowing Him is the reason we were reconciled to Him by the blood of His Precious Son in the first place? And more to the point, how do we come to know Him, and what is the price of this intimate knowledge?

It was Austin-Sparks, that gracious and humble servant of God, who taught that the cross must be basic to all knowledge of the Lord, and that true spirituality, reduced down, is simply knowing God. He also wrote this –

> *"We cannot have the knowledge of the Lord – the most important thing in the mind of God for us – except on the ground of the continuous application of the cross, and that will go right to the end."*

Dear friends, please keep that statement in mind as you read the following passages –

> *Make me know Your ways, Oh LORD*
> *Teach me Your paths.*
> *Lead me in Your truth and teach me,*
> *For You are the God of my salvation;*
> *For You I wait all the day. (Psa. 25:4-5)*

> *For this reason I bow my knees before the Father, from whom every family in heaven and on earth derives its name, that He would grant you, according to the riches of His glory, to be strengthened with power through His Spirit in the inner man, so that Christ may dwell in your hearts through faith; and that you, being rooted and grounded in love, may be able to comprehend with all the saints what is the breadth and length and height and depth, and to know the love of Christ which sur-*

> *passes knowledge, that you may be filled up to all the fullness of God. (Eph. 3:16-19)*
>
> *For this reason also, since the day we heard of it, we have not ceased to pray for you and to ask that you may be filled with the knowledge of His will in all spiritual wisdom and understanding, so that you will walk in a manner worthy of the Lord, to please Him in all respects, bearing fruit in every good work and increasing in the knowledge of God (Col. 1:9-10)*
>
> *For this reason I too, having heard of the faith in the Lord Jesus which exists among you and your love for all the saints, do not cease giving thanks for you, while making mention of you in my prayers; that the God of our Lord Jesus Christ, the Father of glory, may give to you a spirit of wisdom and of revelation in the knowledge of Him. (Eph. 1:15-17)*
>
> *I will ask the Father, and He will give you another Helper, that He may be with you forever; that is the Spirit of truth, whom the world cannot receive, because it does not see Him or know Him, but you know Him because He abides with you and will be in you. (John 14:16)*

To know the Lord of All Life is the beginning of everything isn't it? One can know many things and many persons and many concepts in the course of his life, but only one thing truly matters at the end of the day – and that is to know the Living God; to know our God! Knowing God is the reason we were born, and the purpose for our lives! And we will go on knowing Him as long as eternity persists! Yet to know Him as He intends means so much more than knowing *about Him* through study or investigation or religious pursuit. Consider Job –

> *Then Job answered the LORD and said,*
> *"I know that You can do all things,*
> *And that no purpose of Yours can be thwarted.*
> *'Who is this that hides counsel without knowledge?'*

> *"Therefore I have declared that which I did not understand, Things too wonderful for me, which I did not know." 'Hear, now, and I will speak;*
> *I will ask You, and You instruct me.'*
> *"I have heard of You by the hearing of the ear;*
> *But now my eye sees You; Therefore I retract,*
> *And I repent in dust and ashes." (Job 42:1-6)*

Job's coming to see and know the Lord was no mere intellectual realization, but a blood and spirit encounter; a reckoning borne out of heart-felt repentance and self negation. If this sounds a lot like what Austin-Sparks was describing above – "the continuous application of the cross" – then it is because that is the only way to see or know our God.

And as we also recognize from the passages mentioned, to know the Son ("The image of the invisible God") is to know the Father. This is the fundamental reason any idol or graven image representing God is blasphemous, for it supplants and obscures the one true and legitimate image of the Eternal God – ***the Lord Jesus Christ!***

Further, Ephesians reveals that fruit, borne out of the crucified life, leads to the ever-increasing knowledge of God. If we want to know our God, and to know Him more perfectly, there must be loss, rejection, suffering, pain, loneliness, estrangement; in short an ultimate cost to be paid. For if the Lord Jesus Christ is the singular way to the Father, then only His way can be ours as well. It is a way spotted with blood; where the chorus of the crowd shouts down against the few, where life is brought forth mysteriously out of death. It is ironic that spiritual life can only genuinely begin when one is reduced to the very thing from which the animal life was derived in the beginning – dust.

And so when David prayed –

> *Make me know Your ways, Oh LORD; Teach me Your paths. (Psa. 25:4)*

– we must acknowledge what, in fact, he was asking for and how it would ultimately be apprehended. Not sitting casually at ease in the king's chamber reading the scrolls or discussing theology with his contemporaries. No, where David learned the ways and paths of the Lord was by sharing in the rejection and suffering of the Christ. And it is no different with any of us, dear brethren, all those who would know the Lord God in all of His Wondrous Wisdom and Love and Glory.

How we all need His grace to know Him, and His Spirit and Help to know Him, and how that knowing Him would become the very pivot of our lives, turning us here or there, or wherever He leads us. And I pray that we will see, that as we come to know Him it is not as a God somehow outside of us (out there or up there), but within, abiding within us in real spiritual unity, intimacy and relationship.

Dear friends, I must say sadly and candidly, that there are many in the world and the church speaking for our God who don't actually seem to know Him. They (it would appear anyway) have never actually encountered Him or experienced that moment of reckoning where they see Him as He truly is, and then abandon all else to follow Him unequivocally. There are many more I suppose who have studied the Scriptures to great depth, and have a vocabulary for all of their high-sounding concepts about the Lord (this was me at one time I confess). Yet look around and there is no cross, no thorns, and no blood and no pain and no rejection. In short, the way they have chosen is not the Lord's way. The truth they have accepted is not His truth! And the life they are advancing is merely a religious, ephemeral life rooted in ease and earthly security; it is not a life derived out of death at all.

The path of knowing the Lord is a singular one, and as much as we may prefer the notion of many different roads all leading to the same happy place, this concept is nowhere found in the testimony of Scripture. It is a lie and can only lead to greater blindness and unknowing, the polar opposite of what we are referring to here.

My friends, dear saints of God, we must all come to the place where we are willing to suffer whatever the cost that we might know the Lord God who saves us. Everything else to be known is incidental and relatively worthless. We were created and redeemed that we might know our God who breathed life into us, and is conforming us to the image of His Son. Yes, we can read in the Bible that He is this or that, but our knowledge of Him must be founded on so much more than reading or scholarship (please note that I am in no way devaluing the importance of study in the Word; this should go without saying). We must experience Him in all of His abiding wisdom and love and truth and wonder. And we cannot possibly know Him if we persist in remaining rooted and attached to this present evil world, for He has already judged this world and its god, and found it wanting. Doom, death and destruction is all that remains for this world on its collision course with the Almighty Judge.

Is the price of knowing Him dear? Oh yes, very dear indeed, for the pioneer of our faith showed us the way to the heart of the Father, and look at what it cost Him. Dear brethren, the greatest blessing the Lord has endowed us with is Himself. Let me say that again – the greatest blessing the Lord has endowed us with is Himself. Look how much our Lord loved and honored the Father. Oh what He must have known about Him, such that all else proved merely superfluous. Oh what He must have seen. To know God truly is to love Him. And to know Him is to worship Him as He deserves, with all honor and truth and spiritual praise. Truly He is the most compelling thing in His universe.

> *"This is eternal life, that they may know You, the only true God, and Jesus Christ whom You have sent. (John 17:3)*

My friends, I pray for all of you that you might know the Lord our God, and be willing to pay the price, such as it is in your life, that this might be possible. I can personally attest to the fact that it is not an easy path; that at times it is a bewildering and painful road we are on. But we are all on it together, my brethren, and it leads to the very heart of our Heavenly and Loving Father.

Oh Lord, help us to know You most perfectly in the spirit, for this is eternal life. In Jesus' name, we pray. Amen.

Three Little Words

Just three little words – so astoundingly simple; so wonderfully perfect and revealing.

Just three little words – that represent the colossal sum and substance of all of God's eternal wisdom, causing even the angelic hosts to be transfixed by the heart and mind of their creator.

Just three little words – that transformed a murderous Pharisee named Saul into a life-affirming apostle named Paul.

Just three little words – that represent humanity's only hope, and the destroyer's gravest fear.

Just three little words – that define the immeasurable gulf between some religious puppet animated by strings, and a life breathed unto eternity in the power and presence of the Eternal God.

Just three little words – that enliven and fulfill the whole intent and beauty of God's Holy law, bringing heaven within reach of those who are dust.

Just three little words – that neutralize the flesh in man and the spirit of Adam and antichrist that pervades the world.

Just three little words – that explain how the Divine Shepherd will make this world His foot stool in and through His sheep.

> *To whom God willed to make known what is the riches of the glory of this mystery among the Gentiles, which is Christ in you, the hope of glory. (Col. 1:27)*

"*Christ in you*" – three of the most powerful and earth-shattering little words ever conceived and transacted in all the created universe. Three little words that most churches and supposed teachers sadly negate by their practice, if not their teaching. Three little words that mark that immeasurable and eternal chasm between heaven and hell, truth and the lie, Christ and antichrist, holy and reprobate, heresy and light, doing and being, religion and the hope of glory.

> *However, you are not in the flesh but in the Spirit, if indeed the Spirit of God dwells in you. But if anyone does not have the Spirit of Christ, he does not belong to Him. If Christ is in you, though the body is dead because of sin, yet the spirit is alive because of righteousness. But if the Spirit of Him who raised Jesus from the dead dwells in you, He who raised Christ Jesus from the dead will also give life to your mortal bodies through His Spirit who dwells in you. (Rom. 8:9-11)*

So, are we confident that this describes us? We had better be. For many false and fruitless years I thought it did for me, my friends. I foolishly listened to and followed many who thought they had a better way; that there was somehow more to it; that it just wasn't that simple.

Oh how we have strayed, dear saints. Oh how we have betrayed the beauty and wonder of the resurrected Christ. How we have so readily fallen for that first and vicious lie of the improved man, the transformed man, the actualized man. Where then is the power and the quickening to life? In steps, in programs, in ministry, in might or method or determination or discipline? In good and pure thoughts? In redemptive sacrifice perhaps?

Oh what fools we are, and blind! He told us didn't He? He told us it was better that He returned to the Father; that He would write His laws in our hearts and minds; that we would once and for all find rest in Him? He told us that He was the Bread from Heaven, and the Way and the Truth and the Life? That He was the staff raised by Moses? That unless we ate of His flesh and drank of His blood, we were as good as dead already?

Yet for 2,000 years men have reared themselves up and convinced us that we need them; that we need mediators and priests and shepherds and rites and practices, etc. And now apparently we need humanism, and psychology, and methods and programs and the consumer economy, and everything else that Babylon offers.

Rubbish I say!

Three little words dash all of this to pieces. Three little words are all we need to know to send every one of these lies back to the hell from whence they came.

Christ in you!

Here, let me say it again –

Christ in you!

Did you hear that, my brethren?

Christ in you!

Here alone is the wonder of the Christian life. Here alone is the power over every unclean and unwanted thing in our hearts and lives! Here is the power and the glory – the power to be, to resist, to walk, to stand, to live and love and learn all that the Father intends for us in His Beloved Son. Here is the beginning and the end, the hope of heaven and the hope of glory that no man nor devil shall ever snatch away from us. Here is the tree of life forsaken by Adam in that distant garden, yet offered to you and me today.

So utterly and indescribably simple it seems. So hopeful and affirming to every creature in need of redemption and life.

And yet what have our churches and theologians and gurus done, my brethren? To what have they added to this divine simplicity? Have they not taught every single one of us in so many sordid and sophisticated ways that –

IT IS NOT ENOUGH!!!

That we need to eat also from the tree of the knowledge of good and evil; that it is in ourselves to be acceptable to the holy and awesome Creator who will not suffer the ungodliness of His creation?

This modern generation seems hell-bent on "*doing Jesus*" like they "*do*" so many other things. But He is not merely another thing; He is the *Only Thing*! In the Father's eyes, in fact, there is only His Beloved Son, and all those attached to Him as the True Vine! There is nothing else! Until we come to see this, we will try this and try that, and do this and do that, but it will all be dead.

So then we will add a stirring soundtrack to it, and vibrant colors and lights to make it seem alive. We will attach strings to make it dance around; but only those who want such things will be fooled. I am somewhat amused how we paint the faces of the dead, and put fine clothes on them so that they might be more presentable for the "*viewing*". They even push the corners of their mouths so they appear to be smiling and joyful.

But death is death, and the only life is in the One who came down from heaven as the life of the world, the light of men! Our modern religion is insidious to the Father because it obscures the one and only thing that satisfies His Perfect Heart - His Beloved Son!

I must confess before all of you that I am positively grieved to the very core of my soul that so many of His little ones have fallen for this first and only lie; that so many continue to support churches and teachers who would add or subtract from the divine sufficiency of the Lord Jesus Christ inhabiting His people. All those who belong to Him no longer experience Him as something outside of them, some mere teacher, or prophet - but rather within them, as a force and presence of life and godliness and unity. He has become their living peace with God the Father, the active and inner penetrating fulfillment of every shadow and type presented from Genesis to Malachi.

This is the mystery and hope of the gospel is it not? Is this not what Paul taught and what every true Christian since has embraced as the ultimate essential? The battleground is within you – here alone is where Jesus Christ, that Bright and Morning Star, the Beginning of the Creation of God, the Author and Finisher of our Faith, will take back dominion from that thief in the garden. Here is where all life and death collide; not in Washington or Hollywood or Rome.

Oh my little ones, why then do we follow those who seek to usher in the Kingdom through political activism or cultural change or anything else?

> *My children, with whom I am again in labor until Christ is formed in you— (Gal. 4:19)*

> *For I am confident of this very thing, that He who began a good work in you will perfect it until the day of Christ Jesus. (Phil. 1:6)*

> *You are from God, little children, and have overcome them; because greater is He who is in you than he who is in the world. (1 John 4:4)*

So then –

Is He in you, my brother? Is He really and truly? Why then are we still so dependent and needy, groping for every new thing to come along that tickles ours ears? Why then are there more priests and heretics today than ever before, with fat bellies and thousands following behind them like blind and dumb beasts? Why so many supplements and additions and books and theories and theologies all supplanting that essential and exclusive reality that He in us is all we have and ever will need?

Time is short, my brethren, and this is no small point of doctrine that we can hold loosely. In truth, this is the only doctrine, as absolutely everything promised by our Lord hinges upon Him being the way and the life; the holy and quintessential power abiding within us. Now, at the end of this age, is the time to examine ourselves to determine just who and what is inside us –

> *Test yourselves to see if you are in the faith; examine yourselves! Or do you not recognize this about yourselves, that Jesus Christ is in you—unless indeed you fail the test? But I trust that you will realize that we ourselves do not fail the test. (2 Cor. 13:5-6)*

Here in plain language is the only measure of the authenticity of all those who profess to be Christians! Notice that we see nothing here about anything that we do, or our good intentions toward God.

If Christ is not in you, then you are disqualified, you have failed the test: He will say to you in that day –

'Truly I say to you, I do not know you.' (Matt. 25:12)

And don't take this too lightly either. It matters not if you consider yourself a religious or spiritual person, a person of faith even; a church-goer, steeped in the traditional tenets of the faith. The only way He will really and truly know you is if He lives in you; if He has claimed you as His dwelling place.

Did you accept Him into your life once? Excellent, but is He inside you now, at this very moment – your way and life and truth? Or do you trust in another?

Did you pour your heart out to Him once, in bloody anguish of soul and repentance? Terrific, but what spirit moves you on a moment-by-moment basis now? Is He alone your breathing in and breathing out; your standing up and sitting down? Your very life and essence?

This is not a game to be played, or a suit of clothes to take on and off! This is life and death and the criteria is profoundly clear – Either He actively abides in you and is Lord of your life or He isn't. Either you have chosen life or you have chosen death! What will it be?

My friends, the devil himself and all his demons are not intimidated in the least by our religious exertion, our high intentions, or the self-life rising up in the name of Jesus Christ. There is in truth only one reality that fills them with fear and dread, and that is the one fact in the universe that is divinely positioned to restore all of the dominion currently under demonic control back to the Most High God. Consider therefore, who and what compels you. If you blindly believe you can sit on the fence while all of hell rises up to be judged, then you may just find yourself among them.

Will you not rather withdraw once and for all that He might advance? Will you then stop pretending to be and start being in Him? Will you allow yourself to be emptied that He alone may fill you and encompass you? Will you be reduced that He alone might be increased in you? Will you be sidelined that He – with all His power and ability – may enter the game? Will you stop asserting and presenting yourself that He alone would be revealed, in all of His heavenly goodness and love?

This is our prayer for you, and it is truly the only one that matters. Oh that the world and everyone in it would see the Lord Jesus Christ enlarged and revealed in His holy people. Oh that they would stop seeing only *christians* and start witnessing Christ Himself in all His holiness and glory! Oh that they would no longer be touched by some good-hearted church ministry to the filling of the belly or self-esteem, and be touched by the Lord Himself to the redeeming and claiming of the soul.

Here, my beloved, is the place where Spirit touches bone; where we live in Him, and move in Him and have our very being in Him – solely because He is in us, and all that we are is being appropriated for Himself and His Heavenly Father.

Christ in you – just three little words. But, my friends, this is all we will ever need. Go to Him now if you have never let Him in, or if lately you have shut Him out. And stop your ears from all those trying to convince you that you need anything or anyone else.

If coming to Him to receive Him means departing from something or someone else, then do it gladly and do it quickly, and don't look back. You won't ever be the same again, I promise you.

Oh Mighty and Everlasting Father in Heaven – We pray for all of Your little ones, that no longer would we try to please You in the power of our own life. We invite the Lord Jesus Christ into our lives to reign from within us, to lead us onward as the Captain and Navigator of our souls. Oh righteous Father, that He alone would be magnified and You also for granting Him to us, and us to Him. Let all of the unbelievers and the world see Him, Lord, and not some form of improved or dressed up man; not us merely. Help us to know and understand that He alone is all we truly need; that in Him alone the victory is ours to claim, and that no created thing can prevail against Him and the one in whom He dwells. We thank You Father and love You, for in granting us Your Holy Son You have restored us to wholeness and life. In Jesus' glorious name, we pray. Amen.

If the World Hates You

The Scriptures convey most vividly the idea that those begotten of God by His Spirit represent nothing less than the corporate manifestation of Jesus Christ on the earth. As His *body* we are inseparably joined to Him in more than principle, agreement or religious allegory, but in origin, life and purpose. The Father, in choosing to create a new spiritual man in place of Adam, has formed both the head and body in His beloved Son, Jesus Christ.

> *Now you are Christ's body, and individually members of it. (1 Cor. 12:27)*

> *And He put all things in subjection under His feet, and gave Him as head over all things to the church, which is His body, the fullness of Him who fills all in all. (Eph. 1:22–23)*

> *For the husband is the head of the wife, as Christ also is the head of the church, He Himself being the Savior of the body. (Eph. 5:23)*

As the Lord's manifest body on the earth, we are to represent His presence and purpose in both our individual lives and the corporate life of the "*ecclesia*". If we are to cast any shadow at all, it is only to be His shadow. If we are to demonstrate or reflect any kind of wisdom or purpose whatsoever, then it is to be His wisdom. If we are to proclaim and embody any message, then it must be His message. Having been bought at such a price, we are no longer our own, coming and going and living as we please unto ourselves. We are intrinsically joined unto Him that we might fulfill the Father's eternal purpose in manifesting and magnifying His Son throughout His creation. In choosing to propagate and advance His divine essence throughout the universe, He has graciously called upon a tiny remnant of puny, mortal creatures to share in His work.

Although the Head is currently seated in heaven with the Father, His ministry and witness continues in this present age through His Body – the Ecclesia (or "called out" ones) of the Living God. And it should also be expected that the world (and the current ruler of this world) – that is opposed to God and all His plans and purposes in Christ – would respond to His Body in precisely the same way as it responded to Him – with bitter contempt, hatred and murderous intent.

> *"If the world hates you, you know that it has hated Me before it hated you." (John 15:18)*

> *I have given them Your word; and the world has hated them because they are not of the world, just as I am not of the world. (John 17:14)*

> *"You will be hated by all because of My name, but it is the one who has endured to the end who will be saved." (Matt. 10:22)*

Dear saints, all of this is presented, by way of introduction, that we might present our immediate topic, which is *the tribulation and testing of the saints.* Now this is important stuff here, my friends, for I fear a subtle deceit has been perpetrated upon God's people by many who have taught them to expect something other than what our Lord received in this world. Both the Scriptures and the Spirit suggest otherwise however, as we shall see.

Now there are concepts seldom mentioned today by many Christians, and they are these – *rejection, isolation, suffering, tribulation, trial, persecution, loss, peril, distress, opposition, affliction, martyrdom.* Perhaps there is this general sense that these unsavory topics are no longer relevant or applicable to the sophisticated and pragmatic church of today – those who believe kingdom blessings can come in advance of the kingdom itself and the King. The whole issue of suffering for the glory of God and His Christ has become one of the many unmentionables in the modern church – bad for business one might suggest.

This, of course, flies in the face of our Lord's consistent message that the ill manner in which the world treated the Head would necessarily be applied to the Body, which represents the perpetuation of His presence and ministry on the earth. This also runs counter to the violent manner in which most of the Lord's holy prophets and apostles were treated. Consider Hebrews 11, for example, which grimly catalogs the fate of so many faithful saints of old –

> *Women received back their dead, raised to life again. Others were tortured and refused to be released, so that they might gain a better resurrection. Some faced jeers and flogging, while still others were chained and put in prison. They were stoned; they were sawed in two; they were put to death by the sword. They went about in sheepskins and goatskins, destitute, persecuted and mistreated— the world was not worthy of them. They wandered in deserts and mountains, and in caves and holes in the ground. (Heb. 11:35–38)*

And why should we who serve the Lord today expect anything less? In 2nd Timothy we are assured that "*all who desire to live godly in Christ will suffer persecution*". Not some, not a few, but "all". Why? Again, because of the deep-seated and murderous hatred of the ruler of this world to all things representing the King and His Kingdom. The idea expressed is that anti-christian and predatory forces are literally hunting down all that threaten their very survival and vitality. Elsewhere the Scriptures convey the image of the devil as a roaring lion seeking to devour all who would oppose his earthly dominion and influence. Our Lord prayed to the Father that His sheep would not be removed from the earth, but preserved from this lion seeking to devour them. And Satan essentially employs two means whereby to neutralize opposition – to tempt them into rejecting God's true revelation in His Son, or if they refuse, destroying them.

My friends, this current gospel of an easy and painless testimony in this world is clearly not from heaven but from somewhere else. The body that is legitimized by the world and does in fact experience this kind of relative ease and safety is truly not attached to the Head that is the Lamb of God. The entire message of both testaments is that a colossal war is underway in which the spiritual forces of evil are pitted violently against God, His people, and His interests. This world is and has never been worthy of those who are true, pure, holy, righteous and faithful to the One who saved them out if it. It seeks only to devour and destroy them, and (listen carefully, saints) the wonder of it all is this – our loving God actually permits the righteous to be physically persecuted and even slain. He doesn't always deliver His children from the wrath of the rulers of this world. Even today, in many parts of the world, there are many genuine children of God, who hold the testimony of Jesus and represent His manifest Body on the earth, who are being poured out as a shining sacrifice to the glory of God. The prophetic Scriptures indicate that this will become worldwide once evil is more universally unleashed, and the murderous wrath of the beast and his minions is released against the testimony of the Lamb.

The plain and simple testimony of Scripture is that God nowhere promises us deliverance *from* persecution, but rather deliverance *through* it, and victory *over and above* it. All spiritual growth and maturity requires and meets some form of resistance, as Peter assumed in his prayer –

> *After you have suffered for a little while, the God of all grace, who called you to His eternal glory in Christ, will Himself perfect, confirm, strengthen and establish you. (1 Pet. 5:10)*

Resistance quickens our faith, bringing it to life, maturing it, and deepening it into obedience. Hebrews 5 tells us that our Lord "*learned obedience by the things which he suffered.*"

Brethren, it may be worth repeating that this world is not our world. We are merely traveling through on our way to a better place. And if we are truly bearing the testimony of Jesus Christ in our lives and example, then we represent a spotlight shining on all that is false and unclean in this world. As such, we represent a significant threat to all those (both human and otherwise) who profit and gain from the present state of evil. Rest assured, that all wickedness in high places will hate us and seek our destruction, for the very reasons it hated our Master. As His body, we bear His truth and His testimony – and the world cannot bear it, and must come against us in the only way it knows – with malice and violence.

Here, in a nutshell, is the very reason we are in the world – as a righteous testimony against it. We are witnesses of the Most High God, who is poised to judge this present evil world with righteous judgment and fierce wrath. Our very testimony will play a large part in the Lord's case against this world and all those who support and serve it.

> *For God has not destined us for wrath, but for obtaining salvation through our Lord Jesus Christ. (1 Thess. 5:9)*

No brethren, we are not subject to God's wrath or the execution of His judgment on this world, but neither are we greater than our Master (John 15:20), and all throughout the Bible we are conditioned to expect violence and affliction at the hands of the devil and all who represent him. It is Satan's murderous wrath that constitutes the real physical threat (and it can only ever be a physical threat, affecting the body and soul) to the saints. Through so many forms of trial, tribulation, torment, accusation, violence, loss and deprivation against the body of Christ, Satan seeks always to reduce Jesus Christ, to stamp Him out in some form or another.

Yet, here is the wonder and the power of the testimony of the saints, in demonstration of a wisdom that renders even the angels awestruck — that when violence and even murder comes against the sheep, the Shepherd is not thereby reduced, but increased and magnified to an even greater degree. His glory shines even brighter in the testimony of the slain, whose righteous blood the world is not worthy. Not only are His little ones not ultimately destroyed, but they are deemed "*more than conquerors*" (Romans 8:37).

The same Loving God who has numbered the very hairs on our head, and who encourages and sustains us through much testing, trial, and tribulation at the hands of evil in high places, is forever with us and in us, strengthening and fortifying us in Himself. Recall, dear saints, that remarkable fourth figure in Nebuchadnezzar's fiery furnace (Daniel 3:25), looking very much like the Son of God, and preserving His own in the midst of the oven. No, my friends, we are not, nor ever shall be left alone to endure this world's fiery wrath and indignation. The Body and the Head are one.

Why then do we love this world so, and grip it so tightly, when all that it is and represents is opposed to the Holy One we serve? When it scorned and crucified the only pure and perfect thing that ever entered it? Why do we seek its acceptance and legitimacy, even its love, when our Lord commanded us to follow Him out of this world, to bear His cross, and to die to this world and its ways, to its illegitimate wisdom and purpose? If the Head was not of this world, then must not this also be true of the body? Why then do we seek to align ourselves with all that this world represents in its opposition to God – its politics, its systems, its institutions and even its false, small "c" christianity?

Our Lord's claim on us is an ultimate one, and neither the gates of Hades nor Death, nor the god of this world can ultimately deprive us of what we have been given in Christ. But let us not reduce this assurance to mere physical survival of the body or the preservation of our place in this world. It is the spirit that is inviolable to the gates of Hades and the one who holds its key. And this alone marks the source of our sanctified and prophetic testimony before every false and unholy thing.

The wisdom of this world and its god is to protect, preserve and increase itself by force if necessary. If it cannot convince or otherwise claim something for itself, it will endeavor to destroy it. It is the way of GET! And into this world, the Lord has inserted us to demonstrate another kind of wisdom, adverse and opposed to all that it represents – the way of GIVE. Hereby, we are oil mixed with water, day dividing night, and salt preventing corruption. Only we know that love cannot exist apart from truth, and ours is a message of truth (that the Lord's soon–coming kingdom will ultimately supplant the kingdom of men and devils) that the world cannot possibly bear, for it exposes it and reveals all that is hidden. Ours is a testimony that cannot, and will not, conform to the world's precepts and ways; and yet blind conformity is what it is all about. This is why it hated our Lord and continues to resist all those who live in Him, right up until the very last day, when God Himself will remove His faithful ones before executing His fierce wrath on this evil world.

Most beloved saints, those in whom His very life and spirit abides, we all know the times in which we live, that forces are quickly marshaling to bring about the most wicked state of existence the world has ever known. If we are not being made ready now, then I fear many of us will not resist the dread powers to come. If our lamps are not topped up now, then how shall we fill them then? If we do not have a martyr's faith and a martyr's love now, then from whom shall we get it when those days are upon us? If we have no root in ourselves now, then what shall keep us from being uprooted then? In the very name of Our Gracious Lord and King, I implore and exhort all who read these words to make yourselves ready while there is yet time.

All of our Lord's words are rapidly quickening to life and fulfillment as we prepare our hearts as end–time pilgrims on this earth. Do we indeed love self, family or things more than Him, and how shall we respond when this world threatens to separate us from such? For this is all the devil can really do when you get right down to it, as evidenced by his vicious attack on Job. Indeed, with the Lord's permission, he can separate us from the ones we love, from our physical existence, from our property certainly. Yet –

> *Who will separate us from the love of Christ? Will tribulation, or distress, or persecution, or famine, or nakedness, or peril, or sword? Just as it is written,*
>
> *"FOR YOUR SAKE WE ARE BEING PUT TO DEATH ALL DAY LONG;*
>
> *WE WERE CONSIDERED AS SHEEP TO BE SLAUGHTERED."*
>
> *But in all these things we overwhelmingly conquer through Him who loved us. For I am convinced that neither death, nor life, nor angels, nor principalities, nor things present, nor things to come, nor powers, nor height, nor depth, nor any other created thing, will be able to separate us from the love of God, which is in Christ Jesus our Lord. (Rom. 8:35–39)*

So, do we genuinely and deeply believe this, my brethren? Have we resolved this in our hearts and minds today, in anticipation of a world where we will certainly be marked and rejected? Where everything and everyone will be against us? When we will be scattered and alone, with only God and His promised provision?

Do we believe our Lord when He assures us that – "*In the world you will have tribulation, but be of good cheer. I have overcome the world*"? Do we actually comprehend what the Lord means when He says that judgment will begin with the house of God?

> *Beloved, do not be surprised at the fiery ordeal among you, which comes upon you for your testing, as though some strange thing were happening to you; but to the degree that you share the sufferings of Christ, keep on rejoicing, so that also at the revelation of His glory you may rejoice with exultation. If you are reviled for the name of Christ, you are blessed, because the Spirit of glory and of God rests on you. Make sure that none of you suffers as a murderer, or thief, or evildoer, or a troublesome meddler; but if anyone suffers as a Christian, he is not to be ashamed, but is to glorify God in this name. For it is time for judgment to begin with the household of God; and if it begins with us first, what will be the outcome for those who do not obey the gospel of God? (1 Pet. 4:12–17)*

There is first a refining, a strengthening, a testing, and a building up of patience amongst the saints that must occur before this world is judged. And whether you choose to believe it or not, the clear and certain message of God's Holy Word is that this requires suffering and separation. And God has always used the devil and his world as an instrument of such. All of us must be separated from our idols, violently if necessary, before entering the kingdom. And remember, an idol can be anything or anyone that we love or trust or turn to before the Living God who made us.

Dear saints, our most precious Lord went meekly as a lamb to the slaughter in obedience to the Heavenly Father, suffering the ultimate separation for His Glory. We too, as the Lord's manifest and mystic body on this earth, must be ready and willing and preparing now to experience the same thing for the glory of our God. In this and anything else, there truly can be no greater or higher motivation, than that the God we serve and love will receive the glory worthy of His holy name and eminence! This, and I believe the Lord affirms this, is where we must focus our hearts and devotion and prayers as end–time saints anticipating the days to come!

Oh Most Holy Father, keep us from the lie that we can be made ready apart from loss or separation, that as servants we can expect anything less than that which befell our Master, that maturity can come in a box. Fortify the saints, Oh Lord, in preparation for the testimony of Your purpose and glory before a world that is rushing headlong into depravity and the incarnate rule of the evil one. Turn our hearts singularly to You and Your Son in these last days, and let us not be afraid or thwarted from our steadfast faith and trust in You alone, to help us to overcome whatever comes. Most precious Father, we do indeed love Thee, and know that we can be and do all things in Christ Jesus who strengthens us. In His exalted name, we pray. Amen.

Having Been With Jesus

> *Now as they observed the confidence of Peter and John and understood that they were uneducated and untrained men, they were amazed, and began to recognize them as having been with Jesus. (Acts 4:13)*

No formal seminary education. No letters after their names. No denominational degrees or honors. No standing among the religious leaders of the day. No training, workshops, seminars, correspondence courses. No high-minded vocabulary. No vaunted place among the initiated. No published works. No, none of these, but rather they had been with Jesus. For over three years they had walked with Him, and broken bread with Him, and sailed with Him, and listened to Him, and beheld all of the many miracles He performed.

> *And He appointed twelve, so that they would be with Him and that He could send them out to preach. (Mark 3:14)*

Oh dear friends, how frightfully difficult it is for *religious* men to comprehend those who have truly been with the Lord Jesus. It was that way then and it remains this way today. I dare say I would rather hear three little words from a man who has actually been with Jesus than three million words from the trained and educated man who only has second-hand, hearsay knowledge.

Spend time with Him my friends. Walk with Him and talk to Him, and more importantly, listen to all He tells you. Sit at His feet and subject yourself to His wisdom and discipline. Do whatever He tells you to do and go wherever He tells you to go. Obey His every word and wait on His provision and blessing. Trust that He will never leave you nor abandon you. Ask for greater faith and ears to hear and eyes wide open in the spirit to see what He is doing. Watch Him at work as the Master He is, and be willing lay down everything you know about everything, for He alone is Truth and Light. Oh if only I had learned this lesson many years ago; if only I knew then what I am beginning to learn now.

> *For this reason I bow my knees before the Father, from whom every family in heaven and on earth derives its name, that He would grant you, according to the riches of His glory, to be strengthened with power through His Spirit in the inner man, so that Christ may dwell in your hearts through faith; and that you, being rooted and grounded in love, may be able to comprehend with all the saints what is the breadth and length and height and depth, and to know the love of Christ which surpasses knowledge, that you may be filled up to all the fullness of God. (Eph. 3:14-19)*

To be sure, we live in a world that highly esteems it's professionals and elites, and the church of Christ is, sadly, no exception. The clergy today is made up of highly trained and credentialed professionals who largely honor themselves and have exalted themselves above the people. All that their official distinctions have served to do over the course of 2,000 years is to distance them from their brethren. Rare indeed is the servant whose service simply flows out of his life and fellowship in Christ; his merely being with Jesus.

Peter and John moved the people because they had been with the Lord Jesus and all they were doing was in His name, and in His power; it flowed out of His life within them. They were mere fishermen, untrained and unqualified in the eyes of the religious elites of their day. Yet they moved the people just as the Lord moved the people. No one before or since has spoken as He did, and His disciples had seen and heard and tasted the Lord and this was all that truly mattered in the end.

My sense in the spirit is that there are many Peters and Johns out there today, those who have simply been with the Lord and who know His heart, His plans and purposes, and what He truly feels about all those who have made His precious Church a means of gain and worldly advancement. They know that the time of judgment on the churches is at hand, and that all those who are pretenders and imposters will be exposed and removed.

Perhaps this why so many are leaving the organized church and the denominations, because they are simply hungry to hear from those who have been with the Lord, those who rise early with Him and so remain throughout each day.

Consider, dear saints, these poignant words of T. Austin-Sparks regarding popular Christianity –

> *I am quite sure that many of you will immediately discern that is just the flaw in a very great deal of popular Christianity today—a kind of objective imitation of Jesus which gets nowhere, rather than the subjective learning Jesus which gets everywhere. (from "The School of Christ")*

Brethren, a mature saint should be able to discern almost immediately whether the one writing or speaking this or that has actually been with Jesus Christ. This being the case, why is it that so much of what it written and taught in His name is actually counter too all that He represents? So many books sold, and web sites visited, and men exalted. Blind patronage to be sure, when so few have actually spent time with the Lord in the Spirit.

There is no need to explain this further. Many of you know what I am referring to, having been with Jesus yourselves. For all the rest, just spend time with Him in the Spirit, for He is the Father's greatest blessing.

> *So when they had finished breakfast, Jesus said to Simon Peter, "Simon, son of John, do you love Me more than these?" He said to Him, "Yes, Lord; You know that I love You." He said to him, "Tend My lambs."*
>
> *He said to him again a second time, "Simon, son of John, do you love Me?" He said to Him, "Yes, Lord; You know that I love You." He said to him, "Shepherd My sheep."*

> *He said to him the third time, "Simon, son of John, do you love Me?" Peter was grieved because He said to him the third time, "Do you love Me?" And he said to Him, "Lord, You know all things; You know that I love You." Jesus said to him, "Tend My sheep." (John 21:17)*

Here is great wisdom my friends; this principle that only those who love the Lord Jesus and know Him and have spent much time with Him can be of any real service to His sheep.

Oh Father, help us to know Your Beloved Son most perfectly. In His name, we pray. Amen.

Of Being and Doing

If I speak with the tongues of men and of angels, but do not have love, I have become a noisy gong or a clanging cymbal. If I have the gift of prophecy, and know all mysteries and all knowledge; and if I have all faith, so as to remove mountains, but do not have love, I am nothing. And if I give all my possessions to feed the poor, and if I surrender my body to be burned, but do not have love, it profits me nothing. (1 Cor. 13:1-3)

I must here confess to you all a spot on my heart that the Lord God, by His inexplicable patience and grace, is dealing with. You see, I am by nature and earthly disposition a pragmatist, a doer, a finder and fixer of things broken. And as an Englishman, it may even be brewed in the blood, so to speak, for my people tend to be industrious and activity oriented.

People like me are, by nature, judgmental, harsh, perhaps even seen as cold at times. Yet our intentions are often admirable as the world might judge; to make things better, to restore good where possible. Herein lies the temptation and danger to one who is a child of God and subject to His Lordship. Our holy and righteous God must first reshape us into His likeness before we can be of any spiritual good to Him. It is easy for a man like me to put the cart before the horse and wrongly assume that doing something for God is better than merely being like Him.

The Scriptures rightly place things in their proper order in many places. Let's start with Matthew –

Do not judge so that you will not be judged. For in the way you judge, you will be judged; and by your standard of measure, it will be measured to you. Why do you look at the speck that is in your brother's eye, but do not notice the plank that is in your own eye? Or how can you say to your brother, 'Let me take the speck out of your eye,' and behold, the plank is in your own eye? You hypocrite, first take the plank out of your own eye, and then you will see clearly to take the speck out of your brother's eye. (Matt. 7:1-5)

For someone like me, it is so easy, so natural to see what is wrong in people and things outside of myself. For many years, I wrongly interpreted this moral clarity with God's will, as something of a spiritual gift perhaps. So I did what so many others have done it seems – set up a *discernment ministry* web site. I poured everything I had into it and all along firmly believed that God was behind it all, that it was even His will perhaps. He wasn't, of course, and it fizzled out and left me sorely discouraged. I vowed to myself never again to venture out *in God's name,* when it was really my name and my inspiration behind it.

"First remove the plank from your own eye."

I have since begun to learn that to judge rightly requires far more than just the ability to see what is wrong or broken, but the heart of meekness and love (the very heart of the Lord Jesus) to respond to what you see in a loving and unselfish way. In truth, without such meekness and love, it is questionable whether we can see clearly in the first place. Sadly, I believed that I had the gift of discernment, but true spiritual discernment is to see what our Lord sees, first in ourselves, then others and the world. It not only distinguishes between good and evil, bit even more importantly, between that which is natural (of the soul) and that which is spiritual (flowing out of the life of Christ within us). True, Spirit-inspired discernment begins with a revealing of what is wrong or unchristlike in ourselves, and as such requires a depth of spiritual experience and maturity that we often lack. It is vital that we are able to discern that which is spiritual from that which is purely natural, if we are to grow up unto perfection and in some way serve fellow members of the body of Christ.

For the word of God is living and active and sharper than any two-edged sword, and piercing as far as the

> *division of soul and spirit, of both joints and marrow, and able to judge the thoughts and intentions of the heart. And there is no creature hidden from His sight, but all things are open and laid bare to the eyes of Him with whom we have to do. (Heb. 4:12-13)*
>
> *For everyone who partakes only of milk is not accustomed to the word of righteousness, for he is an infant. But solid food is for the mature, who because of practice have their senses trained to discern good and evil. (Heb. 5:13-14)*

In a similar way, we who are prone to holy, righteous indignation must be careful that we are found in ourselves to be holy and righteous, that there is no unlikeness to our Holy and Righteous Father. It is so easy to start out on some supposedly heaven-sent crusade against the darkness when the blackness of our own hearts has not been adequately dealt with.

A.W. Tozer was often fond of suggesting that one could be a Christian technically, holding to all the creeds and confessions of the faith for example, but not a Christian in actuality and living practice. Indeed, we can do and say all the right things so that other saints may pat us on the head and say "*well done, good and faithful servant*", yet there is a *plank* in our eye and *spots on our garments*, preventing us from living and walking in vital union with He who is pure and perfect. We become little more than "*a noisy gong or a clanging cymbal*", in other words.

It is instructive to study in both the Old and New Testaments, the depth of equipping and preparation required of God's saints and servants prior to them actually *doing* anything for Him. The pattern seems to be plain – first the preparation, then the sending. Often we focus on the sending and the walking, when what is more essential is the bringing of the servant to the point of brokenness and agreement with God in every sense. Often we extol the storming of the enemy's gate without truly appreciating the time spent alone with the Lord in the wilderness, learning to agree with Him, to be loosed from the old man, and to be formed into His likeness.

Invariably, this process of *de-planking* involves the breaking down and stripping away of the old, natural (soulish) man, with all of his pride and identity rooted in self and the world. It is often a long and lonely process whereby we are forced to consider what we truly are, as He sees us. It leads us to brokenness, tearful confession and a sense of being undone as we are brought unceremoniously to the end of ourselves by His loving discipline. The *plank*, you see, represents all things pertaining to the old man and the old life (dominated by the human soul: reason, emotion, self-will, etc) that must come to an end and die.

> *Truly, truly, I say to you, unless a grain of wheat falls into the earth and dies, it remains alone; but if it dies, it bears much fruit. He who loves his life loses it, and he who hates his life in this world will keep it to life eternal. (John 12:24-25)*

Herein lies the mystery of the Christian life and by extension all true Christian service – that out of death, life springs forth; that only from brokenness comes fullness and fulfillment. This wisdom confounds our natural wisdom and reality, I know, but it is God's only way. This is the path whereby He will fill all of His creation with the fullness and likeness of His Beloved Son.

You see brethren, the highest attainment in this new life in Christ is not measured by results and outcomes of an external kind so much, but by how closely we are being conformed to the likeness of He who made us in the beginning. It was for this reason that man was conceived – not to do what God could do Himself – but to be a creature fashioned to enjoy fellowship with God on His terms, according to His nature and holiness.

To coin a phrase – "*To be or not to be*" – this is the only question The *doing*, if it is to flow at all, must flow freely out from the being.

> *As for me, I shall behold Your face in righteousness; I will be satisfied with Your likeness when I awake. (Psa. 17:15)*

Here is one who has found his treasure and purpose in life. Here is one who has his priorities straight, for he has seen the Holy One, and been touched by Him. There is no fear here that he will set out on his own doing his own things for God. He knows why he was created, and this compels him in all things pertaining to life in this world. His likeness doesn't matter any more, for he has died to himself and to everything he trusted in all of his days.

Dear saints, if we believe we can retain ourselves in some manner, being in the likeness of the world and the devil, then we will be sorely disappointed in this Christian walk. For there is only one face our Heavenly Father beholds in which He is well pleased, and that is the beautiful and shining face of His Beloved Son. Jesus Christ never once deviated from the likeness of His Eternal Father! And it is in the Son alone that we discover the only path to that state of being revealed for us in Psalm 17.

Notice what the Apostle Paul conveys in his epistle to the Romans –

> *If we have been united with him like this in his death, we will certainly also be united with him in his resurrection. For we know that our old self was crucified with him so that the body of sin might be done away with, that we should no longer be slaves to sin— because anyone who has died has been freed from sin.*
>
> *Now if we died with Christ, we believe that we will also live with him. For we know that since Christ was raised from the dead, he cannot die again; death no longer has mastery over him. The death he died, he died to sin once for all; but the life he lives, he lives to God.*
>
> *In the same way, count yourselves dead to sin but alive to God in Christ Jesus. Therefore do not let sin reign in your mortal body so that you obey its evil desires. Do not offer the parts of your body to sin, as instruments of wickedness, but rather offer yourselves to God, as those who have been brought from death to life; and offer the parts of your body to him as instruments of righteousness. For sin shall not be your master, because you are not under law, but under grace.*
>
> *What then? Shall we sin because we are not under law but under grace? By no means! Don't you know*

> *that when you offer yourselves to someone to obey him as slaves, you are slaves to the one whom you obey—whether you are slaves to sin, which leads to death, or to obedience, which leads to righteousness? But thanks be to God that, though you used to be slaves to sin, you wholeheartedly obeyed the form of teaching to which you were entrusted. You have been set free from sin and have become slaves to righteousness. (Rom. 6:5-18)*

Sin is moral unlikeness to God (or "*missing the mark*", to be more technically correct), and the Bible from end to end declares it as a way of life, or a pattern of living. It opposes Him as surely as darkness opposes light. It is the very lifeblood and oxygen of the world, just as righteousness enlivens and defines God's Holy Kingdom. And in the context of this message, sin prevents us from seeing clearly and from walking in agreement and fellowship with our God.

Dear brethren, it is not sufficient to behold all that is wrong, worldly, carnal and sinful in other people, even the church, unless and until we discern the same operating in ourselves. Only God's restoring and revealing Spirit can expose all of this death in our hearts, then lead us onward to true confession and victory over sin in Christ Jesus. No, we do not have to reach moral perfection down here in order to make a statement about Christian things, or to be useful to the Lord in spiritual service; but it must be up to the One who searches the heart to determine when we have reached the level of maturity necessary to honorably represent His name and testimony on this earth.

Just recently, I found myself listening to a creaky, old 1950s era recording of a sermon delivered by A.W. Tozer on the omnipresence of God. In it, he spoke of a remoteness that many saints experience in terms of His presence. He contrasted the doctrine of His being near, by virtue of His omnipresence, to that of being "*feelingly near*" in the experience of His children.

Tozer went on to suggest that what most of us saints truly desire is a more personal and powerful manifestation of His presence in our lives. We want to sense Him near to us, in such an intimately spiritual way that we receive all that His life and spirit imparts to us. We are thereby encouraged, edified and refreshed down here in this dark, oppressive world.

Dear brethren, what is it that explains this estrangement from our God, who wants so much to take us into His arms and breathe life into our spirit? In a word, it is our unlikeness – our dissimilarity to Him. He is loving, yet we are not; He is longsuffering and kind, yet we are not; He is genuine and pure in spirit, yet we are not; He gives of Himself constantly and unselfishly, and yet we do not; His is a body of life, yet ours is one of death.

> *"Wretched man that I am! Who will set me free from the body of this death? Thanks be to God through Jesus Christ our Lord!" (Rom. 7:24-25)*

Oh that His penetrating Word and Spirit would pierce the stubborn shell of our old man and bring us constantly to the throne of grace and refreshing. Oh that He would form us anew in His likeness and nature – HOLY, PURE, WHITE, LOVING, UNSELFISH AND UNSPOILED from this carnal and corrupted world.

My friends, it is dreadfully easy to be found busy, supposedly doing this or that for the Lord in His Name. This describes so much activity in this generation and yet how much is genuinely the work of the Holy Spirit? Only God knows of course, but there is much to suggest to those in the Spirit that very little of eternal consequence is actually being done despite all of our web sites and satellite dishes and modern ministry efforts.

Folks, my sense, for what it's worth, is that out there in the shadows at this very moment, out of sight and beyond the view of the world and even the recognizable church, God is actively preparing a small and faithful remnant for this great end times work of proclaiming His lordship and glory to a world speeding blindly towards destruction.

In one sense, this preparation, as has always been the case with all of His saints and servants of old, is merely preliminary. Yet, as we have suggested, this very preparation is an end in itself, pointing to the very origin and intent of our calling as His children.

Dear saints, the imperative is clear for those whose hearts have been pricked by the Spirit of holiness. We must go deeper and we must see more clearly all that we are, deep down to the very root and source. We must hold nothing back nor proclaim anything untouchable to His sanctifying power. The end is clear, for we must see our Lord as He is and be only all that He is. His is a life marked by self-sacrificing love and grace and truth and a devotion to the Father of Life that penetrates and subdues all else. We too must be broken, dear ones. All that we are must fall to the ground and die; and from that cracked and broken shell, a new life must spring forth, released and renewed in holiness, righteousness and meekness. This alone is our spiritual and eternal inheritance. This is why He called to us out of the blackness and futility of our lives and commanded us to "*follow me*" and "*come and see.*" This above all else is what causes demons to tremble and angels to wonder in awe at the unspeakable wisdom of the almighty and uncreated One.

Oh Righteous and Perfect Lord, grant Your grace that we might see all that You see of our hearts and lives. Humble us, Oh Father, allowing us to be exposed for all that we are. It is so easy to see it in the world, in other men, even in the church, yet we need You to remove the plank of pride and selfishness from our own eyes that we might see all that is unholy and ungodly in ourselves. Split us open, Oh Lord, but only in Your mercy, lest we remain broken. Split us open so that a new life may be engendered – that of Your Holy and Beloved Son – the Righteous One, He who has heard and done all that You have commanded Him; He who proved faithful and true. Bring Him forth in us, Oh Father – by Your mighty and mysterious power and glory, that we might live only in You and for You, shaped in Your likeness, forever and ever. In Jesus' holy name, we pray. Amen.

But if it Dies

"Truly, truly, I say to you, unless a grain of wheat falls into the earth and dies, it remains alone; but if it dies, it bears much fruit. "He who loves his life loses it, and he who hates his life in this world will keep it to life eternal. "If anyone serves Me, he must follow Me; and where I am, there My servant will be also; if anyone serves Me, the Father will honor him. (John 12:24-26)

You fool! That which you sow does not come to life unless it dies; (1 Cor. 15:36)

Even though I walk through the valley of the shadow of death, I fear no evil, for You are with me; Your rod and Your staff, they comfort me. (Psa. 23:4)

It is an awe-inspiring truth (as we shall see) that this shadow of death, spoken of throughout the Scriptures, promises the hope and potential of deeper, more abundant life. Although this is undoubtedly man's greatest threat and fear, it is also where God does His finest and most heart-quickening work.

Death, decay, then life – a natural process every tiller of the soil or naturalist knows only too well. From mighty trees fallen and eroding on the forest bed flow all of the ingredients for even greater life and vitality. Here death and life, caught up in a dance only the Creator could have conceived, form a vital connection, the one perpetuating the other in a mysterious and magnanimous circle. Death, decay and decomposition promote a frenzy of micro-organic activity that perpetuates and promotes the continuing life and vitality of the ecosystem.

This is true also of the realm within the human heart where spirit and soul intersect. It is also one of the preeminent themes of the Bible.

> *But when this perishable will have put on the imperishable, and this mortal will have put on immortality, then will come about the saying that is written, "DEATH IS SWALLOWED UP in victory. "O DEATH, WHERE IS YOUR VICTORY? O DEATH, WHERE IS YOUR STING?" (1 Cor. 15:54-55)*

> *Therefore, since the children share in flesh and blood, He Himself likewise also partook of the same, that through death He might render powerless him who had the power of death, that is, the devil, and might free those who through fear of death were subject to slavery all their lives. (Heb. 2:14-15)*

Death – sin, the devil, the way of man.

Life – righteousness, Christ, the way of God.

> *"...but from the fruit of the tree which is in the middle of the garden, God has said, 'You shall not eat from it or touch it, or you will die.'" The serpent said to the woman, "You surely will not die! "For God knows that in the day you eat from it your eyes will be opened, and you will be like God, knowing good and evil." (Gen. 3:3-5)*

Here we find the first, and in many respects, the only lie – "*You shall not die*". Indeed, we will and we must. For it is from the death and loss of the self-life (or the *soul life* as Watchman Nee terms it) that we gain the life of He who is God's precious Seed – Jesus Christ.

My friends, the Kingdom of God does not grow in numbers and vitality through sophisticated and worldly marketing campaigns, fancy facilities or ear-tickling sermons. Nor can the individual Christian life increase in fruitfulness by the preservation of the life of the soul and flesh. God is abundantly clear on this – that life flows only out of death; that unless a seed falls to the ground broken, there can be no promise of fruitfulness and life. Here is one answer to that age-old question of why the devil is among us.

Indeed, we must die (and in fact welcome the death of the self; the old man) and fall to the ground such that the living dynamic of Jesus Christ can be born and developed within us. He is God's precious seed that was planted on the earth such that the life of God would grow and multiply throughout His creation. He was bruised and broken open on the cross only that life might spill out to the many who claim Him by faith alone. Here is how death is swallowed up in victory and the designs of the devil are universally confounded.

> *And I will put enmity between you and the woman, And between your seed and her seed; He shall bruise you on the head And you shall bruise him on the heel." (Gen. 3:15)*

The mortal flesh is merely the shell that contains the promise of life. Yet look at the expense and excess to which human beings go to perpetuate and promote what is essentially only packaging. Look again at how we Christians go to such great lengths to prevent the seed from falling and being broken. Until we love God more than our own life; unless we are willing, as so many saints and martyrs of old, to lay down our lives and risk being broken open and exposed, then the fruitfulness and vitality we preach about and desire will never actually happen.

Why then brethren is the contemporary church still falling for this first and most vicious lie and living for the life of the world in the pursuit of earthly things? We curry its favor rather than boldly preach the truth and risk being persecuted or worse. We look for easy ways of advancing the kingdom that don't require provoking the animosity of the world and its god. We have perverted the Christian message to such a degree that many see it as a means of worldly gain and not loss. Yet the clear testimony of God's word, affirmed by example and the Holy Spirit Himself, is that only those who do not love their lives unto death will truly grow and live and impart life to others. Here again is the power of the cross of Christ on the individual soul, performing the work of reducing that which must be brought to death.

> *"If anyone wishes to come after Me, he must deny himself, and take up his cross and follow Me. "For whoever wishes to save his life will lose it, but whoever loses his life for My sake and the gospel's will save it. (Mark 8: 34-35)*

Dear saints, it should be in no manner offensive to say that to preserve, promote and perpetuate our life is opposed to all things taught in the Bible. Jesus rebuked Peter as Satan's mouthpiece for opposing the purposes of God in allowing His beloved Son to advance towards the cross. Here was the same spirit found in the serpent in the garden when he told the first woman she shall not die. True saints follow their Lord in not loving their lives unto death, and in possessing a perpetual willingness to lay it down. Recall that Paul, writing to the Philippians, expresses his desire –

> *"...that I may know Him and the power of His resurrection and the fellowship of His sufferings, being conformed to His death. (Phil. 3:10)*

Paul knew most pointedly that, until we are conformed to the death of Christ, He could not be raised in us; that death and life were constantly working together to promote the creative and transformative purposes of the Father.

> *But we have this treasure in earthen vessels, so that the surpassing greatness of the power will be of God and not from ourselves; we are afflicted in every way, but not crushed; perplexed, but not despairing; persecuted, but not forsaken; struck down, but not destroyed; always carrying about in the body the dying of Jesus, so that the life of Jesus also may be manifested in our body. For we who live are constantly being delivered over to death for Jesus' sake, so that the life of Jesus also may be manifested in our mortal flesh. So death works in us, but life in you. (2 Cor. 4:7-12)*

The sheer wonder of it all is that the Father's way demands a devil here among those whom He would claim and refashion in His Son. Although the devil, by his very nature, intends our harm and loss, the Creator uses it to build up His little ones in His eternal kingdom. This theme is found over and over again throughout both Testaments of the Bible; that from the laying down and brokenness of one, flows life and abundance to the many. We see this from the garden of Eden onward to that quintessential act of God's precious Son pouring out His life for the life of the world.

Only by leaving his homeland and following his God blindly and vicariously through the wilderness, could Abraham prove himself faithful and become the father of many nations.

Only through tremendous loss and pain, could Job experience the fruitfulness of his Creator's encouraging word and the restoration and increase of all things.

Only by losing his freedom and dignity, could Jacob come to see that with God all things are possible, including reconciliation with his brother.

Only by being debased, broken and stripped of his pride, could Joseph bring life to His family in Egypt during the drought.

Only by being dispatched to the wilderness, and stripped of all of his princely ambitions and attachments, could Moses be prepared as the instrument of salvation to so many.

Only through being maligned, misunderstood and martyred would the testimony and message of the prophets offer hope, comfort and life to those who would come after them.

Only by being reduced and poured out from one end of the Roman Empire to the other, could Paul and the apostles advance the gospel and the kingdom, saying – *"So death works in us, but life in you"*.

Dear brethren, the Bible is replete with examples where Satan or his agents intended evil and destruction, but God used it for good and life. Many new Christians are often confused by the question of why the devil or why pain and death? Yet here is the answer from Genesis to Revelation – that life would emanate from His Son alone – bruised and broken open; that life would spill out to all those who would believe on Him, being conformed to His death, and raised up in His life.

Praise God for this mystery of life and godliness too often kept hidden from the saints. Yet it is the theme of all the Scriptures is it not? In so many types and examples and allusions, all pointing to He who is the ultimate fulfillment and hope of all things.

All so that the *"excellency of the power"* would be of God and not ourselves, lest we might boast. Always death (the cross) and life (the resurrection life of Christ) interacting within us to produce this new man in the image of the Lord of all life, He alone who is worthy before the Heavenly Father. Oh the mystery and majesty of it all, such that even a devil and death itself has a role in the creative workings of God.

Addressing the reason why there is so little fruitfulness and fullness of Christ in the lives of believers, Watchman Nee (who spent many years of His life imprisoned for his faith) wrote –

> *"There is new life in us, if we have received Christ. We all have that precious possession, the treasure in the vessel. Praise the Lord for the reality of His life within us! But why is there so little expression of that life? Why is there an 'abiding alone'? Why is it not overflowing and imparting life to others? Why is it scarcely making itself apparent even in our own lives? The reason why there is so little sign of life where life is present is that the soul in us is enveloping and confining that life (as the husk envelops the grain of wheat) so that it cannot find outlet. We are living in the soul; we are working and serving in our own natural strength; we are not drawing from God. It is the soul that stands in the way of the springing up of life. Lose it; for that way lies fullness."*

Oh, but to lose is not popular in our modern churches. To be reduced or side-lined, perhaps split open and poured out; this is more often than not seen as a sign of infidelity or spiritual weakness, surely not the intimate workings of a loving and heavenly Father with His hand on our lives. In His infinite wisdom, He has ordained that in order for us to live again and anew in His Son, we are to die to sin and the world and indeed all that opposes the life and nature of God and His Son. Paul clearly draws this out for us throughout his epistles –

> *Or do you not know that all of us who have been baptized into Christ Jesus have been baptized into His death? Therefore we have been buried with Him through baptism into death, so that as Christ was raised from the dead through the glory of the Father, so we too might walk in newness of life. For if we have become united with Him in the likeness of His death, certainly we shall also be in the likeness of His resurrection, knowing this, that our old self was crucified with Him, in order that our body of sin might be done away with, so that we would no longer be slaves to sin; for he who has died is freed from sin.*
>
> *Now if we have died with Christ, we believe that we shall also live with Him, knowing that Christ, having been raised from the dead, is never to die again; death no longer is master over Him. For the death that He died, He died to sin once for all; but the life that He lives, He lives to God. Even so consider yourselves to be dead to sin, but alive to God in Christ Jesus. (Rom. 6:3-11)*

Here we see that death is used by the Father to foster even greater life (the life of the spirit) and that by being identified with the death of His Son (as illustrated through the rite of baptism), we also share in the power and dynamic of His resurrected life.

Elsewhere, Paul incorporates the law and sin into the equation, providing even deeper insight into how death is bound up in the plan of God –

> *"For through the Law I died to the Law, so that I might live to God. "I have been crucified with Christ; and it is no longer I who live, but Christ lives in me; and the life which I now live in the flesh I live by faith in the Son of God, who loved me and gave Himself up for me. (Gal. 2:19-20)*

And further –

> *...and in Him you were also circumcised with a circumcision made without hands, in the removal of the body of the flesh by the circumcision of Christ; having been buried with Him in baptism, in which you were also raised up with Him through faith in the working of God, who raised Him from the dead. When you were dead in your transgressions and the uncircumcision of your flesh, He made you alive together with Him, having forgiven us all our transgressions, having canceled out the certificate of debt consisting of decrees against us, which was hostile to us; and He has taken it out of the way, having nailed it to the cross. (Col. 2:11-14)*

> *If you have died with Christ to the elementary principles of the world, why, as if you were living in the world, do you submit yourself to decrees, such as, "Do not handle, do not taste, do not touch!" (which all refer to things destined to perish with use)—in accordance with the commandments and teachings of men? These are matters which have, to be sure, the appearance of wisdom in self-made religion and self-abasement and severe treatment of the body, but are of no value against fleshly indulgence. (Col. 2:20-23)*

> *Therefore if you have been raised up with Christ, keep seeking the things above, where Christ is, seated at the right hand of God. Set your mind on the things above, not on the things that are on earth. For you have died and your life is hidden with Christ in God. When Christ, who is our life, is revealed, then you also will be revealed with Him in glory. (Col. 3:1-4)*

To Timothy, Paul declares –

> *It is a trustworthy statement: For if we died with Him, we will also live with Him; (2 Tim. 2:11)*

Dear brethren, saints of the Most High; clearly the Lord's eternal wisdom and ways are nothing like our own. That which we fear and dread more than anything is precisely what He employs to generate life – real life, His life. And this is no empty mysticism or allegory here. That true spiritual life – the very life of God – can be conferred to mortal beings, who start out life in the material world and the flesh, is a mystery and wonder that only the Spirit can discern.

Death will most certainly be swallowed up in life and victory –

> *He will swallow up death for all time, And the Lord GOD will wipe tears away from all faces, And He will remove the reproach of His people from all the earth; For the LORD has spoken. (Isa. 25:8)*

And so stripped down to bare facts, the Christian reality is essentially about a new (spiritual) life being raised up out of an old (natural) life that has been willingly laid down and broken open. Nothing happens or indeed can happen until this happens. Until each and every one of us come to the point where the life of Christ is more important than our own, then nothing else matters. Not rules, or self-discipline, or the flesh dressed up in church clothes. None of these or anything else can produce the fruit that only life can generate.

Think seriously on this brethren, for so much of what passes for Christianity in this world has little to do with the life of Christ being born out of the death of the fallen Christian. Many are baptized each and every day not really comprehending what it represents: death and resurrection life. The power and ability is in the life, and there is only one life that matters to the Father, and that is the life of His Son. The law only has the power to legislate and condemn; it changes nothing. The existential nature and life of Adamic man has the power only to sin and offend God.

ONLY THE LIFE OF JESUS CHRIST ABIDING IN THE BELIEVER MAKES THE LIVING POSSIBLE!

Everything else is a pretense, and denies the power, as Paul has said. "*But if it dies*", then the promise of life advances. And oh what a life it is, brethren, for nothing in all creation is as awesome and beautiful and worthy as the life of the Son of God. It is a life that is destined by the Father to subsume all the universe, filling every space and soul, bringing the hope of the transcendent glory of God to all created things.

My sense in this hour is that those who would be His witnesses at the close of this age must carry forth that testimony that started with righteous Abel and all who followed him, all those who were martyred for their faithful service to the Lord. We must all be prepared and willing to surrender all that the Lord would require so that the life of His Son would be fully formed and manifested in us. The first generation church did not grow, either in number or spiritual maturity, because of slick marketing campaigns or big buildings, but rather it grew up out of the blood and broken bodies of the apostles and saints; those who lovingly poured themselves out that the life of Jesus Christ would rise up throughout the Roman Empire.

Let's consider this again, recognizing that its meaning is for every single one of us seeking to advance the Lord Jesus and His Eternal Kingdom –

> *–unless a grain of wheat falls into the earth and dies, it remains alone; but if it dies, it bears much fruit. "He who loves his life loses it, and he who hates his life in this world will keep it to life eternal. "If anyone serves Me, he must follow Me; and where I am, there My servant will be also; if anyone serves Me, the Father will honor him. (John 12:24-26)*

Oh Heavenly and Glorious Father - we have been taught many things, and we have believed many lies about how You as the Author of Life perpetuates life. We know that in our fleshly hearts we would prefer an easier, less intrusive way. Yet from the life of one, poured out in love, as a willing sacrifice, flows life to the many. And we pray for just such a heart and spirit, that for You and Your loved ones, we would be ready and willing to lay down our lives, our place or position, or anything else so that much fruit would be formed in us. In Jesus' precious name, we pray. Amen.

The Beauty of Brokenness

The breaking of the outward man is the basic experience of all who serve God. This must be accomplished before He can use us in an effectual way. No one is equipped to work simply because he has learned some teachings. The basic question is still: what kind of man is he? Can one whose inner workings are wrong, but whose teaching is right, supply the need of the Church? The basic lesson we must learn is to be transformed into a vessel fit for the Master's use. This can only be done by the breaking of the outward man. (Watchman Nee, The Release of the Spirit)

And Jesus answered them, saying, "The hour has come for the Son of Man to be glorified. "Truly, truly, I say to you, unless a grain of wheat falls into the earth and dies, it remains alone; but if it dies, it bears much fruit." (John 12:23-24)

I am the true vine, and My Father is the vinedresser. Every branch in Me that does not bear fruit, He takes away; and every branch that bears fruit, He prunes it so that it may bear more fruit. (John 15:1-2)

A time to kill and a time to heal; A time to tear down and a time to build up. (Ecc. 3:3)

Dear reader, there is a profound beauty in brokenness; that process whereby we are in some manner reduced by our Lord's loving and artful hand. By failure perhaps, or persistent, nagging sickness or disrepute, or poverty – all, of course, working to bring us to that ultimate state of nothingness, that His ever-quickening Spirit can be released in us. Notice what Austin-Sparks says in this matter –

> *Then He says that the Cross for Him was the way of release, "How am I straitened, how am I held in, pent up, until it be accomplished!" The passion of the Cross is the way of our release, and if you consider your own spiritual experience, those of you who have any experience of a walk with God, you know quite well that it has been through times of deep and acute suffering that you have found fresh releases; fresh releases in your spiritual life. Is it not true? Yes, we pass into a time of excruciating spiritual and soul suffering. We do not know what the Lord is doing, what He means by this, what He is after, but we know the features of our experience and know what it is that we are suffering, and it goes on. We, of course, ask the Lord to stop it, to bring it to a quick end, to deliver us from it. He takes no notice of us, and it is only those people who get out the other end who say, 'Thank God, He did not take any notice.' In the meantime, we think He is anything but kind and good and doing the right thing, but as we get on under His hand, we begin to see and to sense that He is dealing with something. Maybe He is dealing with our pride, our independence, or our irresponsibility, for example. That is the issue that comes up, and we are faced all the time with something about ourselves that is almost devastating. We would not have believed that that was so strong in us. (from,* The Cross and the Way of Life*)*

How can it be, we wonder? What possible good can come from such humiliation, pain, loss or rejection? Yet the beauty, my friends, lies in the loving wisdom of a heavenly Father who wishes to bless us to all abounding with the lasting riches of His fullest and abiding presence. It is in the stripping away of all that inhibits or corrupts this potential gift, where the truest splendor shines. For brick upon rotting brick must be chiseled away until the foundation is exposed. Only then can our blessed Advocate secure Himself as our sure and solid foundation.

The beauty ultimately lies in the purification of our hearts that results from being exposed to the Refiner's fire. Here is where all the dross of selfish ambition and love of the world is burned away from our lives, leaving a pure and refined saint where a sinner and rebel once stood.

> *He will sit as a smelter and purifier of silver, and He will purify the sons of Levi and refine them like gold and silver, so that they may present to the LORD offerings in righteousness. (Mal. 3:3)*

The beauty also shines forth through the dynamic and living testimony that results, as our wise Counselor and Teacher permits us to prove what He is revealing to us, whether it is a test of our faith in His love, or His trustworthiness. When the devil or his darkness comes at us head on, to tempt or corrupt us, our Lord must know that our light will remain, that we will stand firm as His faithful lampstand.

And always resisting and grinding under it all is the swollen, festering pride of humanity, the *oh that I were a king* presumption that surfaced first in that ancient and sordid heart of the archangel Lucifer. How it loathes failure, defeat and loss of any kind. How it despises dependence on anyone and submission to circumstance. Watch as it writhes and coils under the weight of so many painful setbacks and assaults on our self-sufficiency.

I remember vividly when my wife and I relocated to the Midwestern United States from Canada some years ago. Here I was, with a number of university degrees, a growing career and business, a heart full of my own esteem and importance, unable to find a decent job. Despite numerous attempts, every door seemed to close abruptly on me, as if God Himself and all His angels were against me.

I guess I knew intellectually that we are tested as Christians, but somehow this was different, infinitely more real, and more painful. I was compelled for a number of years to take some menial jobs that I felt were far below my credentials and ability. As a husband, my self-worth started to erode as I was unable to adequately provide for even my wife. I grew increasingly languid and depressed, with seemingly no way to escape. I would pray, sure, but gradually all that was coming out was "*Why Lord why*?" and "*When Lord when*?"

You must also understand that all of this was happening in the mid-nineties at the height of the health-wealth gospel. Every Christian television station seemed to be littered with sharp-dressed showmen pulling out proof text after proof text to convince us that our material success was indicative of our spiritual condition and faith in God. Here I was, ready to go under, and this was effectively like someone throwing me an anchor.

Other Christians meant well too, but after a while I couldn't bear to hear another Bible verse used to convince me that God chastened the children He loved, or the pastor telling me that there was some unrepented sin or idol somewhere in my life, that I might not even be saved. I attempted not to lose heart, to hang on, but it was so terribly hard. The world seemed to be advancing ahead of me and I just couldn't keep up. I was angry and bitter and alone. I felt like something was dying inside me, like I was losing my grip on reality.

And you know what, my friends, that is exactly what was happening; and I have since come to realize that all that I experienced, all of the deep down hurt and abandonment was securely in the hands of a loving Father who was breaking me down in order to build me back up again in His Son.

This is the part that is beautiful, if we have eyes to see. Believe me, I know it is not easy, nor does it appear beautiful while we are right in the middle of it. Yet it shows us vividly how deep our roots run into this world and its self-worshipping spirit.

Recently, I found myself revisiting Watchman Nee's small but immensely powerful book, *The Release of the Spirit*. The theme of the book is the Lord's wise and wondrous work of breaking the individual, such that the life of God might flow forth. Here is an excerpt –

> *"God is at work in our lives unceasingly. Many years of sufferings, trials, hindrances-this is the hand of God, daily seeking to carry on His work of breaking us. Don't*

you see what God is doing in this endless round of difficulties? If not, you should ask Him, "Oh God, open my eyes that I may see Thy hand." How often the eyes of an ass are sharper than those of a self-styled prophet.

Though the ass had already seen the Angel of the Lord, his master had not. The ass recognized the forbidding hand of God, but the self-styled prophet did not. We should be aware that brokenness is God's way in our lives. How sad that some still imagine that if they could only absorb more teaching, accumulate more preaching material, and assimilate more Bible exposition, they would be profitable to God. This is absolutely wrong. God's hand is upon you to break you-not according to your will, but His; not according to your thoughts, but His; not according to your decision, but His. Our difficulty is that as God withstands us, we blame others. We react like that prophet who, blind to God's hand, blamed the ass for refusing to budge.

All that comes to us is ordered by God. To a Christian, nothing is accidental. We should ask God to open our eyes that we may see He is striking us in all things and in all areas of our life. One day, when by the grace of God upon us we are able to accept the ordering of God in our environment, our spirit is released and ready to function."

So often in our lives, the Lord needs to know that, stripped right down to nothing (as the world measures things anyway), we won't abandon Him. He needs to know that if all else has been lost, that He is our sufficiency; that He will be increased while we are being decreased.

Please hear this, my friends, for I believe it is very important –

You and I are only on this earth as disciples of Christ for one reason, and one reason only – to represent a true and effective witness to the soon-coming Kingdom of God. It is through this kingdom and government, that the Lord will "*put all His enemies under His feet*", and subject all things unto Himself (see 1 Cor. 15).

I also encourage you to familiarize yourselves with the concept of the Holy Spirit being sent into the world to procure a bride for the Father's Son, as typified by Abraham's servant being sent to find Rebekah and bring her to Isaac.

And just as this is true, so it is also true that this testimony (the entire sum of our lives as God's witnesses on earth) must be forged in the furnace of His refining fire. There must be no exceptions! You can survey all the pages of the Bible and you will not find one. Wherever there is light, there is bound to be darkness coming against it with all of its hellish fury.

Perhaps this is why the physical birth of a human child is such a violent affair. Where there is newness of life, there is pain and upheaval and tumult – yet look at the wondrous result.

From such crushing and at times bloody denial, the brash heart within us is brought patiently or perhaps abruptly to the point of need. Here is the moment of truth; here is the place where the inner man (spirit) and the outer man (soul and flesh) collide; here is that divine pathway to contriteness and true biblical humility; here is where all things beautiful in the soul of a redeemed human being have their genesis. Truly the grain cannot grow until the seed is made to fall to the ground and die.

Notice how Watchman Nee conveys this –

> *"Anyone who serves God will discover sooner or later that the great hindrance to his work is not others but himself. He will discover that his outward man and his inward man are not in harmony, for both are tending toward opposite directions. He will also sense the inability of his outward man to submit to the spirit's control, thus rendering him incapable of obeying God's highest commands. He will quickly detect that the greatest difficulty lies in his outward man, for it hinders him from using his spirit.*

Many of God's servants are not able to do even the most elementary works. Ordinarily they should be enabled by the exercise of their spirit to know God's Word, to discern the spiritual condition of another, to send forth God's messages under anointing and to receive God's revelations. Yet due to the distractions of the outward man, their spirit does not seem to function properly. It is basically because their outward man has never been dealt with. For this reason revival, zeal, pleading and activity are but a waste of time. As we shall see, there is just one basic dealing which can enable man to be useful before God : brokenness."

The man who would follow Christ must first be loosed from the self, oftentimes painfully, in order that Christ might prevail and assume His rightful preeminence. And just as a broken stallion is both a splendid and useful creature, so the man of God has been brought by his assorted ordeals to be something better and higher; to assume his proper station beneath the Most High.

Here is some further insight from Watchman Nee –

"There is no one more beautiful than one who is broken! Stubbornness and self-love give way to beauty in one who has been broken by God. We see Jacob in the Old Testament, how even in his mother's womb he struggled with his brother. He was subtle, tricky, deceitful. Yet his life was full of sorrows and grief. When a youth, he fled from home. For twenty years he was cheated by Laban. The wife of his heart's love, Rachel, died prematurely. The son of his love, Joseph, was sold. Years later Benjamin was detained in Egypt. He was successively dealt with by God, meeting misfortune after misfortune. He was stricken by God once, twice; indeed, his whole history could be said to be a history of being stricken by God. Finally after many such dealings, the man Jacob was transformed. In his last few years, he was quite transparent. How dignified was his answer to Pharaoh! How beautiful was his end, when he worshipped God on his staff! How clear were his

blessings to his descendants! After reading the last page of his history, we want to bow our heads and worship God. Here is one who is matured, who knows God. Several decades of dealings have resulted in Jacob's outward man being destroyed. In his old age, the picture is a beautiful one.

Each one of us has much of the same Jacob nature in us. Our only hope is that the Lord may blaze a way out, destroying the outward man to such a degree that the inward man may come out and be seen. This is precious, and this is the way of those who serve the Lord. Only thus can we serve; only thus can we lead men to the Lord. All else is limited in its value. Doctrine does not have much use, nor does theology. What is the use of mere mental knowledge of the Bible if the outward man remains unbroken? Only the person through whom God can come forth is useful."

My friends, as we attempt to understand the harsh trials coming upon us, consider the perfect beauty and power of brokenness – how our bruises are working to purify and refine us for an eternal purpose; how our faith and trust in our God is being emboldened and hardened from the testing; and how our love for Him is being purged of all devotion to self and any created thing.

We understand from the Book of Job and other places in the Word how intimately our Loving Father loves us, and is involved in our development and sanctification, and how He was even willing to release His own perfect Son to the same suffering and death that we could be saved entirely - *spirit, soul and body.* What a wonderful thing when we see it in the eternal context of His plan for our lives as His children.

Is it easy? No. Is it often hard, painful and humiliating? Definitely. But is it profoundly beautiful when seen through heavenly eyes? Absolutely.

Oh Father in heaven, we pray for such eyes to see in the spirit; for perfect yet strange is Your discipline of the saints. Lord, we ask this in the name of Jesus Christ our Lord. Amen.

The Peril of Trusting Ourselves

Thus says the LORD,
"Cursed is the man who trusts in mankind
And makes flesh his strength,
And whose heart turns away from the LORD.
"For he will be like a bush in the desert
And will not see when prosperity comes,
But will live in stony wastes in the wilderness,
A land of salt without inhabitant.
"Blessed is the man who trusts in the LORD
And whose trust is the LORD.
"For he will be like a tree planted by the water,
That extends its roots by a stream
And will not fear when the heat comes;
But its leaves will be green,
And it will not be anxious in a year of drought
Nor cease to yield fruit. (Jer. 17:5-8)

Brethren, why do we persist in trusting in ourselves when the long, sordid history of our lives plainly reveals that our ways do not lead to the blessings of God, nor to His eternal purposes being fulfilled?

> *For we do not want you to be unaware, brethren, of our affliction which came to us in Asia, that we were burdened excessively, beyond our strength, so that we despaired even of life; Indeed, we had the sentence of death within ourselves so that we would not trust in ourselves, but in God who raises the dead. (2 Cor. 1:8-9)*

It is His way to bring us to the end of ourselves as in the passage above; to bring us to the very brink of despair so that we might see no way out but to trust in Him wholly and without flinching. You see, the testimony of Christ in His chosen ones does not hinge on human strength or wisdom at all but on His provision and power alone. If our hope is not in Christ but in ourselves or any other created thing, then how can we be sure we are abiding in His will? Is His care not sufficient? Do we foolishly think we need something more?

This is why the Scriptures are literally packed with examples of human beings and angels being confounded with almost unthinkable patterns of deliverance. The utter outlandishness of these stories are often what lead so many to refute the veracity of the Bible itself – Noah's boat, Isaac's altar, Jacob's long and painful pilgrimage to the end of himself, Joseph's unlikely path to savior of his people, Moses' mysterious road to becoming intercessor, the parting of the Red Sea, Jericho's falling walls, Jonah's gargantuan fish, Job's loss and restoration, David's bizarre and winding path to the throne, Esther's night with the king leading to the deliverance of all Israel; God's Son coming into the world by way of a virgin birth; and of course, His reconciliation of that very same world by way of a bloody cross. Yet is it not the case that such unthinkable events actually reveal to us that God is behind them; that His ways are beyond searching; that if we are to be saved or blessed by Him, then He will do it in a manner that refutes all other means, methods, possibilities or explanations?

I have been spending a lot of time in the Old Testament lately, and one theme seems to be rooting itself deeper and deeper into my spirit; and it is this – that the God of the Bible; He who has proven Himself over and over to be faithful to His chosen people; does not think or act or proceed as a man in any way, shape or form. There is a mystery surrounding how He does things that is irreconcilable to our experiences and expectations. He seemingly takes delight in confounding us; in turning our reality on its head. Typically, His deliverance or victory comes in a manner that is inconceivable to our puny little reality trapped as it is in time and space. Often, we really don't have a clue what He is going to do or even what He is doing at the time He is doing it – it is often only after He has accomplished His purposes that we finally and ultimately see the wonder of His ways; and afford Him the praise and glory that is exclusively His to claim.

So often it seems, we not only want God to help us or show forth His grace on us, but we want Him to do it in our way, and according to our logic and schedule. We want to be healed perhaps, or delivered from some circumstance that is discomforting, even painful, and we have it all mapped out how we think He should proceed to help us. Or maybe we have a ministry, and we vainly feel that the Eternal God who sits high above the circle of the earth has an obligation to advance it in some manner. Oh we sowed all these seeds, and have the entire marketing plan all carefully devised according to the ways of men and the world; and yet we somehow think He will automatically bless it and give life to it. Oh what fools we are, dear brethren! Have we not learned what is written in the Scriptures, that His ways are not our ways –

> *Let the wicked forsake his way And the unrighteous man his thoughts; And let him return to the LORD, And He will have compassion on him, And to our God, For He will abundantly pardon. "For My thoughts are not your thoughts, Nor are your ways My ways," declares the LORD.*
>
> *"For {as} the heavens are higher than the earth, So are My ways higher than your ways And My thoughts than your thoughts. "For as the rain and the snow come down from heaven, And do not return there without watering the earth And making it bear and sprout, And furnishing seed to the sower and bread to the eater; So will My word be which goes forth from My mouth; It will not return to Me empty, Without accomplishing what I desire, And without succeeding {in the matter} for which I sent it. (Isa. 55:8-11)*

And that "*no flesh should glory in His presence*"; which is what the unwashed human heart really wants isn't it? Be honest now. It is positively unthinkable that others would look at us as small or foolish, weak or base; an absolute nothing in this world. Do we not, on the contrary, attempt to project what we are out into the world; to appear larger than our true condition?

> *For consider your calling, brethren, that there were not many wise according to the flesh, not many mighty, not many noble; but God has chosen the foolish things of the world to shame the wise, and God has chosen the weak things of the world to shame the things which are strong, and the base things of the world and the despised God has chosen, the things that are not, so that He may nullify the things that are, so that no man may boast before God. But by His doing you are in Christ Jesus, who became to us wisdom from God, and righteousness and sanctification, and redemption, so that, just as it is written, "LET HIM WHO BOASTS, BOAST IN THE LORD." (1 Cor. 1:26-31)*

Does not this confound everything the world teaches about how to get ahead in life; how teams, for example, set about to win at whatever sport they are engaged in; how business goes about competing in the marketplace? Clearly it does, because down here it is all about this or that man seeking glory for himself, and praise from everyone else. "*Look at me*" – he cries in the street! "*Look at what I can do!*" His boast is not in the Lord, and neither is his trust.

The whole divinely twisted concept of a suffering servant, of losing one's life to win it; of the weak becoming strong in the strength of another; of pouring out your own life so that others might live – it almost hurts our brains trying to see the logic of it all doesn't it? And it opposes everything we have been taught from the moment we stuck our crooked little heads into the light. And this modern generation, with all of its emphasis on working and doing and overachieving, and man's seemingly limitless capacity to solve his problems and to advance himself with human initiative and ingenuity – the power of the human will; the boundary-shattering potential of technology and science at both the micro and the macro level – Oh my brethren we are so desperately and grievously wicked aren't we? Oh how fallen and polluted in our hearts we have become. Lord, help us! Lord, have mercy!

I dare say that I more than any am most guilty of this. I wish I could deny my own condition, but how can I when it is what I know so intimately; and have known all my vain, foolish life.

Oh gracious and glorious Father of Life – forgive us, for we have all sinned and fallen short of Your holy purpose. Oh Lord, why will we not forsake our ways? Why do we cling so stubbornly to only that which our minds can comprehend or our hands can accomplish? Why will we not hope in our Lord and Christ, when He is more than willing and able to save and sanctify us to the uttermost?

All throughout his ministry to the gentiles, the Apostle Paul struggled trying to get them not to be ashamed or repulsed on account of his weakness in presenting the gospel to them. In fact, it seems that he was always at any point at the brink of death as he poured himself out for the gospel of Christ.

> *And when I came to you, brethren, I did not come with superiority of speech or of wisdom, proclaiming to you the testimony of God. For I determined to know nothing among you except Jesus Christ, and Him crucified. I was with you in weakness and in fear and in much trembling, and my message and my preaching were not in persuasive words of wisdom, but in demonstration of the Spirit and of power, so that your faith would not rest on the wisdom of men, but on the power of God.*

> *Yet we do speak wisdom among those who are mature; a wisdom, however, not of this age nor of the rulers of this age, who are passing away; but we speak God's wisdom in a mystery, the hidden {wisdom} which God predestined before the ages to our glory; {the wisdom} which none of the rulers of this age has understood; for if they had understood it they would not have crucified the Lord of glory; but just as it is written,*

> *"THINGS WHICH EYE HAS NOT SEEN AND EAR HAS NOT HEARD, AND {which} HAVE NOT ENTERED THE HEART OF MAN, ALL THAT GOD HAS PREPARED FOR THOSE WHO LOVE HIM."*

> *For to us God revealed {them} through the Spirit; for the Spirit searches all things, even the depths of God. For who among men knows the {thoughts} of a man except the spirit of the man which is in him? Even so the {thoughts} of God no one knows except the Spirit of God. Now we have received, not the spirit of the world, but the Spirit who is from God, so that we may know the things freely given to us by God, which things we also speak, not in words taught by human wisdom, but in those taught by the Spirit, combining spiritual {thoughts} with spiritual {words.} But a natural man does not accept the things of the Spirit of God, for they are foolishness to him; and he cannot understand them, because they are spiritually appraised. But he who is spiritual appraises all things, yet he himself is appraised by no one.*
>
> *For WHO HAS KNOWN THE MIND OF THE LORD, THAT HE WILL INSTRUCT HIM? But we have the mind of Christ. (1 Cor. 2:1-16)*

Interesting that we have a generation of believers that, by all evidence, seems heaven-bent on eradicating all weakness and ill health, poverty and discomfort in the lives of the saints, when this appears to be precisely our Lord's pattern of ministry. So ready are we to exchange our sackcloth for silk, and our weakness for the humanist ideal of the shiny, all-together man, that the vast majority of Christian service and witness has become little more than emptiness and futility. If there is one thing new Christians must learn from the first day, it is that life can only spring forth out of death. Oh Lord, help us.

Dear friends, beloved saints of the Lord Jesus Christ – I am not here to condemn anyone, for then I could only begin and end with myself, and who among us could stand? Yet the Lord has impressed upon my heart the utter need for us in this age and generation to be in a posture of readiness and waiting upon Him alone. There is so much mixture and corruption in our midst and this cannot stand. For too long we have been directing our ways rather than letting the Lord direct us in His ways. It matters not what we can do, or would do, or might do given the resources – it matters only what He can do, and what He is doing. And don't pretend to think that you know His ways, for they more often than not turn all of our designs and plans upside down. He must know that we will wait for Him, trust in Him, and hope in Him, and follow Him down that path (the path of the cross) that seemingly makes no sense; that makes us squirm, that compels us to wait until the very last moment until He prevails over the plans of men and the fallen hosts of darkness. Only then does the glory rise up to where it belongs; only then my friends – don't be fooled.

This is so exceedingly important, for what is coming is a time of revealing, of stripping away. All will be made known in the time of shaking that is coming upon this earth. And when His little ones stand up adorned in sackcloth, and presenting only the pure and simple testimony of the Lamb, their every step will be determined and directed by the Lord. They will not so much as sit down or stand up unless His Word directs and equips them. They will appear wretched and failed as humanity beholds them; yet they will command the very might and power of the Creator as they witness for Him against the darkness all around. Like the Son of Man 2,000 years ago, there will be no beauty in them as the world deems beauty, and their words and testimony will make the many want only to kill and destroy them.

Are we ready, my brethren? Have we forsaken all of our thoughts and ways for His? What are our expectations regarding the end of this age anyway? I am sad to say that most of what the church is teaching today is doing little to prepare His people for what will be. In point of fact, by the Spirit of Truth that abides within me, most of the flock is being set up to be deceived by events that will transpire prior to our Lord's return. I pray you will not be one of them.

Yet we must take to heart that the ways and methods of men will not fulfill the purpose of God, nor bring Him the praise and glory He deserves. I too must come to terms with what I think about weakness and distress and despair, and my almost inborn need to eradicate it at all cost. Yes, we are to be strong, but not in our own strength. Yes, we are to do great things by our Lord, but He alone is the author and finisher of our faith and works. The very reality of small and pitiful little human beings doing extraordinary things beyond their ability or scope can only lead the world to consider who they are dealing with; who in fact stands before them. Herein lies the divine judgment of those final days soon upon us, dear brethren. This will not be a time for taking up swords to protect our Lord, or to rely on human reason or instinct or emotion or logic or education or any other known or created thing!

As always and forever, His grace is sufficient for us. Now this in no way means we will understand in advance what He is doing and why He is doing it. Not so, dear saints, for this is the path of child-like faith and trust. When He comes to us and asks us to do something that at once seems bizarre or incomprehensible, that our minds cannot in any way rationalize, here is where we must follow Him in perfect and trusting obedience. And if someone comes into your life or crosses your path; someone lowly and unimpressive to your eyes and human predilection; and yet they come with the very words and spirit of the Lord – do not despise them, but rather give praise and glory to the Father of our Lord Jesus Christ; who causes even the blind to see and the lame to stand and walk. And if perchance the Lord asks you to exchange your comfortable but empty little life for sackcloth and ash; for mourning and witness to the dread of this world and the foul sin in the heart of man – then my brother, don't look back, go forward in His grace and power alone; and be all that He would be in you, and say all that He might say through you; and suffer all that He might permit you to suffer and lose for His sake in this cursed world.

Dear saints of the Most High – no longer must it be that fleshly wisdom defines us and determines our conduct and testimony in this world. This is nothing to be proud of, as attested to by Paul to the Corinthians –

> *For our proud confidence is this: the testimony of our conscience, that in holiness and godly sincerity, not in fleshly wisdom but in the grace of God, we have conducted ourselves in the world, and especially toward you. (2 Cor. 1:12)*

Rather, we must appropriate all that the Lord provides for us through His expansive and ever-flowing grace. Just as our Savior and Shepherd lived breath-upon-breath and moment-to-moment by His Father's care and provision, so must we live in Him, for His gracious provision is more than sufficient for both life and godliness in this crooked generation. We must cease trusting in ourselves, in our quaint little religious urges, our vaunted opinions and positions pertaining to the Christian walk, our empty "the ends justify the means" results-oriented thinking. Both the way and the results belong to the Lord, as does all the glory. All praise and glory is His and must flow from the lives of His children as they forsake their ways for His.

Dear saints, I will leave you with a fascinating and mysterious passage in Ephesians that has always intrigued me personally –

> *To me, the very least of all saints, this grace was given, to preach to the Gentiles the unfathomable riches of Christ, and to bring to light what is the administration of the mystery which for ages has been hidden in God who created all things; so that the manifold wisdom of God might now be made known through the church to the rulers and the authorities in the heavenly places. (Eph. 3:8-12)*

Something ageless and mysterious; something demonstrating the manifold wisdom of God; something involving God's eternal purposes for the church is being played out on this earth and even the angels are watching intently. We must keep this in mind and take it to heart as we look out at the current and seemingly hopeless situation – where the church at large has forsaken her sanctuary and Lord and has become powerless and worldly; where Israel is in her land but is darkness to the gentiles and not God's intended light. He will prevail, my brethren, for His ways cannot fail, and His words cannot come back to Him empty and void. So let us trust Him and go to Him now if need be, and receive forgiveness and cleansing of our pride and self-trust. And each day let us be careful in the Spirit, that we don't fall for the temptation to start taking things upon ourselves as if this was our work and our kingdom.

Oh Heavenly and Eternal Father, keep us from the vanity of our own thoughts, and the emptiness and delusion of our own capacity. Purge us, dear Father, of all secret sin; and the deep brooding lust of glory that is in all of us. Make us ready Father, that we might stand in that appointed day; that indeed we might stand and show forth Your righteousness and truth in this godless and unholy world. Let all things be done for Your glory Oh Lord, by Your wisdom and way. Let it be Your strength and might alone that operates in the lives and testimony of Your little ones. Keep us from all delusion and deception and distraction that prevent Your purposes from being realized in our lives. And please come, Lord Jesus! Please come soon to claim us and to raise us up to where You are for ever and ever. Amen.

The Lord is My Portion

So many delusions and distractions today it seems, diverting the saints of God from essential things – so many forms and shadows that appear useful on the surface, to the natural wisdom, but so decidedly misplaced in terms of where we are in His ultimate plan and purpose.

I was out walking the other night and conversing with the Lord, when out of nowhere I said something like – "*Lord, I want you to be my only portion; I want to be satisfied with you alone.*" He then started to reveal the numerous things in my life that are currently my *portion* – things I trust in and rely upon and cling to. When I got back to my study, I opened the Scriptures because this whole concept of having only God as our share or portion was something that seemed so vitally important.

Consider the following passages –

> *"The LORD is my portion," says my soul, "Therefore I have hope in Him." (Lam. 3:24)*

> *The LORD is the portion of my inheritance and my cup. You support my lot. The lines have fallen to me in pleasant places; Indeed, my heritage is beautiful to me. (Psa. 16:5-6)*

> *One thing I have asked from the LORD, that I shall seek: That I may dwell in the house of the LORD all the days of my life, To behold the beauty of the LORD. And to meditate in His temple. (Psa. 27:4)*

> *O God, You are my God; I shall seek You earnestly;*

My soul thirsts for You, my flesh yearns for You, In a dry and weary land where there is no water. Thus I have seen You in the sanctuary, To see Your power and Your glory. Because Your lovingkindness is better than life, My lips will praise You. (Psa. 63:1)

Whom have I in heaven but you? And earth has nothing I desire besides you. My flesh and my heart may fail, but God is the strength of my heart and my portion forever. (Psa. 73:25-26)

The LORD is my portion; I have promised to keep Your words. I sought Your favor with all my heart; Be gracious to me according to Your word. (Psa. 119:57-58)

Look to the right and see; For there is no one who regards me; There is no escape for me; No one cares for my soul. I cried out to You, O LORD; I said, "You are my refuge, My portion in the land of the living. (Psa. 142:4-5)

But whatever things were gain to me, those things I have counted as loss for the sake of Christ. More than that, I count all things to be loss in view of the surpassing value of knowing Christ Jesus my Lord, for whom I have suffered the loss of all things, and count them but rubbish so that I may gain Christ, and may be found in Him, not having a righteousness of my own derived from the Law, but that which is through faith in Christ, the righteousness which comes from God on the basis of faith. (Phil. 3:7-9)

But He said to them "I have food to eat that you do not know about." So the disciples were saying to one another, "No one brought Him anything to eat, did he?" Jesus said to them, "My food is to do the will of Him who sent Me and to accomplish His work. (John 4:32)

This concept of selling or releasing all that we have such that we can attain the Lord God (not His gifts and blessings, but Himself as the gift and the ultimate blessing) as our portion, and be satisfied is a powerful one in the Bible, touching the very heart of His desire for His children. Consider the hard and horrendous life of Jeremiah, how he was asked to forsake all – his father's house, his calling in the priesthood, his nation, a bride and family of his own, his reputation, everything – all the prophet would be permitted to have was the Lord his God.

"The Lord is my portion."

My friends, perhaps take some time to read the Book of Jeremiah and Lamentations prayerfully, and ask the Lord to lead you to His ever-penetrating conclusions about your need for a prophet's heart and a prophet's conviction.

The times in Jeremiah's day were very much like our own, with anticipation of impending judgment, uncertainty, false and natural religion; an entire generation of believers professing true things but not partaking of the one True Thing; pride and trust in the temple or the church, and the activities of such as though by this the Lord God who sees the whole heart is impressed or satisfied. False prophets abounding with words of peace, peace and the easy way. And all the time Babylon is knocking at the door.

My friends, I really don't know what will happen; what circumstances or losses I will be asked to bear in order that He might know that I love Him, and that in Him as my only portion I will hope and be satisfied. This world means nothing to me, but I do have a wife and son whom I love deeply and dearly. In fact, they have been very much my portion for many years. I secretly fear that perhaps my love for them has often crossed the line into that dangerous area where idolatry begins. This is not a syrupy romantic, natural love as the world might recognize it, but rather a love born of time and dependence and belonging.

Am I ready to give them up if necessary? I can't answer that, only He can. But far greater men than I have been asked to give up far more. Again, consider the 40-50 years of Jeremiah's faithful service to the Lord; where our Lord's words were the prophet's very breath and food keeping him alive. Oh to sell all that we have, to relinquish all that hinders and obscures His purposes in us, to release ourselves completely like a little child falling into his father's arms behind him.

Yes, the oil is His life flowing into us and through us and out of us. In this sense can we ever have enough of His fullness and life. He is the living and flowing dynamic, the spark of divine existence and being, that animates these *jars of clay.*

Is He alone your portion brethren?

Perhaps it is time to go to him quietly now and let Him search all that is in your heart. Are you content with Him alone? Is He your one true desire? Have you discovered Him as the strength of your heart and life? If all else were required of you; all that you love and hold dear; would you let it go gladly that you might have Him, and Him alone? Is He your infinite supply or do you seek something elsewhere – in religion, or community perhaps, in the warm and familiar embrace of loved ones? Would you be willing, as the prophet Jeremiah, to be hated and considered an enemy by your family, your church, your pastor, or your nation – such that you would enter into the love and blessing of the Eternal God?

Why is it brethren that we covet so many things, even GOOD things (of and by themselves), when the very BEST thing is – God Himself.

And here's another thought –

If indeed we were that last generation of faithful servants before the Son of God returns for His own – should He not be the only one we trust and turn to in this darkest hour, when all is being aligned in opposition against Him and His testimony on the earth? If this world and even the "church" of His day utterly and brutally rejected Him, then will we be willing in this day also to suffer that rejection with Him, when no man would know Him or "*care for His soul*"?

> *Look to my right and see; no one is concerned for me. I have no refuge; no one cares for my life. I cried out to You, O LORD; I said, "You are my refuge, My portion in the land of the living." (Psa. 142:5)*

Dear saints, try to imagine if you will that everyone, and I mean everyone, including friends, family, fellow church members, has abandoned and rejected you; that they have cut you off from among them, then spoiled your goods, and left you festering on some dump heap somewhere to die. You had nothing, it would seem, as the world reckons it. Penniless, friendless, naked, alone – What would you have at that very moment? Would all be lost? Would you be as Job and curse the day you were conceived? Would you reckon your life's account to have a zero balance?

> *I WILL NEVER DESERT YOU, NOR WILL I EVER FORSAKE YOU. (Heb. 13:5)*

Oh dear ones, why does it seem that He is never enough for us? How fouled and wicked are our hearts, that He whom we should love the most, and be satisfied with above all else, is the one portion that we esteem so lightly? So many people and things and activities and pursuits that we always seem to so easily and naturally put before Him. Amazing isn't? Astounding! Oh Lord, save us from ourselves and our blind and covetous hearts.

Here is a spiritual insight that I hope and pray you will receive, my friends, and it is this –

True godly contentment can never be attained unless and until the Lord Our God becomes our only portion.

And here is a very serious question that I believe we would do well to answer honestly once and for all – Is prayer merely a means to an end for us, or is the time we spend in intimate fellowship with our Lord the ultimate end in our life? Do we seek Him or His blessings in other words?

Hmm.

"*The Lord is my portion*", wrote Jeremiah and the psalmist. "*My food is to do the will of Him who sent Me and to accomplish His work*", affirmed our Lord. If all we have is the Lord God, brethren, will that be enough for us? What now is our portion in this life? Are we willing to suffer the loss of it, whatever it might be, such that we might gain Christ in all His fullness and provision?

Oh Heavenly Father – we give praise and glory and honor to You and for Your most precious Son; so hard and deep are such thoughts oh Lord! Oh that in Your beloved Son we might enter into Thee as our only portion and provision; into all Your grace and fullness, into all Your ever-abounding life and blessing. Food indeed, we have beside meat for the natural body – and that food and vitality is Thee. Grant that we might have the oil of overcoming – the life that flows from Thee – flowing and moving in us as Your little children. Claim us as Your own, dear Father, claim us from the world and the evil one and all others who might seek to steal us away from Your heart! Make us ready and worthy for all that is coming to test the hearts of men – whether they truly love Thee or not. Forgive us, oh Father, for so weak and feeble are our hands and our hope. Make us holy in Thy Son; that all the world might see Your glory, Your splendor, Your beauty and Your ever-righteous judgments! In Jesus' name, we pray. Amen.

All That I Am

Dear brethren, precious and beloved of our Heavenly Father, I thank our Great God and the Lord Jesus Christ for all of you *out there* in the wilderness who regularly visit these pages and pray for this effort and the one sharing these thoughts. We are commanded to love one another by our Master who first loved us, and I can think of no deeper way to express this love than to bring each other before the throne of grace and help, and to join with one another in the spirit in prayer and patient petition.

The truth of the matter, brethren, is that we are all broken and in need of repair (or more accurately, *replacement*). Every single one of us, by virtue of all that we are and have become, is an offense to the Sovereign Creator and Judge who is infinitely holy and perfect and complete in every way. Oh how wondrous it is that when He considers us, when He looks down upon us, He sees His beloved and righteous Son, and not our filthy rags, and the leprosy of sin that cleaves to our very being.

Yet He has also sent forth His Holy and All-Searching Spirit into our hearts to reveal what we are at the root and core. And little ones, it ain't pretty to be sure. In fact, lately I must confess that I am being stripped bare of all that I am, as He shows me just how utterly wicked and thread-bare I really am. The mirror is nothing less than the Christ Himself, and my unlikeness to Him is positively appalling.

Please pray for me, brethren. Not that my life would be easy and smooth in this world. Not that He would grant me a new position somewhere where I can be a somebody with a face and a name. Not that I would be able to enjoy a pain-and-suffering-free existence in this world. Not that I would have the *abundant and over-flowing life* they talk about on Christian radio and television. Not that my family would enjoy uninterrupted good health and blessing continuously.

No, not that, my friends. Not that at all. But rather that He would do something mighty and miraculous with my loose tongue, and impulsive nature; That He would confound my stubborn pride and self-will. That over forty years of doing things *my way* and *for myself* would finally and ultimately come to an end; that I would learn once and for all to trust Him completely, and stop trying to navigate this life by my instincts and intelligence and soulish wisdom; that I would once and for all stop listening to men, and start learning to discern His voice and His direction alone.

Oh brethren, I am broken more than you can ever know. Yet I know, for I live inside this mind and this heart every single moment of every day. I want so much to be useful and profitable to Him, but something keeps getting in the way – and it is always ME! And everything that I am and have become in this life!

Perhaps you have read many of the high-sounding sentiments I have shared over the years and have supposed that this author is somehow further down this road than you are; that I have drunk deep and long at the heavenly fountain. Funny isn't it, how we human beings tend to do that. Yet we should know better as disciples of the Lord Jesus Christ.

Have you ever wondered how the Bible seems to make a point of revealing the errors and weaknesses of the saints? Noah getting drunk on wine. Abraham lying about His wife to Pharaoh. Jonah running away from his post. Peter denying the Lord three times.

Please pray that He would help me; that He would break me down such that He can build me up again in His Son. All or nothing. In one respect, it matters little to me that I have been saved or redeemed or baptized or any other religious sounding thing. What I want more than anything now, dear ones, is to be holy as He is holy; to be righteous as He is righteous; and ultimately to be something from which He can derive even some small measure of glory and honor.

Brethren, you know it really doesn't matter how we became what we are – nature or nurture, genetics or environment. The only thing that matters is that all that we are is of positively no use to God unless and until He can reshape us into His very image. It is this image we see as we gaze upon the Holy One – *the Bright and Shining Star!*

In the end, we are either a good tree or a bad tree, and our fruit gives us away, regardless of how religious or Christian we try to appear before others.

> *So every good tree bears good fruit, but the bad tree bears bad fruit. A good tree cannot produce bad fruit, nor can a bad tree produce good fruit. (Matt. 7:17-18)*

> *"I am the vine, you are the branches. He who abides in Me, and I in him, bears much fruit; for without Me you can do nothing." (John 15:5)*

My friends, I must confess before you that for most of my Christian life I have attempted to bring forth good fruit, even though I am, in every sense of the word, a *bad tree*. I am sure many of you know how this works. It is like draping a shiny new suit of clothes over a filthy body; yet at some point the fruit must give us away and reveal us for what we truly are.

So please pray that the Lord would make me a good tree, with good roots and good branches and good fruit. And the hard truth of the matter is that there is really only one Good Tree, as John 15 affirms.

Like many others, I have made the fatal mistake of wanting to do something meaningful for the Lord at the end of this age. Strange isn't it, how we so readily presume that He actually needs us flawed and puny human beings to restore this earth to agreement with Him, or put all of His enemies under His feet, or accomplish anything of eternal consequence?

Strange also, how we seem to so readily see the mysterious New Man in Christ, and what this presents to us individually, as merely a means to a larger end. Perhaps this is why the church spends a million dollars to save one single human being, and only a penny to teach them what this means. Incidentally, I have often compared this to companies selling products, who spend 99% of their budget on marketing (getting the customer) and only 1% on customer service (keeping the customer) after the fact.

The bottom line, at the end of the day, is that we have all been saved that we might become holy! And if that is not our underlying hope or intention then perhaps we are better off back in the muck and mire of the world, scratching and clawing, without hope and without God!

Brethren, please pray that He would do whatever it takes, that I would be conformed to the image of His Son. That the same precious blood that washed me thoroughly and brought newness of life into my dead spirit, would cleanse me of my unclean lips, my self-indulgent ways, my impulsive and foolish nature, my faithless heart, and my seeking after a place in this world.

This means a lot to me, believe me. I need you just as much as you need me. This is what it means to be one in the spirit; to both gain and suffer as the entire body gains and suffers. We really have nothing to hide from each other, as we all know (or should anyway) what the human heart truly looks like. I have always thought that the more we abide with each other in our weakness and need of cleansing, then the more intimately we will abide in He who is the True Life of the Body. I hope that makes sense. I am learning these things too, my friends believe me, and often in my case it is the hard and long way. Let us learn the lesson of the Apostle Paul, and not be ashamed of our weakness in this world.

> *And He has said to me, "My grace is sufficient for you, for power is perfected in weakness." Most gladly, therefore, I will rather boast about my weaknesses, so that the power of Christ may dwell in me. (2 Cor. 12:9)*

Thank you, and may our gracious and mighty Lord bless and establish you at the end of this age. He is coming soon don't you know? The hour is late, and the time is short brethren. Let us not turn back, as did Lot's wife, to the foul, yet familiar stench of Sodom, but let us go forward into His Glorious Kingdom! Amen.

To Taste and See

As the deer pants for the water brooks, So my soul pants for You, O God. My soul thirsts for God, for the living God; When shall I come and appear before God? (Psa. 42:1-2)

O God, You are my God; I shall seek You earnestly; My soul thirsts for You, my flesh yearns for You, In a dry and weary land where there is no water. (Psa. 63:1)

We have elsewhere alluded to the reality that, as spirit-born children of a Heavenly Father, only God Himself can truly satisfy the thirst He has given us. David, in particular, recognized this reality and wrote about it often, stretching even language to its breaking point. Those who are truly His, living and breathing and abiding in the fullness and life of the Son, can affirm this intimately, for to taste the *Bread of Life* even once is to desire more; this is a living principle and how the Father of Life has ordained it.

Here, we would like to pursue this concept of heavenly food even further, as the Spirit permits, for it represents to us the essential things such as sustenance and survival and healing. Without nourishment the body will weaken and die; this is as true in the natural realm as it is in the spiritual.

In Ezekiel, we learn that one like David himself will be established as the true and faithful shepherd over the Lord's people –

"Then I will set over them one shepherd, My servant David, and he will feed them; he will feed them himself and be their shepherd." (Eze. 34:23)

Of course we know this to be none other than the Father's Beloved and Faithful Son, Jesus Christ. And later, in the New Testament, we see this responsibility extended and fulfilled through His first disciples –

> *So when they had finished breakfast, Jesus said to Simon Peter, "Simon, son of John, do you love Me more than these?" He said to Him, "Yes, Lord; You know that I love You." He said to him, "Tend My lambs." He said to him again a second time, "Simon, son of John, do you love Me?" He said to Him, "Yes, Lord; You know that I love You." He said to him, "Shepherd My sheep." He said to him the third time, "Simon, son of John, do you love Me?" Peter was grieved because He said to him the third time, "Do you love Me?" And he said to Him, "Lord, You know all things; You know that I love You." Jesus said to him, "Tend My sheep." (John 21:15-17)*

> *"Be on guard for yourselves and for all the flock, among which the Holy Spirit has made you overseers, to shepherd the church of God which He purchased with His own blood." (Acts 20:28)*

> *Therefore, I exhort the elders among you, as your fellow elder and witness of the sufferings of Christ, and a partaker also of the glory that is to be revealed, shepherd the flock of God among you, exercising oversight not under compulsion, but voluntarily, according to the will of God; and not for sordid gain, but with eagerness; nor yet as lording it over those allotted to your charge, but proving to be examples to the flock. And when the Chief Shepherd appears, you will receive the unfading crown of glory." (1 Pet. 5:1-4)*

So what, in fact, is this food that this Shepherd will provide for His hungry sheep. Let's consider this further, for our very survival and development in the Spirit rests upon both the One who feeds and the food itself.

In Genesis we see that the Creator speaks life into existence; that all of His creation responds to His Word. In this sense then, it is a creative and sustaining Word – a Living Word. And it is a faithful word because it never returns to Him void or empty.

> *So will My word be which goes forth from My mouth; It will not return to Me empty, Without accomplishing what I desire, And without succeeding in the matter for which I sent it. (Isa. 55:11)*

It always fulfils precisely what He purposes for it. This may sound familiar for there was another to whom this describes –

> *Meanwhile the disciples were urging Him, saying, "Rabbi, eat." But He said to them, "I have food to eat that you do not know about." So the disciples were saying to one another, "No one brought Him anything to eat, did he?" Jesus said to them, "My food is to do the will of Him who sent Me and to accomplish His work. (John 4:31-34)*

Just as the Creator's Word spoke the heavens and the earth (and all things in them) into existence in Genesis, Jesus Christ is the Living Word whose food is to do the will of the Father and to finish all the work that He has purposed. In fact, this very same Word is one and the same from the beginning, as John affirms for us –

> *In the beginning was the Word, and the Word was with God, and the Word was God. He was in the beginning with God. All things came into being through Him, and apart from Him nothing came into being that has come into being. In Him was life, and the life was the Light of men. (John 1:1-4)*

What sustained our Lord on the earth, as His food and sustenance, was actively pursuing the will and work of His Father in Heaven. And as the living and dynamic Word that expresses all life into being, He in turn represents the food we need to live and grow in Him. Often we hear teachers tell us that the Scriptures are the food we need to remain spiritually healthy and to grow up in the faith. This is only partially true of course, as the Lord Himself is the Living Word and Expressive Truth that encompasses all of the Father's creative will and purposes.

The physical manna falling daily in the wilderness was a wondrous and miraculous source of life and health for the people of Israel. Yet it was not provided or intended to satisfy the hunger that only the Bread of Life could satisfy.

> *"He humbled you and let you be hungry, and fed you with manna which you did not know, nor did your fathers know, that He might make you understand that man does not live by bread alone, but man lives by everything that proceeds out of the mouth of the LORD." (Deut. 8:3)*

Notice how David expresses this –

> *Trust in the LORD and do good; Dwell in the land and cultivate (or feed on) faithfulness. (Psa. 37:3)*

> *O taste and see that the LORD is good; How blessed is the man who takes refuge in Him! (Psa. 34:8)*

To feed on something, to literally take it into your mouth so you can taste it, is a form of apprehension and experience that goes deeper than sight or touch or even hearing it with your ears. Only when this food gets inside you, and becomes part of you, can you know it truly, and only then will its life-sustaining energy begin to work. All the while the Israelites were constantly worrying about food and physical survival, and experiencing the faithfulness and goodness of the Lord's miraculous provision, they were failing to learn the lesson that they were to feed on the Lord's faithfulness; to taste that He is good and trustworthy, that "*life is more than meat, and the body [is more] than raiment.*"

Sadly they were more like those described by Paul –

> *For many walk, of whom I often told you, and now tell you even weeping, that they are enemies of the cross of Christ, whose end is destruction, whose god is their appetite, and whose glory is in their shame, who set their minds on earthly things." (Phil. 3:18-19)*

Like Esau before them, they hungered only for the earthly pottage that fills the body for a time, and not for the Living Bread who represents true life and fullness for the spirit in man.

We would do well to heed this lesson brethren, for the very fact that most of them did not enter into the promised land represents a harsh lesson for us. We must be careful if we are so convinced in ourselves that we are standing in the Lord, lest we fall in our delusion.

> *"Blessed are those who hunger and thirst for righteousness, for they shall be satisfied." (Matt. 5:6)*
>
> *Jesus said to them, "I am the bread of life; he who comes to Me will not hunger, and he who believes in Me will never thirst." (John 6:35)*
>
> *...for the kingdom of God is not eating and drinking, but righteousness and peace and joy in the Holy Spirit. (Rom. 14:17)*

Yes, this spiritual food includes biblical teaching and doctrine (*milk*), but the real meat (*solid food*) that the Father wants us to sink our spiritual teeth into is Christ in all His fullness and life. It literally broke the Apostle Paul's heart that he could not take these *babes* deeper into the provision and sufficiency of the Lord Jesus Christ, as our All and Everything; as the food that will ultimately satisfy us for all eternity. This is where all of these natural and physical shadows and types in the Old Testament lead. He alone is the conclusion of the matter; the moral of the story if you will. Ever so painfully and slowly it seems I am starting to learn this wondrous principle.

> *Brothers, I could not address you as spiritual but as worldly—mere infants in Christ. I gave you milk, not solid food, for you were not yet ready for it. Indeed, you are still not ready. (1 Cor. 3:1-2)*
>
> *For though by this time you ought to be teachers, you have need again for someone to teach you the elementary principles of the oracles of God, and you have come to need milk and not solid food. For everyone who partakes only of milk is not accustomed to the word of righteousness, for he is an infant. But solid food is for*

> *the mature, who because of practice have their senses trained to discern good and evil. (Heb. 5:12-14)*
>
> *Jesus answered and said to them, "This is the work of God, that you believe in Him whom He has sent." So they said to Him, "What then do You do for a sign, so that we may see, and believe You? What work do You perform? "Our fathers ate the manna in the wilderness; as it is written, 'HE GAVE THEM BREAD OUT OF HEAVEN TO EAT.'" Jesus then said to them, "Truly, truly, I say to you, it is not Moses who has given you the bread out of heaven, but it is My Father who gives you the true bread out of heaven. "For the bread of God is that which comes down out of heaven, and gives life to the world." Then they said to Him, "Lord, always give us this bread."*
>
> *Jesus said to them, "I am the bread of life; he who comes to Me will not hunger, and he who believes in Me will never thirst. "But I said to you that you have seen Me, and yet do not believe. "All that the Father gives Me will come to Me, and the one who comes to Me I will certainly not cast out. "For I have come down from heaven, not to do My own will, but the will of Him who sent Me." (John 6:29-38)*

So what about you and I? Is He our daily bread? Do we feed on the strength, wisdom and righteousness of the Lord Jesus Christ? Or, are we actively seeking to be filled by some other means? He does indeed save us but He is so much more than a Savior. He does indeed justify us, but He is so much more than merely a Justifier. He certainly sanctifies us, but He is by no means limited to that. You see brethren, these are mere doctrines, and although they do hold a place, they can only be touched or handled, never *tasted*. Better that we understand and apprehend Him as the Bread of Life, and the Living Water, and the flesh and blood of the Lamb slain from before the foundation of the world. The life is in the food and the feeding. Oh that He would impress this on His people! Oh that we would be so much more than theologians or Bible scholars – and savor the sweetness of the Living, Creative Word!

My friends, in this context there are really only three groups of people on the earth today. The first care nothing of the things of God and generally go about their little, natural lives "*sitting down to eat and drink and rising up to play*" (Exodus 32:6). They want only to fill their bellies, much like Esau, who forsook his birthright for a bowl of soup to appease his carnal hunger.

The second have a taste for spiritual things, perhaps attend church regularly, even consider themselves well-schooled in the truths of Scripture. Many in fact are what they would consider fundamentalist or conservative in their understanding and approach to the Christian faith. Yet, because the soul has not been brought under the subjection of the spirit, they know only the theological word (*milk*). A such, they remain babes; born again to be sure, but stunted in growth, not walking and pressing deeper into the life and provision of God's Heavenly Bread. Satisfied only with milk, they know little of *hungering and thirsting for righteousness*; of eating the body and drinking the blood of the Lamb of God. When they read things like David wrote in the Psalms, about "*tasting and seeing*" the Lord's goodness, and "*feeding on (or cultivating) His faithfulness*", it is more poetry than a living dynamic marking the difference between life and death; between divine life and humanly-sustained religion.

The third group has grown faint in this world, feeding for a time on its food and philosophy and religion. Yet, they have come to the point where they are no longer satisfied with the enriched white bread of man's pursuit of God and meaning. They are tired of eating and drinking and still feeling empty and wasted. They have perhaps sampled many different foods on their journey, yet each leaves them even more empty. They hunger for something real; something substantial; something that will finally satisfy the longing in their spirit. After tasting the sweet manna of the wilderness, they desire the true *Heavenly Bread* sent down from the Father. And for the very few who have partaken of this Bread, their lives have been changed and enriched forever. They have partaken of the fruit of the Father's glorious provision of life, and its taste is sweet and full in their mouths. It sends out strength and healing and victory over the *old man*, and all that is sickly and weak within them. And they are forever one with Him whom they have partaken. Finally, they have come to see that life can only flow from the Living Word that is inside them. To derive life from Him, then to live and move in the power and energy of that life, is what the Creator had always intended for them.

I recognize, with all frankness and humility, that there are elements of each of these in every one of us, my brethren. At least I can say this of myself even on my best days. But I also recognize that "*in Him we live and move and have our being*" and that He is the very fullness of God because He is the very food of God. There is no other. Believe me, as someone who has spent many years on this earth sampling this or that delicacy, hoping it will appease my hungry soul, I can confess honestly and completely that He is indeed the only One. Everything else is junk food, which is no food at all.

My hope and prayer is that each of us would feed on the Lord's faithfulness; on His strength and fullness; and that we would taste and see that He is good and trustworthy, and that His Word never returns to Him empty or void. It is the very creative voice of God, and the Son, and only until we develop an appetite for this Heavenly Bread will we ever hope to be truly satisfied. Don't be fooled by anything else, dear ones. And if you feel like you have been on milk for far too long, the time to go on to Him is now. Ask Him for the meat that is the *Lamb of God*, and He will not disappoint you.

By His grace and power, let us partake of the Prince of Life, and grow thereby in all ways pleasing to our Heavenly Father! Let us pray daily for one another as the time of His appearing draws near. Let us present ourselves before Him as a living sacrifice pleasing to the Father, no longer living and being for ourselves but for Him and His Glorious Kingdom. Let us forsake the cares of this world, the love of self and pleasure and money and getting more, more more! He is all we need my friends; all we need in every sense! Let us draw further into the Light as the darkness of the pit rises up with all manner of wickedness and deceit and violence against the household of God! Most of all, let us come to Him meekly as little children, acknowledging our absolute dependence on Him for all things pertaining to the life of the body and the Spirit.

In Jesus' precious name, we pray. Amen.

Let There Be Light!

Before we begin brethren, please pray for one another as the revealing of the saints draws near, as the kingdoms of this world become the Kingdom of our Lord and of His Christ. Pray also that His will be done on this earth as it is in heaven. I pray for all His little ones every day – that our dear and heavenly Father will bring you to glory in His beloved Son.

I am deeply grateful for all of you, so few yet so genuine, who frequent these pages, and have determined to press ever deeper into all that the Father has for us through His Son. I know we can seem at times scattered and isolated here in the wilderness, but we are closer than we think in the true measure of spiritual intimacy and relationship. We are one in Him, and bound spiritually to each other with a bond that nothing in this world, nor time or space can separate. And soon, brethren, very soon (I can almost feel it in my spiritual bones) we shall be forever together with He who has formed us together in Himself.

What I would like to share in this message is something the Lord has been affirming to me lately, and that is the reality that in His eyes, as He beholds this world and everything in it, there is only darkness and light (night and day), and all authority and activity is represented by either one or the other. Here are some passages, in no particular order, that bear this out –

> *For He rescued us from the domain of darkness, and transferred us to the kingdom of His beloved Son. (Col. 1:13)*

> *For our struggle is not against flesh and blood, but against the rulers, against the powers, against the*

world forces of this darkness, against the spiritual forces of wickedness in the heavenly places. (Eph. 6:12)

But you, brethren, are not in darkness, that the day would overtake you like a thief; for you are all sons of light and sons of day. We are not of night nor of darkness. (1 Thess. 5:4-5)

"You are the light of the world. A city set on a hill cannot be hidden; nor does anyone light a lamp and put it under a basket, but on the lampstand, and it gives light to all who are in the house. "Let your light shine before men in such a way that they may see your good works, and glorify your Father who is in heaven." (Matt. 5: 14-16)

This is the message we have heard from Him and announce to you, that God is Light, and in Him there is no darkness at all. If we say that we have fellowship with Him and {yet} walk in the darkness, we lie and do not practice the truth; but if we walk in the Light as He Himself is in the Light, we have fellowship with one another, and the blood of Jesus His Son cleanses us from all sin. (1 John 1:5-7)

In Him was life, and the life was the Light of men. The Light shines in the darkness, and the darkness did not comprehend it. There came a man sent from God, whose name was John. He came as a witness, to testify about the Light, so that all might believe through him. He was not the Light, but {he came} to testify about the Light. There was the true Light which, coming into the world, enlightens every man. (John 1:4-9)

Then Jesus again spoke to them, saying, "I am the Light of the world; he who follows Me will not walk in the darkness, but will have the Light of life." (John 8:12)

But you are A CHOSEN RACE, A royal PRIESTHOOD, A HOLY NATION, A PEOPLE FOR God's OWN POSSESSION, so that you may proclaim the excellen-

cies of Him who has called you out of darkness into His marvelous light. (1 Pet. 2:9)

Dearest saints, sons of the day, are we truly aware of what occurs when He claims us for Himself; that indeed, we are spiritually transferred from a domain of darkness ruled by a liar and a pretender, into His Glorious Kingdom of Light in which the true Light of the world (John 8:12), Jesus Christ, is King. All physical realities, elements and forces that shine forth light into darkness, such as the sun and the stars and flame, are merely figments and shadows of the One who is the True Light of the world. And the glorious truth is that His marvellous and penetrating light can shine forth in us who live and walk in Him. He is that Bright and Morning Star who brings the dawn and daylight to a dark world cursed with perpetual night.

Notice again in John 1, where it says that "*In Him was life, and the life was the Light of men.*" It is nothing in ourselves – our wisdom, works, intellect, good intentions, morals or religion – that represents this "*light*" in us, but His very life working in and through us. In coming freely and humbly to Him, we come out of darkness and into light; revealed for the first time, seeing clearly for the first time, exposed for the first time, alive and seeing the dawn of day by that *Bright and Morning Star.* For God is Light and in Him there is no darkness. Only He can enlighten us; and He does so by His eternally creative command – "*Let there be Light*".

Brethren, this too must be our deepest intent and desire, that true light would enlighten us, radiating outward everywhere we go in this dark, shadow-filled world. There is no clearer distinction than light and darkness; day and night. And even the smallest, most insignificant light will always dispel the darkness.

So then, my beloved, just as you have always obeyed, not as in my presence only, but now much more in my absence, work out your salvation with fear and trembling; for it is God who is at work in you, both to will and to work for His good pleasure. Do all things without grumbling or disputing; so that you will prove yourselves to be blameless and innocent, children of

> *God above reproach in the midst of a crooked and perverse generation, among whom you appear as lights in the world, among whom you shine as lights in the world. (Phil. 2:12-15)*

> *Therefore do not be partakers with them; for you were formerly darkness, but now you are Light in the Lord; walk as children of Light (for the fruit of the Light consists in all goodness and righteousness and truth), trying to learn what is pleasing to the Lord. Do not participate in the unfruitful deeds of darkness, but instead even expose them; for it is disgraceful even to speak of the things which are done by them in secret. But all things become visible when they are exposed by the light, for everything that becomes visible is light. For this reason it says,*

> *"Awake, sleeper, And arise from the dead, And Christ will shine on you." (Eph. 5:7-14)*

Nothing wrought of ourselves, however high or noble in nature will shine forth as His light. Only the *marvelous light* of Jesus Christ – the True Light – shining in us will scatter the darkness of this world and bring glory to the Father. Anything less is simply advancing darkness and death. Even the capacity to see what is wrought in the Light is itself evidence that we have this *Light of Life*.

There are indeed many in the world today who say that they have fellowship with Him and yet *walk in darkness*. This is a serious thing brethren, as only a dark and deluded heart could think this to be so. For the Son of God is Light, and only those who walk in this Light truly abide in active fellowship with Him. In Him there is no darkness whatsoever, and all the world and everything contained in it is shrouded in secrecy and darkness. Nothing is as it seems. All is built on a lie, and to the degree that believers abide in this world, we represent and advance the darkness. Dear brethren, this should not be so –

> *For He rescued us from the domain of darkness, and transferred us to the kingdom of His beloved Son. (Col. 1:13)*

We need to pray always that He would show us the darkness that is even within us, and infuse us with His marvelous light, the *Light of Life* that is in Himself.

Another aspect of this is found in Matthew 6, where our Lord teaches us that to see spiritually requires light –

> *The eye is the lamp of the body; so then if your eye is clear, your whole body will be full of light. But if your eye is bad, your whole body will be full of darkness. If then the light that is in you is darkness, how great is the darkness! (Matt. 6:22-23)*

If the Light of God is in us, then we will be able to discern between spiritual light and spiritual darkness, just as our physical eyes do in the material realm. As it is through the eyes that we take in all around us, it is essential that our spiritual eyes be equipped to see clearly. It is not enough to judge things by our physical eyes, for all is a deception in this world, and even the devil can make himself appear to be an angel of light –

> *But I am not surprised! Even Satan can disguise himself as an angel of light. (2 Cor. 11:14)*

Again, nothing in this world is as it seems, as many of you know, dear saints. The world is darkness because the god of this world is the personification of darkness. All is rooted in a age-old lie that has been concealed in the shadows since that first dawn. That man can live apart from the one who made Him, and formed Him for Himself and His Glory – this is the dark lie that has been foisted so viciously on those still under the cover of night; those who have yet to come into the Light.

Yet the blessed wonder of it all is that, by His grace, we have been given the gift of sight; able to behold that which is real and true by the Light of He who is Truth! Praise God, for in Him now we can *practice the truth* and thereby enter into His Light! And perfect revelation demands that there will be no darkness (*deception, dishonesty, craftiness, guile, impurity, etc.*) in us whatsoever; that there will be no unlikeness to the One who is the pure and perfect and all-revealing Light.

Oh gracious and wise Father, please show us where there is darkness and shadow in us. Expose and reveal all of the secret places in our hearts where we even deceive ourselves of our real condition and need for illumination. Dear Lord, let the all-penetrating Light of your Beloved Son shine on us, and from us ever brighter, even more constant and true. Help us, Father, not to love the darkness or rely on it to cover up what we truly are. Oh Lord, bring us into Your Glorious and Eternal Light that we might see clearly, once and for all. Amen.

In Proverbs we read –

> *But the path of the righteous is like the light of dawn,*
> *That shines brighter and brighter until the full day.*
> *(Prov. 4:18)*

And so what is the "*path of the righteous*" if not the very life of the Son, the Lord Jesus Christ? Did He not say that He was *the way and the truth and the life*? This is the true Light, my friends, and nothing else claiming to be enlightenment or illumination or anything else will do. He is the divine spark of life that has come into the world to enlighten each and every one of us who has received Him by faith. Of course, "*the powers…* the *world forces of this darkness*" despise this Light, for He exposes their ways as evil, and reveals all for what it truly is. Nothing can hide from He who is the Light of the World, and the *night* is always threatened by the *day* that will bring a swift end to its shadowy reign.

Precious saints, if indeed we are of the day and not of the night, then why do so many us still walk in darkness? Why do we still trust the dark designs of those who obscure the perfect ways and wisdom of our God? Why do we so often live in the shadows rather than coming forward into His magnanimous Light? Why are we more often blind than seeing what we need to see; what His Light alone reveals – first in ourselves, and then in everything else? Do we not understand that in Christ alone we who were "*formerly darkness*" have been transferred from a "*domain of darkness*" into a Kingdom of Light?

Now there are many things that promise great things and big results, even in this Christian walk. Yet if anything, even a good thing in itself, obscures the Lord Jesus Christ, the Light of the World, in any way, then it is darkness and must be stamped out and rejected.

Can we actually see this brethren, with spiritual eyes wide open? Can we see that He alone is the Light that lights our way; that He is the Sun around which all things *live and move and have their being*? Can we see that it is His life in us, *eternal life*, that brings glory to the Father and blessing to others? Can we see that anything or anyone that promises to provide illumination, that does not center around Christ Jesus, are not lights at all, but merely expressions of darkness? I dare say, quite solemnly in fact, that there is much darkness, even in the Christian church. Oh Father have mercy on us! May Your Son shine on all of those still in darkness; especially those who love the darkness and the shadow.

Dear children of the morning, as we approach this final Day of the Lord, His day of reckoning and judgment, let us take to heart these words –

> *"This is the judgment, that the Light has come into the world, and men loved the darkness rather than the Light, for their deeds were evil. "For everyone who does evil hates the Light, and does not come to the Light for fear that his deeds will be exposed. "But he who practices the truth comes to the Light, so that his deeds may be manifested as having been wrought in God."* *(1 John 3:19-21)*

We too, dear saints, represent His Light by which those in the world who love the darkness will be judged. No doubt they will respond to us as they did to the One who is the True Source of all Light. They will try to quench His Light in us lest they be exposed for what they are. Yet in persecution and death, His Light will shine even brighter in His witnesses, just as His Light has never been quenched from the hill of Calvary and never will.

Oh glorious and Wonderful Father, *Most Ancient of Days* – let there be Light in your children! Let the precious light and truth and life of Your Son fill us and surround us completely. Let His Light shine forth radiantly from Your little ones as a testimony to You and the *Bright and Morning Star* who is the Life of the World. Oh Lord, there is darkness and death all around us in this hour; in our families and workplaces; in our churches and institutions, in all the lies and false assumptions that undergird everything. Lies and deception and mistrust at every level of society, from top to bottom, with so many loving the lie, and advancing the darkness all around them.

Oh Father, let us shine forth for Thee and for Thy Glory. Scatter all darkness within us, even if it means pain and loss and the shattering of all of our idols. Let Your Son's Glorious Light fill us throughout, emanating out from us in our words and works wrought only in Him! Oh Beloved Father, please, please, *Let there be Light*! In Jesus' name, we pray. Amen.

Not as the World Gives

Dear saints, beloved of the Lord, these past few weeks have been simply agonizing for me, full of confusion, turmoil, anguish, sleeplessness, blindness, bewilderment and questioning. I have come face to face with the world in its rawest form and its bitter hatred of those who belong to the Lord Jesus Christ. Yet our Heavenly Father, in His illimitable wisdom and love, has deemed me worthy of such suffering and persecution. It seems the self in me has a long way to go before it will willingly lay down and die as it ought; indeed, as it must so that He might rise up out of the ashes of this fallen flesh. So much easier it is to read about turning the other cheek and deferring to His will than actually doing it when confronted with malicious betrayal and the very depths of hell seem to be rising up against us.

At times like these, as I am sure many of you understand, we find ourselves stumbling in the dark, trying to comprehend what is happening; why events don't make any sense. We can't seem to turn our mind off, to keep it from spinning and replaying the same things over and over again. We are powerless, and nothing we do appears to offer comfort or resolution. We are so utterly disoriented that it begins to be clear what the Scriptures mean when they refer to us as aliens and sojourners in this world.

I must confess that many of my responses of late were nothing more or less than the soul in all of its ugly and defiant pride, trying to defend and assert itself in this world, to protect myself and my reputation against the torrent of lies, confusion and attack. So very sad, and I am not feeling very Christian right now. I didn't even want to return to these writings, as I felt so very hypocritical.

Like Job and Jacob, I felt like I was wrestling with God spiritually and mentally. I wasn't at all sure why these things were happening, how He could permit them. I couldn't pray for a couple of days, and when I did all that came out was self-pitying and self-justifying whining. Sound familiar? I couldn't actually concentrate on anything for any length of time. I would open the Bible, but there seemed to be a thick wall inserted between me and the words.

Disillusioned, disheartened, and feeling alone and rejected, it was as if I had died, that my heart had stopped. I cried out to Him for He is all I have. I have no one else. All that the Lord has been showing me over this past many months; the depths of His ways and wisdom summed up in His Beloved Son. All these high-minded prayers about going further and deeper and letting it all go. All became fuzzy and twisted as the gentle hand of His comforting Spirit seemed to be lifted from my life.

Although I kept crying out to Him for understanding and meaning (why Lord, why Lord), this was not really what I needed at all, and He knew that perfectly as only He can. At that very moment where I couldn't possibly endure another second, His voice broke through from Heaven, deep into my very being. It was like an anvil had been lifted from my chest.

> *"I have allowed this my son. I will carry you through it. You are not alone."*

Peace. Unspeakable peace and comfort. Just as our Lord assured us –

> *"Peace I leave with you; My peace I give to you; not as the world gives do I give to you. Do not let your heart be troubled, nor let it be fearful." (John 14:27)*

> *"These things I have spoken to you, so that in Me you may have peace. In the world you have tribulation, but take courage; I have overcome the world." (John 16:33)*

Dear friends, my heart was troubled and I was very much afraid. I thought I was going out of my mind. Nothing made any sense, as I mentioned. So what does He mean by this assurance of peace?

Here we see that His peace is not necessarily the absence or mitigation of tribulation or conflict, as this is what the world means by peace. The world is always talking about and pining for peace, but the history of the world and the shattered condition of the human experience reveal how utterly empty and powerless such sentiment has become.

To the world, peace infers the absence of conflict, enmity, distress, animosity; the free and easy life in other words. Yet our Lord's peace is something altogether different, as I am slowly and painfully discovering. He has pretty much guaranteed, has He not, that in the world, we will have trouble, tribulation and conflict (the absence of peace as the world would see it)? The world hates Him, and so it only follows that it will hate us also. The destroyer is constantly seeking our destruction and will stop at nothing to achieve it. The spirit of antichrist that pervades all the world and those aligned to it is enmity to the Spirit of God and His Christ.

> *"I have given them Your word; and the world has hated them, because they are not of the world, even as I am not of the world. "I do not ask You to take them out of the world, but to keep them from the evil one. "They are not of the world, even as I am not of the world. (John 17:14-16)*

Yet, our Lord's desire is not that we would be removed from the world, either physically or by a conflict-free existence, but rather kept in His peace here in the middle of it. Here in the world is our proving ground; the place we need Him and His peace the most. We are to remain present in this world, and in many respects subject to it, as a stunning and vital testimony to Jesus Christ and His Kingdom.

Our Lord's promised peace is quite different from the kind offered by the world isn't it? Although we would certainly appreciate it sometimes, it does not involve in any manner the absence of antagonism and tribulation, but the assurance of His presence in the midst of it, banishing worry and anxiety even though difficult people and situations provoke them. In fact, it is often the case that He would have us venture forth into circumstances that will place us at risk, provoke conflict with the world, and leave us with only Him (and His strength, peace and comfort) to fall back on. "*He who is in us is greater than he who is in the world.*" – Indeed, and the world will discover this whether it wants to or not.

And how does His peace come to us? Those who have spent anytime in the Word, know that the Father does not grant anything good to His children apart from Jesus Christ. He alone is the essence of all simplicity and fulfillment. Every heavenly provision is embodied and made available in Him. The granting of His peace is no exception. John 16:33 reminds us that "*in Me you have peace*", meaning that peace is not some emotional attribute or quality of mind that He provides apart from Himself. His peace is made possible only by Him abiding in our hearts, as we abide in this world. He alone is our peace, here in the midst of pressure, persecution and the spirit of enmity that pervades the world. The Lord's promise of the Comforter was the promise of His Holy Spirit. Peace, as with any other divine attribute is synonymous with the Lord Jesus Christ. He is the true vine from which all heavenly fruit is derived. He alone is our "*peace, quietness, rest, and unity*" as is embodied in the Greek word for peace – "eirenē".

> *Be anxious for nothing, but in everything by prayer and supplication with thanksgiving let your requests be made known to God. And the peace of God, which surpasses all comprehension, will guard your hearts and your minds in Christ Jesus. (Phil. 4:6-7)*

He has promised to guard our hearts and minds "*through Christ Jesus*" – to be our ever-present peace and provision in the midst of the world and the devil's animosity. As such, we are not in any way to allow people or circumstances to separate us from our God, who promises to fortify us in the center of every storm.

Rest assured, brethren, that if you are a true *remnant child* of the Most High, you can expect to be misunderstood, maligned, falsely accused, targeted, antagonized, persecuted, ostracized, isolated, confounded, and even betrayed by those whom you believed to be your friends or advocates. On a human or rational level, nothing will seem to make sense. Your soul will go crazy trying to seek answers to it all. You may wonder what you could have possibly done to deserve this kind of treatment. You may even be tempted to do everything in your power to *make it right*.

Yet, the world's kind of peace involves compromise, conformity and agreement, and in this sense we can never truly be at peace with this world. Peace at any cost such as this is not applicable to citizens of the heavenly kingdom. And our Lord will undoubtedly use such hard conditions and testing to bring us to the point where we love and trust Him above anything or anyone else. His way, more often than not, leads directly through conflict and separation. It forces a collision with the very heart of darkness and the spirit that is behind it all. Light and darkness cannot coexist peacefully, nor can life and death. There is no middle ground, nor can there be. Just as righteous Abel, and all the holy prophets leading up to and including our Lord, we represent an ever-dangerous threat to all fallen principalities and powers that have dominion over this world. Attempting to make peace with the world is a fool's game for the Christian.

No, it is not the world's peace we need, but the peace summed up and personified in the Prince of Peace. He is the true reality for which everything else is artificial and unreal. He is the Shining One who penetrates the lies and thick darkness of this evil world, and shines as a piercing light on all that is dead and dying. If you have ever gone out at night with a flashlight and lifted up a decaying log you will kind of get the idea. All manner of crawling things will scatter from the presence of the light.

> *For He Himself is our peace, who made both groups into one and broke down the barrier of the dividing wall, by abolishing in His flesh the enmity, which is the Law of commandments contained in ordinances, so that in Himself He might make the two into one new man, thus establishing peace, and might reconcile them both in one body to God through the cross, by it having put to death the enmity. (Eph. 2:14-16)*

The world would have us compromise and get along; to do anything and everything possible to mitigate conflict and foster agreement. Dear saints, this is no peace at all, but a satanic ploy designed to swell the ranks of hell. To live in opposition to the world, animated by the life of Jesus Christ, is to invite enmity and opposition. The Father knew this when He sent down His beloved and perfect Son, and He confirms it still as He sanctifies us here in the midst of it. Yet we are not alone, for our Lord is ever present to settle and secure us, to comfort us and guard our hearts and minds from the impact of being at times despised and rejected.

I am still very much trying to make sense of this, and falling into the wisdom of His ways and purposes for us here. More often lately I stumble and fall. Clearly, I have so much more to learn, as all of my natural instincts attempt to get me to worry, to fight back, to defend myself, to try to fix the situation, to apply soulish human insight or wisdom. Please believe me when I say that I am not sharing this as someone who is very far along in the understanding of it. These truths are still being very much fleshed out in my life, as so many situations have arisen lately to shatter everything I have relied on to secure myself in this world. He must loosen my grip from every manner of coping and surviving in this world that do not center on His Son abiding in and strengthening my spirit.

The Father assured me ultimately that it was His will that all of this madness enveloped me; that He actually permitted it. Not to hurt me, or see me squirm (and believe me I have been doing a lot of this), but to help me to appreciate how His provision of peace in His Son is all that I need. Not a worry-free existence, nor a hassle-free life. Not a day without conflict and opposition – just His Son who is all the peace I will very need.

I tried in vain for many days to affect the peace of the world, to make things right. Oh how I exhausted myself trying to achieve this; how I rethought every possible course of action – but no, this was not the way at all. "*Not as the world gives do I give to you*" said our Shepherd.

Friends and brethren, the last days are assuredly upon us, and I sincerely believe with all of my heart that the hard and deep things we are learning as His children will equip us for what is coming, and for what will be required of us. We must die to this world and its ways, and any part of us still cleaving to it must be released and set free. This is most often bitter and painful, as death can only be. But our Lord must separate us to Himself, and bind us to His provision. We must come to see that we can only be contained and sustained in Him alone.

Eternity awaits, with joy unimaginable, but before that there is an altar and a cross to bear; there is death and the laying down always before the rising up. Oh, how I wish it were not so, that there was another way, but not so my friends.

Our Lord has called us to follow Him, yet He has left us here in the world; a world that is becoming increasingly the expression of the spirit of antichrist. He prayed to the Father that we would be kept from the evil one. Well, the keeping is in Him alone, as He has promised to guard our hearts from failing; to secure and strengthen our resolve in His faith and truth; to comfort and settle us when storms and conflict rage all around. This, dear brethren, is His peace, and by His grace will be sustained in it to the bitter end.

Oh Mighty Father, how we at times hurt so bad, rejected by men, and encompassed by enemies. Yet our Lord, too, was despised and rejected, spit upon, and hung on a cross. Oh how the madness and brutality of the world seems too much at times; how our hearts so quickly fail and we want to run, or fight back, or be tempted to make peace with the world. Keep us from such responses, dear Father. Keep us in Your Beloved Son, in His perfect peace, by the comfort of Your Holy Spirit. Keep us, Oh Lord, in the name of Jesus Christ our hope and provision. Amen.

Reconsidering Prayer

Andrew Murray, in humble consideration of prayer, touches on the idea that when we pray we can only ever really do so *in and through Christ Jesus* upwards to the Father who stands apart from every unholy thing, in perpetuation of an eternal dialogue of sorts. Here are his thoughts –

> *"Just as the Sonship of Jesus on earth may not be separated from His Sonship in heaven, even so with His prayer on earth, it is the continuation and the counterpart of His asking in heaven. The prayer of the man Christ Jesus is the link between the eternal asking of the only-begotten Son in the bosom of the Father and the prayer of men upon earth. Prayer has its rise and its deepest source in the very Being of God. In the bosom of Deity nothing is ever done without prayer—the asking of the Son and the giving of the Father."*

Now is it just me or doesn't this positively shatter all of our ideas and concepts about just what it means to *pray*, and the preeminence of Christ in our personal interaction with the Father.

Murray elaborates -

> *"It is only thus that the believer will be able fully to approach and rightly to adore the glory of God's grace; and only thus that our heart can intelligently apprehend the treasures of wisdom and knowledge there are in redemption, and be prepared to enter fully into the highest note of the song that rises before the throne: 'O the depth of the riches both of the wisdom and knowledge of God!'*

> *In our prayer life this truth has its full application. While prayer and faith are so simple that the newborn convert can pray with power, true Christian science finds in the doctrine of prayer some of its deepest problems. In how far is the power of prayer a reality? If so, how God can grant to prayer such mighty power? How can the action of prayer be harmonized with the will and the decrees of God?*
>
> *How can God's sovereignty and our will, God's liberty and ours, be reconciled?—these and other like questions are fit subjects for Christian meditation and inquiry. The more earnestly and reverently we approach such mysteries, the more shall we in adoring wonder fall down to praise Him who hath in prayer given such power to man."*

Dear brethren, a most important question facing all of us in Christ is exactly that: *How can the action, and even the content of prayer be harmonized with the will and decrees of God?* Is it merely enough to submit our prayers in Christ's Name when in fact we are asking that our wishes and desires be fulfilled? Surely this cannot be what it means? As Andrew Murray suggests, our Lord is no mere means to an end that we devise, but He is the personal link that binds us to the Father in spiritual unity and life. He alone represents any hope that our prayers will be answered according to the Father's will.

When we pray have we ever truly considered that what we are doing is participating in a conversation that has gone on between Father and Son through all eternity? True spiritual prayer effectively draws us up and into their world and their reality.

Perhaps sharing a personal episode will help us to understand this a little better.

Some time ago, my young son was up all night crying and in pain with a severe ear infection. Without question, this represented the severest and most prolonged pain the little guy has ever had to endure. The poor little thing was in such agony, as anyone with an ear infection knows. As I held him and wiped his tears I wanted so much for it to stop. I would have gladly changed places with him as any parent would. I felt so helpless and I prayed unceasingly that the Lord would relieve His suffering, that He would simply take the pain away or let him sleep. He chose not to, and my son wailed and sobbed and hurt most of the night.

This is so hard as it challenges everything we think we know about God; His love and mercy for those He loves; His compassion and loving kindness; His knowledge of what we can endure. We know He can help and heal at will, that nothing is beyond His capability. Yet there is this little boy in sheer agony and his helpless, blubbering father crying out, just wanting it to go away. With so many questions probing the love and wisdom of God. *Why? Why Lord?* It is even more difficult when our little ones, whom we have taught about God's love and mercy and power ask the question – "*Why doesn't He listen, daddy? Why doesn't He hear and take the pain away?*"

You think you are a good Christian. You may even have a ministry of sorts devoted to spiritual things. You believe in Him and think you know a little about what He is and represents. Yet there in the wee hours of the morning you have a little boy with tears that won't end, with questions that you can't really answer with any satisfaction.

And so what is prayer, my friends? Does it not bring us into His heavenly chambers where everything we know or think we know no longer serves us or informs our reality. Do our prayers not often collide head-on with His wisdom and love being played out all around us. We may not have any grand agenda in mind, no desire for riches or fame, only that a little child would be relieved of suffering, only that his tears would stop. Do our prayers not test us even, our faith and understanding about what God is doing, our trust in His ability to reach down into our material reality and circumvent His own physical laws to deliver His loved ones?

As mentioned, my son suffered with an ear infection recently, and spent a dreadful night awake and in excruciating pain. The Lord's response to all of our prayers and supplication was seemingly – No, I will not take away this pain but you will endure with my grace and help. You have something to learn through this.

Now once we were through this I was discussing the whole matter with my son, and trying to help him understand the whole dynamic of prayer and God's mercy and wisdom. I fumbled of course, trying to reduce it down to a level I assumed he could grasp. Then he interrupted me – "*Sometimes He needs to test us, daddy, to know that we will love Him even when we don't really know what he is doing*". I was floored, and his little words echoed in my head and spirit for days, churning up so much that needed to come to the surface in my own faith and understanding. The simple truth is that, for the most part, we just don't know specifically what He is doing; how whatever it is we are suffering through relates to His larger plans and purposes. Here is where we either trust Him or we don't. Here is where we learn through deep experience that "*faith is the assurance of things hoped for, the conviction of things not seen*" (Hebrews 11:1).

Indeed, for in that sweet miracle of self-releasing and self-reducing prayer, we mortals encounter all of the mystery and wonder that is God. We momentarily leave all that we are in this world behind, and enter into His reality, His world, His wisdom, and all that He represents, wills and desires. It is a world that Father and Son have occupied for all eternity. Here is the place where prayer and God's purposes intersect. In this kind of true and trusting prayer He allows us to share in Him all that He sees and desires and wishes for His creation, out of the vast depths of His loving heart. A child sees this quite naturally, but why can't we? Why is our reflex to think prayer is somehow about us, or for us? Or that it in some manner gets God to share in our world, and to see our lives and reality as we do? What fools we are if we think this is the dynamic of spiritual prayer; that it draws the Most High down to the earth.

> *In the same way the Spirit also helps our weakness; for we do not know how to pray as we should, but the Spirit Himself intercedes for us with groanings too deep for words; and He who searches the hearts knows what the mind of the Spirit is, because He intercedes for the saints according to the will of God. (Rom. 8:26-27)*

> *And when you are praying, do not use meaningless repetition as the Gentiles do, for they suppose that they will be heard for their many words. "So do not be like them; for your Father knows what you need before you ask Him. (Matt. 6:7-8)*

My friends, often when I am out walking alone, I may not actually be saying much, but I do feel that the Father is walking beside me, perhaps directing my thoughts to this or that, or helping me to reconsider things in a new light. I am not praying aloud so much (talking to Him) but this time of sharing is invaluable. Scripture suggests that He in fact knows everything we need, and everything we are going through and wrestling with, even before we ever bring it to Him. If this is true, then perhaps the content of our prayers is not as important as *religion* has made it to be. Perhaps it is more important to merely be real, open, honest, sincere, and accessible to God such that He can further impress Himself and His *business* (what He is doing all around us) on our spirit.

At times, when the words or thoughts don't come, I simply cry out for help and mercy, or say somewhat exasperatingly -

> *"You know, Lord. You know all that I am and need. You know how I completely responded in the flesh and not the spirit and wasted an opportunity to manifest Your Son".*

I am starting to see that when we come before the Lord in true sincerity, completely exposed for what we are, it often expresses a desire for His mercy and grace more than anything. For we begin to apprehend in the spirit that anything less than Christ in us is simply not enough. It is the measure of the Lord Jesus being added to us that ultimately matters. Everything else is secondary.

We also begin to realize that whatever we need or ask for, the response and provision on the part of the Father can only ever be the same – *more of His Perfect and Beloved Son*! Do we see this brethren, with eyes wide open in the spirit? Do we see that the Father's answer and response to everything is His Son, Jesus Christ? More of Him, such that He, in time, would come to represent the fullness and sum of all things. This is true within ourselves, on a personal level, just as it is also true for the creation as a whole.

Oh Most High and Holy Father; Oh Lord, Mighty and Loving God – You do indeed know all things, our beginning and end and all points in between. You know our absolute limits Lord, and by Your loving wisdom You sometimes choose to let us reach them. But oh that You would strengthen our feeble hands and spirits that crumble and droop, and our faith in Thee. Perhaps we will never truly understand on this side of heaven why You allow us or the ones we love to suffer. But let us not lose heart in prayer Lord, even if it leads to the sweating of blood, and all that we know or think we know about You falls to the ground. Hold us up Lord, in Your Son. We remember that You sent Him down to us that He too, in such perfect and divine innocence and grace, would suffer pain and rejection and torment and the anguish of death; and that through it all there was a divine purpose and blessing to be realized.

Oh Heavenly Father; our Most Excellent Glory – let Your will alone be done on this earth as it is in heaven so perfectly. Grant that we would rest in Thee, Oh Lord, even when, and especially when, our puny minds wrestle with so much that is unknown or incomprehensible. In Jesus' perfect and precious name, we pray. Amen.

On Worship Pleasing to the Father

> *"Our fathers worshiped in this mountain, and you people say that in Jerusalem is the place where men ought to worship." Jesus said to her, "Woman, believe Me, an hour is coming when neither in this mountain nor in Jerusalem will you worship the Father. "You worship what you do not know; we worship what we know, for salvation is from the Jews. "But an hour is coming, and now is, when the true worshipers will worship the Father in spirit and truth; for such people the Father seeks to be His worshipers. "God is spirit, and those who worship Him must worship in spirit and truth." (John 4:20-24)*

"In Spirit and in truth" – So this cuts to the heart of genuine Christian worship, the worship that pleases the Father, the kind that He is seeking, the quality and substance of worship that identifies *"true worshipers"* from false. But is it not the case today, dear friends, that what seems more important is the attainment of a professional *worship leader* or *worship team*; charismatic and talented individuals who can stir a congregation to great emotional heights, rouse the senses, and impress with their vocal and instrumental ability? Has not the church suffered the worldly temptation of permitting the worship of the Almighty and Eternal God to be reduced to mere fleshly indulgence? It seems to this observer (and forgive me for generalizing to advance my point) that the focus on worship today is primarily on its institutional expression, or corporate worship, rather than the intimate and personal expression of adoration as the Holy Spirit reveals all the Lord is and represents.

We discover in this Scripture a distinction being made by the Master between "*true worshipers*" and false, between worship that is sought by the Heavenly Father and that which is not. So it follows then, that not all forms or manifestations of worship, even that directed *in name* to Him, is pleasing and acceptable to Him. Not all of those who say they know the true God of creation and the Bible are in fact known by Him.

> *"Not everyone who says to Me, 'Lord, Lord,' will enter the kingdom of heaven, but he who does the will of My Father who is in heaven will enter. "Many will say to Me on that day, 'Lord, Lord, did we not prophesy in Your name, and in Your name cast out demons, and in Your name perform many miracles?' "And then I will declare to them, 'I never knew you; DEPART FROM ME, YOU WHO PRACTICE LAWLESSNESS.' (Matt. 7:21-23)*

> *No, but I say that the things which the Gentiles sacrifice, they sacrifice to demons and not to God; and I do not want you to become sharers in demons. You cannot drink the cup of the Lord and the cup of demons; you cannot partake of the table of the Lord and the table of demons. (1 Cor. 10:20-21)*

> *"For while I was passing through and examining the objects of your worship, I also found an altar with this inscription, 'TO AN UNKNOWN GOD.' Therefore what you worship in ignorance, this I proclaim to you. (Acts 17:23)*

Modern, Big-Church Spectacle vs. True Worship

This devil-wrought delusion whereby individuals are led to believe they are worshiping and serving the True God when in fact they are worshiping and drinking from the cup of demons is a dangerous one indeed. We must be completely sure that such Scriptures are not referring to us. Are we?

What then, is true worship? Is it only what has come to be known as the *worship service* that precedes the sermon or teaching session? Is it the highly charged entertainment portion every Sunday morning or Friday night; the part that seems so much more enthralling to the soul and senses; the *singing down* of God from His heavenly throne; the praising the roof off? Important questions indeed, brethren, for have we not ultimately been called and saved to worship, serve and adore our Lord and God? Is worship not the natural response of a creature who has been so mercifully spared from eternal judgment and brought near to the very heart of the Creator?

From the Scriptures, we discover that true worship is that which is spiritual (springing from the renewed spirit in man and directed by God's Spirit) and truthful (directed at the true God as He truly is). In this we see that there is no contradiction, as the same Holy Spirit that enables us to apprehend spiritual things, is also the Spirit of truth, the Counselor and Helper without whom the twice-born child of God can attain nothing of eternal consequence. True worship can never be rooted in group ritual or isolated from the truth of almighty God as revealed in His Word. It can never find its inspiration beyond the individual spirits of those who have dedicated their lives to seeking and following the God of the Bible. If one does not enter into worship with a worshipful heart, then all the loud praises and singing and music in the world will not draw one nearer to the presence of God.

Sadly, much of what is called worship in the church today seems contrived and external; a slick combination of Broadway-style production and old-fashioned big-tent mood manipulation. Just as Hollywood has fine-tuned the art of rendering audiences to emotional reaction at will, so the modern church has discovered the assorted tricks and techniques for reproducing such results in the pews. But is it worship, my brother? Does it rise to the level of worshipful expression seen in the Psalms and Prophets for example? Does it represent a sincere prostration of the individual heart before a Being of extraordinary and inestimable power and glory? Is it a personal and powerful expression of homage and reverence directed at the true God, the only God, the very Father, Son and Holy Spirit found in the pages of the Bible – as He is and can only be? And finally, has such an expression, however wrought, been informed and shaped by the Spirit and Word of God, and not the soulish energies or machinations of men?

Idolatry of the Heart Prohibits True Worship

> *Then some elders of Israel came to me and sat down before me. And the word of the LORD came to me, saying, "Son of man, these men have set up their idols in their hearts and have put right before their faces the stumbling block of their iniquity. Should I be consulted by them at all? "Therefore speak to them and tell them, 'Thus says the Lord GOD, "Any man of the house of Israel who sets up his idols in his heart, puts right before his face the stumbling block of his iniquity, and then comes to the prophet, I the LORD will be brought to give him an answer in the matter in view of the multitude of his idols, in order to lay hold of the hearts of the house of Israel who are estranged from Me through all their idols."'*
>
> *"Therefore say to the house of Israel, 'Thus says the Lord GOD, "Repent and turn away from your idols and turn your faces away from all your abominations. "For anyone of the house of Israel or of the immigrants who stay in Israel who separates himself from Me, sets up his idols in his heart, puts right before his face the stumbling block of his iniquity, and then comes to the prophet to inquire of Me for himself, I the LORD will be brought to answer him in My own person. "I will set My face against that man and make him a sign and a proverb, and I will cut him off from among My people. So you will know that I am the LORD." (Ezek.14:1-8)*

Perhaps I am mistaken here (and I sincerely hope I am), but do we not see today a church at large estranged from God in their hearts while at one and the same time swept up in what we may accurately call *praise and worship mania*? Can a true and estimable God, demanding sincere and exclusive devotion as He does, present Himself to a people beset by competing loyalties, idols and even abomination? I think not. Rather, as we read in Ezekiel, there is a resulting separation and alienation from God and the things of God.

No amount of singing, dancing, arm-waving, and hooting and hollering will alter this. No talented and dynamic worship leader can change this. And no perpetual ruminations of revival, without individual, heart-level change – *spirit, soul and body* – empowered by the Holy Spirit and informed by the Holy Scriptures, will amount to anything but idolatry and false worship. Indeed, if all of this is so, then one must wonder who is benefiting or being blessed from this unsanctified worship. Is it God or men, in other words?

Bad Doctrine Equals Vain Worship

> *'THIS PEOPLE HONORS ME WITH THEIR LIPS, BUT THEIR HEART IS FAR AWAY FROM ME. 'BUT IN VAIN DO THEY WORSHIP ME, TEACHING AS DOCTRINES THE PRECEPTS OF MEN.'" (Matt. 15:8-9)*

These are perhaps the most severest words spoken by our Lord, my brethren. And yet by all accounts there are few who take them seriously. Worship today is more often a soul-seducing and contrived thing than the spirit-touching-bone reality acceptable to God. It is often allowed by church leaders to become an orchestrated and unquestioned experience, rather than the spontaneous and profound expression of praise, thanks and wonder that grips the regenerated spirit at the revelation of pure life and light.

Doctrine and Scriptural relevance of any kind is seen by many carnal believers as confounding and limiting to such an expression. Yet our Lord permitted no such demarcation between doctrine and worship. In His eternal wisdom, bad doctrine implied vain worship, for one cannot truly worship what one doesn't know. Definition is, as we observe, important after all. It is not all we have certainly, but it serves to inform and structure all that we pursue in the faith, before God and each other. It contains emotion when emotion spills over into the unprofitable and unholy. Mere sentiment or sensation is so much like the impetuous teenager who sees a sweet face and cries out "*I love you*" with great passion and spontaneity. For one to argue that it is the passion or the spontaneity of this moment that proves the integrity of the love would be erroneous. And yet, this is precisely what is going on in the modern *Praise and Worship* movement. We need to be sure that anything representing the true worship of our Lord is not based on the soulish inclinations of men or *big ministry* mood manipulators who deal more in brash spectacle than the truth and reality of Almighty God.

Only Holiness Can Make Worship Real

> *"First, seek the heart of the Lord, and then you will possess a heart after God, passionate and sincere, unencumbered by man-ordained traditions and religious pretense." - unknown*

It seems the theme of the hour in *Christian* circles is worshiping God; and every church, pastor, teacher and denomination in North America has their own take on the most effective and "anointed" manner in which to carry this out. May I be so bold therefore as to suggest that there can be no true worship of the Most High and Holy One without holiness in the life of the worshiper?

For all those with ears to hear and eyes lit by the light of God, the Spirit affirms the integral bond between holiness in the life of the believer and the worship of a Holy God. For without the one, you cannot truly have the other. Holiness makes worship happen as naturally and as automatically as the wind kisses the water to make the wave. It is not some mechanical or compelled response, nor can it be.

Many have tried to define *holiness* both biblically and otherwise, and truly it is an onerous task. Personally, I have most benefited from a series of sermons delivered by A.W. Tozer on the attributes of God, one of which offered a wonderful examination on His holiness. Humbly and with the greatest of gravity, Tozer probed behind the veil to enlighten his audience as to what in fact makes God *holy* and unlike us in every moral and spiritual aspect.

> *God's holiness is not simply the best we know infinitely bettered. We know nothing like the divine holiness. It stands apart, unique, unapproachable, incomprehensible and unattainable... Holy is the way God is. To be holy He does not conform to a standard. He is that standard." (from, The Knowledge of the Holy)*

Holiness then, is God's standard. Beyond the Heavenly Father and the Holy Spirit, it is fulfilled only in Christ Jesus. To be holy is to be like Christ; like God. And one could suggest that it involves both an uncompromised moral quality and spiritual purity. It was the state Jehovah intended for ancient Israel, and it is clearly presented in the New Testament as the standard for the Church of Christ.

Holiness can, in another sense, be defined as – *the state of being when a life is totally divested of self and wholly dedicated to the plans, purposes and character of God.* Holiness asks –

- *What matters to God?*
- *What is in His heart?*
- *How would He have me relate to Himself and other human beings?*
- *What does He think about this?*
- *What does He love and approve of?*
- *What makes Him smile?*
- *What fills His heart with joy and gratification?*
- *What does He want for my life, my time, my resources?*

And I hope you see that what we are talking about is what could be called a very *practical holiness,* not merely the mystical and sentimental variety being stressed in many churches today. It grieves me to see that so much of what is called worship in the church today amounts to little more than a soulish (based on feelings, desires, emotions) religious zeal; more psycho-social hoopla than a spirit-informed and loving response to the Lord. Dear saints, do we not know that mere sentiment, without living spiritual reality, amounts to little more than magic and self-gratifying religion, not God-glorifying, God-gratifying holiness?

The most natural expression of holiness in the human spirit is obedience, which is driven perpetually and powerfully by a spirit-borne desire to be conformed to the personification of holiness, the Lord Jesus Himself. To be holy is to be a purified and consecrated thing, dedicated solely and unequivocally to the purposes and character of God. This is what holiness meant to the Israelites and it is, I believe, what Peter was thinking when he wrote –

> *As obedient children, do not be conformed to the former lusts which were yours in your ignorance, but like the Holy One who called you, be holy yourselves also in all your behavior; because it is written, "YOU SHALL BE HOLY, FOR I AM HOLY." (1 Pet. 1:14-16)*

"*Holy in all your conduct*" – this sounds most practical to me, real spirit-touching-bone stuff. It may also be helpful to remember what was engraved on the vestments of the Levite priests in the Old Testament: *Holiness to the Lord.* We, too, are a type of "*holy priesthood,*" representing our Lord, who is quintessentially and perfectly holy.

In 1 Chronicles 16:29 and elsewhere, David sang – "*Oh worship the Lord in the beauty of holiness.*" In Zechariah 14:20-21, it is written that – "*In that day 'Holiness to the Lord' shall be engraved on the bells of the horses,*" and that "*every pot in Jerusalem and Judah shall be holiness to the Lord of hosts.*" How perfect and wondrous the creation will be when every person, beast and thing will again be dedicated exclusively to the design and integrity of the infinite and perfect God, when order is restored to this most tangled and inhospitable garden.

The gospel delivered through Paul is a message promoting holiness throughout. In Romans 12:1, he beseeches believers everywhere to –

> *...present your bodies a living and holy sacrifice, acceptable to God, which is your spiritual service of worship. And do not be conformed to this world, but be transformed by the renewing of your mind, so that you may prove what the will of God is, that which is good and acceptable and perfect. (Rom. 12:1-2)*

Dear ones, our lives are to be consecrated to the service of God. From the moment we accept Jesus Christ as savior and shepherd of our lives, we cease to live for ourselves so that we might live solely *in Him* and *for Him*. Our *bodies* are the vehicle for all moral activity, through which we fulfill our identity as either self-serving, godless creatures or *true worshipers* of the Living God. And it is holiness that is the clearest mark of a life devoted to God. And holiness can never rightly be measured by esoteric or ritual observance, but in the discipline and duty of everyday moral experience. This is the true worship of God, when we finally remember that we have been chosen by Him as ambassadors and representatives of His high and holy kingdom.

So we can conclude that holiness is founded on the fact that, as Christians, we represent Jesus Christ, who is Holy and who is God. Holiness then, is a mark of identification, a badge or seal, communicating to all the world that we belong to, and represent the Holy One.

> *For just as you presented your members as slaves to impurity and to lawlessness, resulting in further lawlessness, so now present your members as slaves to righteousness, resulting in sanctification. (Rom. 6:19)*

Often in the New Testament holiness is coupled with righteousness, and portrayed in combination as the sign of the new birth. Jesus taught at great length about the conduct required of the "*new man*," about the need for exclusive devotion to the Holy Father, about where our heart-felt commitments should lie. Many other passages present holiness and righteousness as fruit of the sanctified life. Moral purity, sanctity, cleanness in the "*inner vessel*," integrity of word, motive and conduct; all these represent what one is. They do not operate at the level of feelings and emotions, although they do influence the realm of the soul, where emotions reside.

Hebrews 12:14 goes so far as to pronounce that without holiness – "*no one will see the Lord.*" Serious business, this thing called holiness. Which is why it is so strange that in modern Christendom it is more often represented as a kind of garb that we put on, much like a pair of pants or shoes; why music and song and chanting and every form of mass emotive experience is seen as being able to arouse worshipful qualities in those participating; why sanctification is defined as some kind of split-second, on-the-spot transformation rather than the life-long, moment-to-moment, often quiet transformation of a heart committed to a Holy God.

"*Instant Holiness Now Possible*" is the banner message of the hour, differing little from the claims of instant weight loss or a happy marriage. Or perhaps even more subtle and subversive to the truth are the countless *christianized* psychology messages emphasizing the need for layered or step-by-step behavioral change. *Seven steps to experiencing God, three things you must do order to be physically healed, twelve steps to breaking the chain of addiction* – all so neat and tidy, my brethren, but none of it Scriptural, none of it ordained by the *Author and Finisher of our faith.*

Beware, dear reader, for holiness can never come in a bottle or a manual, but only from the Holy One Himself. And it returns to Him, and glorifies Him, as others see His holiness reflected in all that you say and do and represent. It flows from the very life of the Holy One, transforming your life in very practical ways, and it leads you to your knees and to that quiet contemplation of all that He is and represents. When the Bible refers to the "*beauty of holiness*" it knows of what it speaks, for indeed holiness is beautiful, more beautiful than anything in this sin-blemished world.

It is, after all, holiness that makes worship real and honest. All of the wonderful spirit-breathed sentiment springing forth from a reconciled heart, the peace and consolation, the unrecognizable joy, the priceless order that results as our lives become synchronized with the original plan, the passion of meaningful service – I for one will take all of this over the artificial and momentary arousal being peddled in the big church on the corner. For I need no drunkard's morning-after, and the hollow sense of longing that it brings. I need no drug-like stupor with all of its carnal side effects and insatiable need for more. What I need is to be holy for He is holy, and this, my friend, should be true for all of us.

Oh Most High and Holy Father – Help us, dear Lord, to see how much You are blessed when Your children present themselves to worship You in spirit and in truth; when all of our lives reflect Your holiness and purity. Grant, dear Lord, that no longer would we settle for anything else or less than what pleases You and Your Beloved Son in whom You are well pleased. In His Holy Name, we pray. Amen.

Behold the Lamb of God

Dear saints – as we push further and deeper into the limitless mind and heart of our God; as we seek sincerely to comprehend and internalize the exceedingly great wisdom of His ways and plans; as we commit to laying aside all religious convention and human insight, we inevitably come naked and alone to He who is known preeminently as the *Lamb.* All else is eclipsed and marginalized as we gaze upon and ponder He who represents the express sum of all of God's grace and truth and wisdom. Every false and self-sustaining thing can only attempt in so many pitiful ways to reduce Him, and every fruit that does not spring forth from out of His life and purpose can only fall to the dust and die. False prophets can only fabricate some other thing, some vain counterfeit, some anemic reality so easily revealed for the emptiness it holds. Yet the Spirit of God knows only the Christ of God. The Father of the Lamb, Peter's "*Most Excellent Glory*" reveals only His Son.

He alone is the mystery, the truth, the wisdom and the life recorded in the Scriptures and confirmed by the very testimony of the heavens and the earth. He is our only object, and only in Him will everything good from the Father flow down to us. Only He was sent to heal the brokenhearted, and to loose the chains of captivity from the human spirit. Only He can comfort those who mourn and lift the spirit of heaviness that bears down on the human condition. Only He can plant trees of righteousness in a forgotten and barren wasteland. Only He can reconcile a universe cut off from the divine intent of its Maker.

And so have you come, dear Christian? Have you stood naked in that most holy place where only you and He stands alone, stripped of your most sacred notions and arguments, all of your man-sized categories and concepts? Or do you turn away from so weak and seemingly pathetic a thing? Does everything it represents prick and unsettle everything you have learned while living and breathing in this dark world? The very survival instinct within you, flowing into you with your mother's milk, is smashed to superficiality by everything that He represents. Clearly, this is some other wisdom, my friends, and please don't be tempted to reduce it to some generalized martyr's zeal, for this was no temporal political or social cause for which our Lord allowed Himself to be poured out and consumed. There are, and have been, many martyrs, but only one *Lamb of God*. There have been countless causes and wrongs to be righted, but only one universe held bondage to the sin of the serpent and his children.

Consider for a moment that most biting and loathsome language employed in Isaiah's Suffering Servant (Isaiah 53) –

- *despised and rejected by men*
- *a man of sorrows, well acquainted with grief*
- *stricken, smitten, afflicted*
- *wounded, bruised*
- *"the Lord has laid on Him the iniquity of us all"*
- *oppressed and afflicted, yet "He opened not His mouth"*
- *"led as a lamb to the slaughter and as sheep before its shearers is silent, so He opened not His mouth"*
- *"it pleased the Lord to bruise Him, He has put Him to grief"*
- *"He poured out His soul unto death, and He was numbered with the transgressors"*
- *"He bore the sins of many and made intercession for the transgressors"*

Now when John the Baptist laid eyes on Him, he did not declare "*Behold your King!*" or "*Herald the Champion of the People!*" Instead, he saw a lamb and cried –

> *"Behold the Lamb of God who takes away the sin of the world!" (John 1:29)*

Let that settle in deep for a moment, folks; let it stir around and swell up inside you. Let the transcendent, spiritual wisdom of it stretch beyond everything that this faith has become in this age, to so many superficial proselytes and pretenders. Let it assimilate and supplant every vain and peripheral notion that so readily consumes so much of His church these days. Let it sift, settle and lie where it may, for this wisdom is unlike anything we have known or can know from any created thing, at anytime or anywhere. To call it *religious* is a mockery. To allegorize it away is practically heresy. And to affirm any other wisdom from any other source is outright apostasy. For here is the Christian way in a nutshell and a heartbeat. Here is God's Wisdom and God's Way. Here is where spirit touches bone.

> *"Worthy is the Lamb that was slain to receive power and riches and wisdom and might and honor and glory and blessing." (Rev. 5:12)*

Whereas the world and its wisdom eschews weakness and esteems the mighty, the true path to glory, honor and power lies elsewhere. The seldom mentioned thrust of the gospel is that our God accepts us only in the context of our rejection at the hands of this world and its wisdom. We will only truly and ultimately find life in Him when we forfeit our lives here and now in this world. Only by releasing it do we attain it. Only by letting it go do we pick it up again. Here is the faith and testimony of the saints, those who love not their lives in this world, and are not afraid to lay it down for their Savior and Lord.

Let me ask you this, dear ones – when our Lord asked you to follow Him, what was He asking? What could He have possibly meant? I think you know the answer, my brethren. His way is the way of the lamb, of death unto life, of losing to gain, of falling to the ground and being broken so that others may live, of being opposed, rejected, and wrongly accused; of being judged and found guilty for crimes you did not commit; of the spilling of innocent blood while the Father weeps and the heavens roar.

Now I dare say this with all boldness – if any preacher, man or angel himself knocks on your door and offers you anything less than this, slam the door and bolt it tight, for the gates of hell have come knocking!

Oh how we have twisted the message my friends. Oh how we have believed that first lie of easy believism. Oh how we all need to rededicate ourselves to His Way and His Wisdom, regardless of the cost. Please help us Lord. Heaven help us.

And before you start assuming that the one sharing these words has already attained to this wisdom, and is shouting down to you from atop the mountain – think again, dear friends. I confess sadly that my disposition has always been that of a fighter, one who scratches and claws to assert himself in whatever way he can, shaking his little red fists at the world. No, like you, I am looking up to He who has ascended, and is forever worthy. My wisdom is perhaps even further from that of our Lord and Master.

Please pray that the Lord's grace and life will spill out into all of us here in such a measure as to demonstrate the wisdom of the Lamb to a world that knows nothing of it, and indeed wants nothing of it.

His very own people rejected Him at His first coming because He was not the *Samson-esque* deliverer they wanted and expected. And I fear in my heart that the church (especially here in the West) has already rejected Him for their own worldly and political savior. May our God deliver us and in His mercy help us to behold the Lamb.

Oh Merciful and Beloved Father – Great and Glorious God – so pampered and needy are we in this generation. Forgive us, Father, and let the sustaining wisdom of Your Son shine forth in us as a witness to Your ultimate and eternal glory. Not because we are in any manner worthy, but merely because we are emptied of every other kind of wisdom, Oh Lord. We praise and honor You as God, and by Your grace we will have no other. In the name of the Lamb, we pray. Amen.

The Good Shepherd

In Ezekiel 34, we see the Lord's brutal indictment against the shepherds in the land who were not fulfilling their charge by adequately feeding, tending for, and protecting the sheep. Rather, they were devouring them and getting fat off of them.

> *Then the word of the LORD came to me saying, "Son of man, prophesy against the shepherds of Israel. Prophesy and say to those shepherds, 'Thus says the Lord GOD, "Woe, shepherds of Israel who have been feeding themselves! Should not the shepherds feed the flock? "You eat the fat and clothe yourselves with the wool, you slaughter the fat sheep without feeding the flock. "Those who are sickly you have not strengthened, the diseased you have not healed, the broken you have not bound up, the scattered you have not brought back, nor have you sought for the lost; but with force and with severity you have dominated them. "They were scattered for lack of a shepherd, and they became food for every beast of the field and were scattered. "My flock wandered through all the mountains and on every high hill; My flock was scattered over all the surface of the earth, and there was no one to search or seek for them."*
>
> *Therefore, you shepherds, hear the word of the LORD: "As I live," declares the Lord GOD, "surely because My flock has become a prey, My flock has even become food for all the beasts of the field for lack of a shepherd, and My shepherds did not search for My flock, but rather the shepherds fed themselves and did not feed My flock; therefore, you shepherds, hear the word*

> *of the LORD: 'Thus says the Lord GOD, "Behold, I am against the shepherds, and I will demand My sheep from them and make them cease from feeding sheep. So the shepherds will not feed themselves anymore, but I will deliver My flock from their mouth, so that they will not be food for them." (Ezek. 34:1-10)*

Dear saints, does this look at all familiar to any of you as you look out on the Christian landscape?

Given the situation then, what does the Lord decide to do, replace the wicked shepherds with others perhaps? Hire new shepherds maybe? Read on –

> *For thus says the Lord GOD, "Behold, I Myself will search for My sheep and seek them out. "As a shepherd cares for his herd in the day when he is among his scattered sheep, so I will care for My sheep and will deliver them from all the places to which they were scattered on a cloudy and gloomy day. "I will bring them out from the peoples and gather them from the countries and bring them to their own land; and I will feed them on the mountains of Israel, by the streams, and in all the inhabited places of the land. "I will feed them in a good pasture, and their grazing ground will be on the mountain heights of Israel. There they will lie down on good grazing ground and feed in rich pasture on the mountains of Israel. "I will feed My flock and I will lead them to rest," declares the Lord GOD. "I will seek the lost, bring back the scattered, bind up the broken and strengthen the sick; but the fat and the strong I will destroy. I will feed them with judgment. (Ezek. 34:11-16)*

Astounding! Did you see that? The Lord will not replace the shepherds with others (*hired hands*) but He Himself will personally become their Shepherd. He will directly assume responsibility for feeding and protecting (the two primary tasks of a shepherd) the sheep.

And, as in everything else, we see this fulfilled and realized in the Lord Jesus Christ, the Good Shepherd –

> *"I am the good shepherd; the good shepherd lays down His life for the sheep. "He who is a hired hand, and not a shepherd, who is not the owner of the sheep, sees the wolf coming, and leaves the sheep and flees, and the wolf snatches them and scatters them. "He flees because he is a hired hand and is not concerned about the sheep. "I am the good shepherd, and I know My own and My own know Me, even as the Father knows Me and I know the Father; and I lay down My life for the sheep. "I have other sheep, which are not of this fold; I must bring them also, and they will hear My voice; and they will become one flock with one shepherd. "For this reason the Father loves Me, because I lay down My life so that I may take it again. "No one has taken it away from Me, but I lay it down on My own initiative. I have authority to lay it down, and I have authority to take it up again. This commandment I received from My Father." (John 10:11-18)*

My friends, please hear in the spirit what this speaks to us – the Lord alone is our Shepherd. Never again will men assume this role. The Lord God, in the eternal and heavenly counsel of His wisdom, has determined this. Jesus Christ is charged with feeding, protecting (and even ultimately judging) the Father's flock. He alone has been deemed worthy. This is the command and the authority He has received from His Father.

In practical terms then, what does this tell us about God's care for His sheep, and even perhaps church leadership? In I Peter we read –

> *Therefore, I exhort the elders among you, as your fellow elder and witness of the sufferings of Christ, and a partaker also of the glory that is to be revealed, shepherd the flock of God among you, exercising oversight not under compulsion, but voluntarily, according to the will of God; and not for sordid gain, but with eagerness; nor yet as lording it over those allotted to your charge, but proving to be examples to the flock. And when the Chief*

> *Shepherd appears, you will receive the unfading crown of glory. (1 Pet. 5:1-10)*

Ah, so there are elders who are tasked with shepherding God's flock, but this is not an official or titular role. They are not *"the Shepherd"*, but rather workers in the field, with shepherding duties. (In actuality, they too are sheep). It has already been made clear that no longer will "*hired hands*" ever assume primary care over God's sheep. It is the Chief Shepherd that exercises primary care over the sheep. The Lord Jesus Himself used this language frequently during His time on earth, to convey His loving concern for the sheep who were routinely left to the ravages of predators.

He will feed, protect, shelter, lead to pasture, and in every manner nurture the sheep who represent the Father's flock. And not one of them will He lose or abandon; this is made clear in many Scriptures. He is the Good Shepherd for this very reason. While other shepherds enriched their lives off of the sheep, He lays His down for them. Consider David, an Old Testament figure of the courageous, self-sacrificing shepherd –

> *But David said to Saul, "Your servant was tending his father's sheep. When a lion or a bear came and took a lamb from the flock, I went out after him and attacked him, and rescued it from his mouth; and when he rose up against me, I seized him by his beard and struck him and killed him. "Your servant has killed both the lion and the bear; and this uncircumcised Philistine will be like one of them, since he has taunted the armies of the living God." (1. Sam. 17:34-46)*

Brethren, our spiritual sustenance and survival are contingent upon no man, not even ourselves. Let us look to the Good Shepherd of Our Souls, in living and abandoned faith, to provide every good thing in Christ. He knows His sheep perfectly doesn't He? And He loves them perfectly. While we may learn from one another, as His life and truth flow out from one vessel to the next; while we can indeed edify and encourage one another in the faith, setting a pure example among the saints (as Peter indicates), these are such small things compared to what the Good Shepherd must represent to us intimately and exclusively.

We are all merely sheep, aren't we, whether we are mature saints or newly born. Have you ever seen sheep following a *lead* sheep, who seems to know the location of good pasture and water? Have you ever observed a really tough *bodyguard-like* sheep defending the flock from a pack of hungry wolves? Now I don't pretend to know a great deal about sheep, and there may be exceptions, but I think you see my point here. The sheep are essentially helpless without a Good Shepherd! And the Lord is our Shepherd!

> *The LORD is my shepherd, I shall not want.*
>
> *He makes me lie down in green pastures; He leads me beside quiet waters. He restores my soul;*
>
> *He guides me in the paths of righteousness For His name's sake.*
>
> *Even though I walk through the valley of the shadow of death, I fear no evil, for You are with me; Your rod and Your staff, they comfort me.*
>
> *You prepare a table before me in the presence of my enemies; You have anointed my head with oil; My cup overflows.*
>
> *Surely goodness and lovingkindness will follow me all the days of my life, And I will dwell in the house of the LORD forever. (Psa. 23)*

Hallelujah! The Lord Jesus Christ is our Shepherd! In Him we shall want for nothing. In Him alone we have peace and rest and comfort. For He is our provision and protection, and He will never abandon us for forsake us for His own self interest.

We don't need to follow or trust any mortal man anymore. Only He who is the Son of Man! We will never need to entrust our spiritual lives to any hired hand, only He who is our Eternal and Loving Shepherd.

The lesson is clear, my friends. Two-thousand years of sordid church history marks this testimony to be true. Oh, how so many false shepherds have scattered and devoured so many little ones, when they should have rightly protected and nurtured them. Rather than lead them to the House of the Lord, they led them into the barren wilderness, estranged and alienated from God.

Praise God that we have that Good Shepherd who will never leave us nor forsake us! Praise God indeed!

Father, oh Father, what riches and wonders we discover in Your Beloved Son, the *True Shepherd* who will bring us to pasture in Your eternal kingdom; who protects us faithfully and vigorously from perils without and within; who feeds us with the heavenly bread of His very life and life-giving streams of living water! Forgive us Father, for seeking shepherds other than the *Good Shepherd*; hired hands who care only for themselves and not for Your little ones. Oh that we would hear and know His voice as He calls to us here in the field of this world, to draw us near unto Himself, and to all His care and provision. This we pray as it is Your will, in His name. Amen.

The Voice of the Shepherd

> *"Truly, truly, I say to you, he who does not enter by the door into the fold of the sheep, but climbs up some other way, he is a thief and a robber. "But he who enters by the door is a shepherd of the sheep. "To him the doorkeeper opens, and the sheep hear his voice, and he calls his own sheep by name and leads them out. "When he puts forth all his own, he goes ahead of them, and the sheep follow him because they know his voice. "A stranger they simply will not follow, but will flee from him, because they do not know the voice of strangers." (John 10:1-5)*

> *"My sheep hear My voice, and I know them, and they follow Me;" (John 10:27)*

Following our Lord requires that we recognize and hear His voice. It is a distinct voice, unlike any other, and our very survival in this living walk depends on our capacity to recognize the true voice of our Shepherd. Notice that it is His *voice* mentioned here, and not His *words*, or what He says. Certainly what our Lord says is essential, but we begin by identifying that it is He who is communicating with us; that it is indeed *His voice.*

Recognition and familiarity comes with spending time together. Friends who fellowship together on a routine basis are readily able to recognize each other's voice immediately. The telephone rings, and even before the caller says, "*It is _*", we know who it is, merely by their voice. Children, from the earliest stage of life recognize their mother's voice, perhaps even from within the womb itself. And there are many examples in nature where even the dumbest creatures are able to survive because they recognize the voice of the mother or father calling them to safety.

Recall the incident of the lad Samuel, who was awakened by the voice of the Lord, yet he wrongly assumed it was his master Eli. After a few times, Eli directed him to listen, for it was the indeed the Lord, and to respond "*Speak, for Your servant hears.*"

The lesson for us here is that it does take time and exposure to recognize our Lord's voice. Yet, from that point on, Samuel came to know the voice of his Lord and God, and he ultimately proved faithful in carrying out everything spoken to him.

There is also the account of Mary at the Master's tomb in John 20, which reads –

> *But Mary was standing outside the tomb weeping; and so, as she wept, she stooped and looked into the tomb; and she saw two angels in white sitting, one at the head and one at the feet, where the body of Jesus had been lying. And they said to her, "Woman, why are you weeping?" She said to them, "Because they have taken away my Lord, and I do not know where they have laid Him." When she had said this, she turned around and saw Jesus standing there, and did not know that it was Jesus. Jesus said to her, "Woman, why are you weeping? Whom are you seeking?" Supposing Him to be the gardener, she said to Him, "Sir, if you have carried Him away, tell me where you have laid Him, and I will take Him away." Jesus said to her, "Mary!" She turned and said to Him in Hebrew, "Rabboni!" (which means, Teacher). (John 20:11-16)*

Note the fact that it was only when our Lord spoke her name, did she recognize immediately that it was Him. There was no doubt. Even her grief could not mask the fact of His identity.

The question presents itself to us then: Are we able to recognize the voice of our Shepherd when He calls to us in the spirit? Of all the voices in our world, both human and otherwise, calling us to do this or do that, are we able to discern the one voice that is calling us to faithfulness, to service, and to Himself?

The Spirit of truth affirms that God, the *Logos*, is communicating to us; yet we are instructed to test all spirits, as the deceiver can also communicate (see Eve in the garden). Jesus said the sheep would know and hear His voice. A helpful principle regarding greater revelation from God, is that He doesn't ever provide it apart from Himself. Only as we venture deeper into His heart and holiness through surrendering faith and obedience, will we start to hear from Him in the ways we all desire and need.

My own personal experience is that His voice is deep, and still and that you know that it is Him and no other. I wish I could explain it in words but I cannot. Just as with a human being, the voice of our Lord is distinct and recognizable. He speaks directly to the spirit and to the heart of His friends, just as He promised when He left this earth. Recall, that He said that it is better that He goes away. Yes, the original twelve heard and knew His audible, human voice, but we too can hear Him, deep down where spirit meets spirit, at the very center of our being.

My friends, expect to hear His voice. We need to hear His voice. It is essential for following Him. When you pray is it you who does most of the talking? Be still. Be silent. After you ask Father a question, expect that He will answer; What father wouldn't respond accordingly to his beloved child?

But more importantly, whatever He asks or requires of you, do it immediately. Do it faithfully.

"*Speak, for Your servant hears*", said the child Samuel.

You will know if it is Him, not only by what He says, but by His voice, which is unlike any other. And please do not confuse this with some empty mysticism, or psycho-spiritual experience involving inner voices, urges or impulses. Like every pure and perfect thing, the devil and his world has their counterfeits. God's Spirit will communicate with our regenerated human spirit, and with time, experience and familiarity, we will come to know that it is Him speaking. As we abide ever deeper in Him, and learn the life of the Vine and the branches, we will begin to know Him and His voice in ways that are wonderful and certain.

This will only make sense to those breathed on by the spirit. If you are not, then you will hear many voices, and nothing will be discernible. Confusion will result. You will become one of those religious crazies who go around saying that God told them something that every child of God knows He would never say. "*The Lord told me that He wants all of you to send me a million dollars so I can build my castle here on earth*", or something like that.

The Lord's voice instills peace and direction. It settles us, and chastens us at times. It never ever confounds the truth of Scripture, because He inspired every word and thought found there. If the voice directs you in ways or concepts that defy the revealed Word, then it is a false voice and to be rejected entirely. My sense is that, over time, you will know that such voices are false, almost immediately. Jesus promised this.

> *"My sheep hear My voice, and I know them, and they follow Me;" (John 10:27)*

The evil one can do impressions, but children born of the spirit will recognize his vain impersonations.

Our Lord's voice is truth, and power, and love; it is sharp and often cuts deep into the hidden chambers of the heart where idols sit proudly on a stolen throne. It fills us, and sometimes consumes us. There are many places in the Scriptures where mere mortals have been undone by the voice of the Almighty. It is the only voice in the created universe that truly matters. Let us be deaf to all others so that we may hear Him, and recognize Him, and respond with trusting obedience and service.

Dear Father, please help us in the spirit to hear You and Your Son and all that You are saying to us. Please give us ears to hear that we might follow our Good Shepherd wherever He leads us, and to prove faithful to His voice in this desperate hour at the end of this age. In Jesus' name. Amen.

Believing, Hearing and Following

> *While he was still speaking, a bright cloud overshadowed them, and behold, a voice out of the cloud said, "This is My beloved Son, with whom I am well-pleased; listen to Him!" When the disciples heard this, they fell face down to the ground and were terrified. (Matt. 17:5-6)*

> *The next day He purposed to go into Galilee, and He found Philip. And Jesus said to him, "Follow Me." (John 1:43)*

"*Hear Him!*" Oh how this is the need of the hour, my friends. How we so desperately and urgently need to submit ourselves to hearing the One sent down to us by the Father. Oh that we would hear Him amidst all the noise and distortion emanating from so many of our gurus these days. Oh that His voice and His voice alone would be all that we hear. And that we would follow Him wherever He goes, as He fulfills His Father's business.

As Christians, we sincerely desire the blessings of God but we often want them on our terms, don't we? Yet the Heavenly Father has once and for all declared that all heavenly blessings, without exception, will flow through His beloved Son. "*Hear Him!*" thunders the holy voice from above, reducing the disciples (and us if we are paying attention) to quivering floor mats.

Life in the spirit has not been pretty for me lately, I am sad to confess. So much of me wants to go deeper into Him and His life, and yet so much resists also. Oh what faith we need to release ourselves vicariously into His loving care. To go deeper, to loosen our grip on our own lives and this world. Oh that He would be increased in this vessel, and everything that I am reduced – that I would simply *believe* Him, and *hear* Him, and *follow* Him. So much unbelief. So little trust. So many man-sized and earth-bound thoughts. Oh Lord, increase our faith!

I have been discovering – quite painfully, in fact – that it is not enough to fill our heads with the works of those who have ventured deep into spiritual reality; the *Taylors*, *Murrays*, and *Nees*, and *Austin-Sparks*, for example. They can certainly offer us their own insights from beyond the veil, but we must apprehend it for ourselves before we can experience true spiritual life, and kiss the hand of the King. Even further study of God's written word means little until we abandon all that we are, that we might believe and hear and follow further and deeper. The Spirit is always beckoning to us to do exactly this dear saints. But will we go forth, will we press on deeper and further into Him as our *way and truth and life*?

My friends, by my very nature I am a pragmatist, a doer, someone who wants to instantly grab hold of something and go with it. These are my natural instincts and tendencies – how I am hard-wired. I am a problem-solver and a man of action, accustomed to taking life by the reigns and steering it this way or that by force of will, design and intellect. This is ingrained in me, and runs deep into everything I am, think and do. All of my life I have learned to trust such instincts; for survival and self-protection in this world, for success (albeit worldly success), and for that feeling of control that I have always thought I needed.

But here again thunders the diving voice from heaven, piercing into the very heart of everything I am –"*Hear Him.*"

Oh that I would and that I could. So many voices in my head. So many experts offering this or that advice. So many supposed shepherds of God telling me to listen to them, to follow them!

Oh Father – silence them all that I would hear only Your beloved Son! That I would follow Him to the cross and beyond, into Your heart and into Your kingdom!

"*How do we work the works of God?*" asked the people of our Lord in John 6.

I have asked Him this same question myself many times: "*How does it actually work?*"; this sanctifying, this shedding of earthly things, this taking on the mind and nature and power of the Son of Man?

Our Father's answer is still the same – "*This is the work of God, that you believe in Him whom He sent*" (John 6:29). And that we hear and follow Him.

Hmm – so I can work the works of God be merely believing in His Son? There are no steps to be taken, activities to be engaged in, disciplines to be developed and cultivated, things to do in fact? Here is the wonder of John's gospel, the mystery of godliness summed up in this awesome being known as the Christ, the Light that came into this dark, sun-less world.

But what about me? What about my need to contribute something? Surely these are worth something! No, my friends, they are not, and until we get our minds around this then all we will have is our earthbound, man-sized religion. We will not experience the life of God coursing through our beings. We will not glimpse heavenly things. There will be no peace, nor victory, nor any other God-sized blessing or outcome we can hope for or imagine.

First comes *believing*, then *hearing*, then *following*. These are the Father's terms for all those who would have true life, for those who want so desperately to experience the reality of the Spirit.

But again, Lord – nothing in and of me that actually seems to help in this world will advance the works of God?

But, but –

Our Lord's very first recorded miracle was to turn water used for ritualized washing (*the outside of the cup*) into wine (*life*) that gets inside the cup. And to think the people at the wedding feast were merely thrilled to have more and better drink to satiate the flesh even more. Here were many of them, already intoxicated perhaps, when He was illustrating dramatically how man would be restored to life in Himself; how His very life can get inside these jars of clay.

And throughout John's gospel we are confronted with this Life spilling out and over into people's lives – the only true thing the earth has ever known, the Life that was the Light of the world, the Light of men, come down from heaven. This was what John was compelled to remember in the Spirit when he wrote down his impression of those events. And by so many ways and forms and words, our Lord kept repeating this mysterious fact, that the Life must get inside us somehow; only then will we be able to work the works of God. No amount of washing or tending to physical things will achieve this. Nothing that we bring with us from the old life can serve us here. We need the wine inside of us, flowing through us, flowing with His very life! Here is the wonder of the New Covenant – that the life of God must get within us.

Notice how Andrew Murray emphasizes this –

> *'Within you! Within you!' This twice-repeated word of our text is one of the keywords of the 'New Covenant.' 'I will put my law in their inward parts, and in their heart will I write it.' 'I will put my fear in their hearts, that they shall not depart from me.' God created man's heart for His dwelling. Sin entered, and defiled it. Four thousand years God's Spirit strove and wrought to regain possession. In the Incarnation and Atonement of Christ the Redemption was accomplished, and the kingdom of God established. Jesus could say, 'The kingdom of God is come unto you;' 'the kingdom of God is within you.' It is within we must look for the fulfillment of the New Covenant, the Covenant not of ordinances but of life: in the power of an endless life the law and the fear of God are to be given in our heart: the Spirit of Christ Himself is to be within us as the power of our life. Not only on Calvary, or in the resurrection, or on the throne, is the glory of Christ the Conqueror to be seen, -but in our heart: within us, within us is to be the true display of the reality and the glory of His Redemption. Within us, in our inmost parts, is the hidden sanctuary where is the ark of the Covenant, sprinkled with the Blood, and containing the Law writ-*

> *ten in an ever-living writing by the Indwelling Spirit, and where, through the Spirit, the Father and the Son now come to dwell.*
>
> *(from, The Spirit of Christ. Referring to Ezekiel 36:26-27 – "A new heart will I give you, and a new spirit will I put within you. And I will put my Spirit within you.')*

Okay, but how then? How to get this life inside us? What to do? Herein is the rub isn't it?

Believe. Simply believe in the One sent by the Father claiming to be that Life! Then listen to Him and follow Him wherever He goes and in whatever He tells you to do. Sounds simple, right?

No, no cries the pragmatist in me, there has to be more, there has to be something He's not telling us.

My friends and brethren, I have since discovered by His grace, that there is no more, that this is all there is, because He is All there is. In the Father's view, there is only His Son, the Christ. He is the promise and fulfillment of all life, because He is that Life. Our journey begins and ends with Him, and He is all of our provision throughout. He is the *Author and Finisher of our faith*, as only He can be!

He is the Life that banishes death, and the Light that scatters the darkness! He merely walked among us for a short time and look at how He divided and scattered the darkness, how He put death on the tracks. The dividing line is drawn and it is this – that we either believe and know Him or we don't. We either have Life in Him or we don't. We are either of the Light or of the darkness that still doesn't comprehend Him because it is incapable of doing so.

Consider here, brethren, what Austin-Sparks has offered, pertaining to that most mysterious phrase: "*The Law of the Spirit of Life in Christ Jesus*" in Romans 8 –

> *The longer one lives and the more one thinks about things, the surer one becomes that the supreme issue*

> *which governs everything between God and man is that of life. Our Scripture says here that life is a law, and it further says that that life is in the hands of the Holy Spirit – "the law of the Spirit of life...".*
>
> *A law is a fixed and established principle. It has potentialities. It means that, if you are adjusted to it and governed by it, certain results are inevitable; that the potentialities which it contains will most surely find expression when that law is established. So that, what we have here is, that the mark of things being of God the Holy Spirit is life. If anything is of God the Holy Spirit, it will live; its chief characteristic will be life. That is a law, an established principle. What is according to God lives, having God's own life in it, and that is, as a principle, a rule of guidance. It is a principle for the direction of the people of God.*
>
> *But there is another thing we must notice at the outset. This is that, in the matter of life as a fixed principle, the life is in Christ Jesus: "The law of the Spirit of life in Christ Jesus." Upon that fact, the Scriptures are more than emphatic, that all that is of God is in Christ Jesus; and inasmuch as the mark of all that is of God is life, then life is in Christ Jesus and in Him alone. (from, The Law of the Spirit of Life in Christ Jesus)*

Did you get that, dear reader? All bound up in life, and not just any life; the life of Christ Jesus. Oh how I wish this supreme truth might pierce you through and through, such that every lesser thing; every other thing, would be cast away forever!

Have you ever noticed that it really didn't matter what the Apostle Paul started to talk about in his epistles, he ultimately came back time and time again to the centrality, the surpassing wonder, the exceeding excellence found only in Jesus Christ? And the book of Hebrews, which indicates that even from that fateful beginning, it was all about the Son, and our need of Him, and His central place in the Father's heart and plan? He has placed His seal on Him. He has sent Him down from that holy height. He has invested all of creation's hope in Him! And He commands that we hear Him. And *only* Him! Only He perfectly satisfies the heart of the Father!

This clearly does not bode well for most Americans, as we are a nation of independent-minded doers, aren't we? The kind that rolls up our sleeves, sucks in our gut, and goes off to fix the problems of the world. I dare say that there is more works-based, man-sourced, man-serving Christianity being taught and practiced in America today than ever before. So much of our fruits indicate beyond any shade of doubt, that we have stopped believing, and as a result we can no longer hear the spiritual voice of the Master, let alone follow Him. The result is nothing less than humanism, the exaltation of the natural, soulish energies and works of man; the unwashed fruit of the *knowledge of good and evil.*

I see so many Christians today more concerned with *doing* rather than simply *being*, when the truth is that the doing springs forth quite naturally from the being. All of God's terms for salvation and sanctification are bound up exclusively in His Son. We begin with Him, because only in Him do we "*live and move and have our being*".

Oh how I wish we would get this, folks. We want so much to do something for our Heavenly Father, to glimpse the deeper life even, when all He wants is for us to come to His Son, and drink from His cup.

Brethren – let us return wholly in heart, fidelity and focus to this Beloved Son. Let us honor the Father of Life by coming to His Son in simple faith, and hearing Him alone. Then let us follow Him in heartfelt and trusting obedience. He is our way now, and nothing we were before is of any value to us on this path. His is a Living Way, and the way leads directly home to the heart of the Father.

This is what we are attempting to convey here – this is really all we have to say. I am sorry if it wearies you, but we will not apologize for magnifying Him above all else, for narrowing our vision to the Only True Thing in all the universe.

So very many things; so many lesser things; have occupied Christians for so many generations. Today, it seems we are consumed by service and ministry; so much running around trying to single-handedly usher in the kingdom of God by our natural energies. It's no wonder growth and results have become an idol to so many groups and individuals. It's no wonder that humanistic psychology has largely replaced the mystery of godliness found in Christ. It's no mystery why we have reverted to man's methods and measurements as we carry out what we believe to be His work. We want His blessings on our terms, don't we? We want results and we want them now. Clearly this is the religion of Micah (Judges 18) and not Jesus Christ or the Apostle Paul.

My brethren, what we need is the Spirit of Christ enlivening us and increasing the measure of the Father's Holy Son in all the parts (*spirit, soul and body*) of our lives. Only then will we discover how He so wondrously keeps bringing us back to Him; to His preeminence; oh the purity and simplicity found solely in Jesus Christ and His ever-flowing and abounding life!

Can we ever be reminded too much of our need for this? Heavens no! For it is the soulish mind of man and the devil that naturally seeks to usurp the majesty and glory of the Son of God. Can we ever have too much of Him? No, my friends, we can never be truly filled with Him, for He will spill up and over from our lives into the lives of others, ultimately filling all things in this universe with Himself. This is where the story ends, with the Father inserting all created things with the life of His exalted and glorified Son!

Oh Father – dear Father; we thank You for this most precious gift, come down to us as Life from heaven. We thank You for all that He represents and embodies for us, that indeed, He is now our life and living. Forgive us for our unbelief, and for our dullness of hearing, and indeed for our disobedience in following other voices. We ask for faith, that we might come to Him. We ask for ears wide open in the Spirit that we might hear Him. And we ask for trust, that we might follow Him all the way back home to You. By Your grace alone we stand, and we ask that all these things might be enacted and enabled by Your mighty Spirit, that the Lord Jesus Christ would be magnified in each of us, that Your perfect will would be done here on earth as it is in heaven. In Christ's precious name, we pray. Amen.

The Perfect Law of Liberty

For the Law was given through Moses; grace and truth were realized through Jesus Christ. (John 1:17)

It was for freedom that Christ set us free; therefore keep standing firm and do not be subject again to a yoke of slavery. (Gal. 5:1)

"Come to Me, all who are weary and heavy-laden, and I will give you rest. Take My yoke upon you and learn from Me, for I am gentle and humble in heart, and YOU WILL FIND REST FOR YOUR SOULS. For My yoke is easy and My burden is light." (Matt. 11:28-30)

For the law of the Spirit of life in Christ Jesus has set you free from the law of sin and of death. (Rom. 8:2)

There is a growing trend among evangelical Christians to start toying with adding certain Old Testament practices (*days, diets, disciplines, patterns, etc.*) to their newfound freedom in Christ. I find this more than a little disheartening and offer my own testimony in support of the position that this is a foolish and even destructive course of action.

My understanding and experience, from many years in a sabbath-keeping group that abided by many of the Judaic holy days, is that the laws and ordinances given to Moses actually kept me at arms-length from my God. It was not necessarily that the law was flawed or imperfect, but it was my weakness, my inability that led to such failure and frustration.

So then, the Law is holy, and the commandment is holy and righteous and good. (Rom. 7:12)

Yet the *Law* never drew me into the life of His Son, the immense depth of His grace, or the mystery of godliness revealed in the gospel. It never discipled me, nor induced me to love the Father, Son and Spirit, or empowered me to fulfill His eternal purpose for my life.

It even did not – and this may shock you – lay down complete moral truth or the ultimate answer to man's dilemma as a fallen creature. This may seem strange as was not the law supposed to inform our moral values, teach us wisdom, and lead us forward into how God Himself perceives life.

This is true, my friends, to a degree, but the problem with the law on its own is that it imposes a burden that we cannot ever hope to bear on our own. Then gradually over many years of heaviness, it is this weight that grows to occupy our attention. The law reminds us constantly that we are captive to sin, and captivity is never a desirable condition for the human spirit, which was created to be free.

Sure the law legislated my time, and diet and speech. Yet it never seemed to be able to go deeper to the root of my hopeless condition – the blackened heart, the corrupted mind, the defiant will. It could not, in the end, *save my soul*. It was, as the Apostle Paul suggests, absolutely powerless to do anything but alter outward behavior. It created habits and a disciplined regimen, monitored constantly by myself and others; it contained an enforceable code that could be policed from without or within. But were these positive things? Is this all there is to this newness of life in Christ Jesus?

What the Mosaic code actually did was to reveal that the sum and total of my life amounted to a "*body of death*". This makes sense, as this is fundamentally the purpose of the law, to convince us of our need for a savior –

> *For I know that nothing good dwells in me, that is, in my flesh; for the willing is present in me, but the doing of the good is not. For the good that I want, I do not do, but I practice the very evil that I do not want. But if I am doing the very thing I do not want, I am no longer the one doing it, but sin which dwells in me. I find then the principle that evil is present in me, the one who*

> *wants to do good. For I joyfully concur with the law of God in the inner man, but I see a different law in the members of my body, waging war against the law of my mind and making me a prisoner of the law of sin which is in my members. Wretched man that I am! Who will set me free from the body of this death? (Rom. 7:18-24)*

Indeed! Who or what could effectively save me from this desperate condition? Condemned under the law, and worthy of death, to whom could I turn?

Paul records the answer in verse 25. I am sure it is familiar to most of you.

> *Thanks be to God through Jesus Christ our Lord! So then, on the one hand I myself with my mind am serving the law of God, but on the other, with my flesh the law of sin. (Rom. 7:25)*

After many years of law-keeping, I remained for the most part unchanged and still very much the *old man*. There was no newness of life but a growing desperation. As Paul indicates, we sincerely want to be good, but we are unable. We are powerless, and although we dress up in our sabbath-best, smile at church and nod our heads at all the religious platitudes, we are nonetheless *unsaved*, or still very much dead. After many years of this pretense, what we experience is the polar opposite of all that is promised in Christ – LIFE, FREEDOM, POWER, VICTORY, REAL CHANGE, HOPE, THE HEART-CHANGING LOVE OF GOD!

My friends, I knew many people who died in this situation, ignorant that the real hope of the law was the *Author of Life*, the *Bright and Morning Star* who brings a new day and a fresh hope to those fallen at the alter. How sad! That all they were left with was a changed diet and a new suit of clothes.

"*I am the way and the truth and the life*", pronounced our Lord. Now the law may point the way, and hint at truth, and provide a glimpse of newness of life, but it can never actually fulfill or empower any of this. Only by following Christ Jesus and living each moment in Him will we experience God's ultimate and living hope for humankind.

Recall that the first tablets of stone were smashed to pieces, reminding us that a code written on anything but the heart is fragile and fleeting. Religion loves and needs and multiplies rules, as this is how it controls and manages people.

Yet, relationship and true life in the body of Christ needs only grace and truth and life, which not only changes behavior, but penetrates to the inner core of the old man. It engages the heart and infuses the spirit of man with the moral life of a holy God. It begins to restore the Creator's originally intended order of *spirit, soul* and *body* that was lost in Eden.

The good news of the gospel of grace is not that we have a set of rules that work, but that we have found LIFE. *Real Life*. Life flowing out through the wonder and person of the Creator of all Life, the *River of Life*! The Inventor and Author and Champion of Life! The Healer and Restorer of Life!

But some may ask –

Is it not the law that informs our conscience of right and wrong? Must we not refer to it to know how to attain a holy life?

There are, I believe, 613 listed do's and don'ts in the Torah. As a spirit-breathed disciple of Jesus Christ, and redeemed child of a Heavenly Father, are these alone what inform my conscience regarding good and evil, sin, and righteousness? I reject that my brethren. Although the moral truth contained in the Torah is inherently good, as Paul and John affirmed, it is also incomplete. "*Grace and truth*" came only with the incarnation of the divine into the world of men. Paul indicates that his gospel, revealing the complete picture, the mystery of godliness (the indwelling life of God within a man), the hope of God's love flowing in us – all of this – solves the problem that the law defines.

Where, for example, does it say in the Torah that we are to lay down our life for our friends? Does love stop at the 613th point?

How does the law guide me into the love of Christ that empties itself for the glory of God and the good of others?

Consider the fact that the reality and perspective of God now resides and abides within us through the medium of the indwelling Spirit of truth. It is He (one of the Holy Three of the Divine Trinity) that is now the informer of our conscience. My friends, take a few moments and consider the incredible enormity of this truth – that at this very moment, behind your eyes, and residing in your regenerated spirit, is the Author of All Life and Truth, the pre-existent One, the very first, the loving Shepherd of our souls!

We now not only have the rules but the *Rule Giver.* We not only have the end but the living, breathing fulfillment of that end. Everything the Law (and the prophets) pointed to, and hinted at, and symbolized, and foreshadowed; all that it meant to God when He created them – embodied and finalized in His Beloved Son – this is what we now have brethren. Read all about it in the book of Hebrews and Galatians. Read it and rejoice for now we have real hope, power, life and freedom.

The law also has no inherent power beyond condemning one to death. In a crude sense, it is like a speed limit sign that cannot prevent anyone from exceeding the posted speed, or a stop light that is routinely violated.

Like the Jews under law, we are free moral agents, but now we have something most of them did not – moral power, or moral life, if you will. We have the *holiness of God* - Jesus Christ! The power is in the life, you see, not in the understanding of what to do. Even Paul indicated that it is not merely enough to know what to do or even desire to do it –

> *For what I am doing, I do not understand; for I am not practicing what I would like to do, but I am doing the very thing I hate. But if I do the very thing I do not want to do, I agree with the Law, confessing that the Law is good. So now, no longer am I the one doing it, but sin which dwells in me. For I know that nothing good dwells in me, that is, in my flesh; for the willing is*

> *present in me, but the doing of the good is not. For the good that I want, I do not do, but I practice the very evil that I do not want. But if I am doing the very thing I do not want, I am no longer the one doing it, but sin which dwells in me. (Rom. 7:15-20)*

The freedom from, and power over sin and death comes from the spirit of life residing in all those who are twice-born or born again. Nicodemus, an expert in the law, couldn't quite get his mind around this concept, and yet it was key to Messiah's first coming. This is why it is taught that the law paved the way, or led to Christ. It was a signpost with all arrows pointing directly to Him.

It is most enlightening that Jesus' first directive to His new disciples was "*Follow Me*". Is this not what we are to do also, follow Him? If the law was an end in itself, then why didn't our Lord say to Peter and John and Andrew "*Follow Moses*". Clearly, in my humble opinion, this is an *either or* decision.

John then goes on to record Jesus' teaching that we are to imbibe Him (partake of His flesh and blood as food necessary for vitality), through the ceremonial fellowship of the Lord's Supper. Why is this necessary if the law is sufficient of and by itself? This makes no sense really, and defies the complete testimony of the Spirit over both old and new covenants.

Legalists of every age, from Paul's day to today, will promise you many things, dear saints, but one thing they can never actually deliver is life. This is only possible when the creature is restored to perfect moral unity with the Creator; when the child is brought home, there in that heavenly place where mortal spirit is infused with immortal spirit.

This is life we are talking about here – real life. The life is in the blood, not in the stone. Please don't make the mistake I made, my friends. I wouldn't be writing any of this if I had no experience to back it up.

I have heard the argument before, that the various laws and ordinances flesh out, or define sin for us, so that we can better adhere to it. Yet, this is still an intellectual thing, an act of knowing, and even though we may sincerely desire to please God by keeping such imperatives so narrowly, it still does not address the *how* of it all.

Now brethren, you are free to do whatever you think is helpful to you under the liberty of the New Covenant (Romans 14). Paul, a Jew, chose to abide by some (not all, and this is key, because if you break one part of the law you have broken it entirely) practices from His heritage, such as the Passover and certain Nazirite vows, for example. Yet he rejected those Jewish believers who were trying to reinstate the Mosaic code on gentile followers of Jesus Christ. This is equivalent to those today and in every age who attempt to reinstate or exalt the Torah in the lives of Christians.

Now what each of us determines to be helpful is entirely up to ourselves and the Lord. It is a personal thing, much like our devotional life. I must confess that I rarely pray on my knees, but rather I prefer to walk when conversing with the Lord. Religionists (those who consider form equal to or more important than reality) will say that I am showing disrespect to the Lord. To date, the Spirit has not yet aligned my conscience with this. I trust Him entirely, and would hope that I would change course immediately once I was convicted of this or anything else.

The problem with law-keeping however, is that human nature and the soul (*the mind, emotions and will*) kick in and we start projecting our personal norms and preferences on other people. I have seen it over and over again, and the history of the church over many years testifies of it.

This, incidentally, is what I believe is wrong with much of the *method-driven* and *step-by-step* ministry we see today. I may have a number of patterns or disciplines that I consider helpful for me, but the minute I tell you that these *seven steps* will produce the same fruit in your life, I have started imposing my relationship with God onto you, and this seldom edifies anyone over the long term. Most parents with multiple children will tell you that each of them is unique and distinct; that one style of parenting cannot be readily applied to all. This is true of God's spiritual children, and it is what makes the church a dynamic and vibrant family.

We must understand that we are all on the same path, but that our Lord relates to us quite differently as His children. Some are stronger or weaker in the maturity of the faith, and giving them some method or regimen may be entirely counter-productive to what the Head of the Body is hoping to do with that individual. For some, one side of the soul is stronger – *the reason, or the emotions, or the will* – so we cannot apply the same methods and imperatives equally. We are all susceptible to the *lust of the eyes and flesh and the pride of life* (all expressions of the soul), but not in the same degree or measure. Only the Lord Himself, who searches the heart, knows what His children require individually.

Please take this to heart, my friends, and be careful of those who will try to convince you that somehow your life in Christ is incomplete. We need no supplements, for He is the All and the Everything for us now. The Law given to Moses is still doing what it was created to do when the holy finger of God engraved it in stone. Yet, let us not confuse this with the "*law of the Spirit of life in Christ Jesus*" that now governs and empowers us as God's beloved children. This is now the active and animating principle of life for all those in Christ Jesus.

> *Therefore there is now no condemnation for those who are in Christ Jesus. For the law of the Spirit of life in Christ Jesus has set you free from the law of sin and of death. For what the Law could not do, weak as it was through the flesh, God did: sending His own Son in the likeness of sinful flesh and as an offering for sin, He condemned sin in the flesh, so that the requirement of the Law might be fulfilled in us, who do not walk according to the flesh but according to the Spirit. For those who are according to the flesh set their minds on the things of the flesh, but those who are according to the Spirit, the things of the Spirit. For the mind set on the flesh is death, but the mind set on the Spirit is life and peace, because the mind set on the flesh is hostile toward God; for it does not subject itself to the law of God, for it is not even able to do so, and those who are in the flesh cannot please God. (Rom. 8:1-8)*

Repentance As a Way of Life

> *The root of all evil in human nature is the corruption of the will. The thoughts and intents of the heart are wrong and as a consequence the whole life is wrong. Repentance is primarily a change of moral purpose, a sudden and often violent reversal of the soul's direction. The prodigal son took his first step upward from the pigsty when he said, "I will arise and go to my father." As he had once willed to leave his father's house, now he willed to return. His subsequent action proved his expressed purpose to be sincere. He did return. (A.W. Tozer, from True Religion is Not Feeling but Willing)*

I dare say I am troubled, my friends, by the general manner in which repentance is presented to us today by our modern Christian teachers and guides. I take issue with the fact that much of the current emphasis barely takes issue with sin, or the inborn depravity of man's condition, or the ageless reality that the God we serve is a high and holy being who cannot dwell with evil.

> *For You are not a God who takes pleasure in wickedness; No evil dwells with You. (Psa. 5:4)*

In much the same way that many other foundational doctrines of the faith are being re-packaged by this new, veiled humanism, such is the case with repentance. Here, too, we discover that at its core, repentance is presented as having to do with fallen man's behavior and need for affirmation, rather than his unlikeness to a Holy Maker who will not abide with darkness and impurity.

I love the way Tozer paints the vivid word picture of repentance as an "*often violent reversal of the soul's direction*", and how he targets the human will as the real source of man's corruption. We do not, according to Tozer, slip morally because we are having a bad day, so much out of character, but rather because the carnal and dark heart within us stands in open defiance of our Father's loving purpose. The will, which animates the human soul, the very soul that must be saved (won over to the Lordship of Christ Jesus), must be brought under the active dominion of the regenerated human spirit, which alone receives the divine things of God, and the power unto righteousness.

"*I have sinned against the Lord*", cried David, accurately portraying his infidelity and murder as an offense against the Most High. All sin, whatever it looks like, or whoever it hurts or destroys, is an offense against God simply because it defies His perfect and creative purpose on the earth. True repentance acknowledges what God is as much and perhaps more than what we are. It stems from the stark and spirit-inspired sense that the chasm between the Creator and the created is wider than we could ever have imagined.

When the first man Adam tasted of that forbidden fruit, and all the creation groaned on that darkest of days, it was the will of man that was then and there corrupted and sealed in his offspring. And ever since it stands with clenched fists in open and violent defiance of the Maker.

Those whom the Bible calls the children of light will see this most clearly. Those who view sanctification as little more than an improved self, or a fancy suit of clothes draped over dead men's bones, will not; indeed, they cannot.

My friends, when we repent, we do so not only for the evil that we have committed (our behavior), but for the evil that our entire existence represents in relation to God (our condition). We repent in dust and ashes for what we are, as we gradually come to see Him for what He is. And as this unlikeness and inequality becomes ever more evident to us, as He draws us into Himself, we begin to see what Job saw when he cried –

> *"Therefore I retract, And I repent in dust and ashes."*
> *(Job 42:6)*

or the Apostle Paul, when He enjoined us to –

> *"Abhor what is evil; cling to what is good."*
> *(Rom. 12:9)*

At the most essential level, as the Holy Spirit is turning our moral world upside down and inside out, we begin to see how absolutely loathsome and helpless we are. Then, flowing out of this is a heaven-sent desire to be rid of it, once and for all and forever. This is what Paul was driving at when he tells us to "abhor evil." The Jews of his day would be very familiar with Old Testament directives to separate themselves from what was unclean or unholy. To abhor implies a desire to be removed or separate from it.

Yet the humanistic religion of our day is quick to nod its happy head and suggest that *"nobody's perfect, my friend. Just say you're sorry to God and all will be well. After all, He loves you and understands that you are only flesh and blood."*

Do we not see how this trivializes it all away into vapor, and why so many supposed Christians never actually grow in Christ, or come to see life from God's perspective. I must confess here that this has been an apt description of my Christian walk for most of my life. I repented for what it did for me; or what I wanted it to do for me, not because it affirmed the moral perfection of my God.

I have since begun to ask the Lord to show me what He sees in me, warts and all, and to help me to treat repentance as a way of living this new life, not something I do only when I stumble morally at some point in time. As we draw further into the light that is Jesus Christ, we will see more clearly and vividly what He sees, and that our need for cleansing and forgiveness is a constant necessity as long as we are here in the flesh.

> *If we say that we have fellowship with Him and yet walk in the darkness, we lie and do not practice the truth; but if we walk in the Light as He Himself is in the Light, we have fellowship with one another, and the*

> *blood of Jesus His Son cleanses us from all sin. If we say that we have no sin, we are deceiving ourselves and the truth is not in us. If we confess our sins, He is faithful and righteous to forgive us our sins and to cleanse us from all unrighteousness. If we say that we have not sinned, we make Him a liar and His word is not in us. (1 John 1:6-10)*

The Bible teaches, and experience confirms, that our behavior (or what the Scriptures call fruit) springs forth from what we are. I sin because, plainly and simply, I am a sinner. I lie, not due to some momentary lapse of truthfulness, but because I am a liar. I steal, not because I temporarily stumbled, but because I am thief. If the well has been polluted, then the water will be undrinkable. Jesus came, suffered, died, then rose on the third day, not to change what we do, but what we are.

> *Everyone who practices sin also practices lawlessness; and sin is lawlessness. You know that He appeared in order to take away sins; and in Him there is no sin. No one who abides in Him sins; no one who sins has seen Him or knows Him. Little children, make sure no one deceives you; the one who practices righteousness is righteous, just as He is righteous… (1 John 3:4-7)*

The humanist tendency today is to refuse to be defined by what we are, to consider the human condition as essentially good, yet prone to weakness. This explanation, false to its core, tramples on the truth of what Adamic man really is, and ultimately degrades the cross of Christ.

To repent in Biblical terms, is to turn away from the sinfulness we abhor, and toward our pure and perfect Redeemer. Repentance is the ongoing expression of the truth that the Holy Spirit is exposing about our foul condition. Yes, when it surfaces in the form of rotten fruit and hurts others, it becomes even more exposed, but repentance has a persistent role in our transformation.

> *"Therefore bear fruit in keeping with repentance…" (Matt. 3:8)*

We repent also because we have veiled the testimony of our Lord to this sin-stained world. Rather than magnify our Lord Jesus Christ, we have covered Him over in the dark shroud of the old carnal self. Rather than shine forth His pure and heavenly light, we have only added to the darkness. In place of salt, we have scattered-sugar, and the rot and decay of evil has advanced, unrestrained by the power of God in us.

Repentance marks a commitment to turn, a redirection of the will back toward the One who has begotten us; He who is drawing us out of the darkness and depravity of this world into His marvelous light.

> *For all that is in the world, the lust of the flesh and the lust of the eyes and the boastful pride of life, is not from the Father, but is from the world. (1 John 2:16)*

It is not an intellectual or even strictly moral thing at all, but it flows out of the illumination of the human spirit. It is a heart-deep revelation of our profound uncleanness, and a God-sent obsession to be eternally cleansed and pure.

True repentance is nothing more than seeing clearly, as the Lord sees. It is seeing *unlikeness, impurity, disorder* (the human soul, with all of its natural energies and inspiration, governing the human spirit, rather than the other way around, as intended by the Creator), *worldliness, carnality* (the lustful energies of the physical body governing both soul and spirit). In short, we repent of anything that is less than Christ, and anything put in place of Christ; even things that are not necessarily bad or evil in themselves. Only as we begin to truly and clearly see the Lord Jesus in all of His divine fullness, with eyes wide open in the spirit, do we begin to see ourselves and all that we represent. Only then, will repentance bring forth the fruit of a transformed life, pleasing to the Father.

We repent, my friends, because we do not love Him as He has loved us. We repent because He is pure and holy, and we are not. We repent because we see with eyes wide open in the spirit, what He sees. We repent because He who is innately worthy has stooped to help we who are not.

> *For the sorrow that is according to the will of God produces a repentance without regret, leading to salvation, but the sorrow of the world produces death. (2 Cor. 7:10)*

Indeed, part of the godly sorrow that surfaces and sometimes threatens to consume us, may even flow out the realization of how utterly unworthy we are of any good thing from the Master's table. He has stooped to wash our feet, yet we persist in wanting to be dirty. I*dolatry, impurity, uncleanness, selfishness, worldliness* – oh that we would be free my brethren; oh for the day when we will be free!

May our Holy and Perfect Father lead each of us further along this path into His light and truth. May the tears that flow from the recognition of our own uncleanness and unfaithfulness render the fruits of righteousness and holiness in our hearts and lives. May we begin to see all things as only He sees them, abhorring that which is evil, and turning to He alone Who is good. In Jesus' perfect and holy name. Amen.

Proof Text Christianity

> *But realize this, that in the last days difficult times will come. For men...holding to a form of godliness, although they have denied its power; Avoid such men as these. (2 Tim. 3:1-5)*

I must confess that for many years I was little more than a *proof text* Christian. What I mean is that I could skillfully swing the sword of truth at anything or anyone at the drop of a hat, to advance my particular view or position. Christianity for me, during this time, was little more than an intellectual argument to be won, not a life derived *moment-by-moment,* in and through Jesus Christ.

Looking back, I can see now that in many ways I loved studying God's Word more than, and even in place of, the Author of my faith. Understanding and learning became an end in itself, a soulish exercise, rather than a means to discovering my need for newness of life, found solely in the Savior of my soul. And just as with every zealous disciple who starts down this path, I burned and fizzled out like a wasted firecracker on the 4th of July.

Interesting how this works really, and how subtly it distances us from the real object of our faith, the only true source of power. Proof text Christians are masterful at weaving together Scriptural tenets to support this or that theological position, and on the surface it appears they may even be further down the road in their spiritual walk than the rest of us. They will never admit it openly, but in living practice they equate the spiritually endowed gift of teaching with higher-level mastery of Strong's Concordance or other Bible study aids.

I know brethren, for I was there. I am writing from experience here. And you know something, it was all nothing but vanity and emptiness; a vain attempt to appear holier and godlier than everyone else – mere religious exhibitionism – and it was as cold and lifeless as a box of rocks.

Go to many Christian forums and biblical discernment websites today, and you will see evidence of this in abundance. People trying desperately to impress each other with copied and pasted proof texts, believing that this is all that the Bible means by discernment, or "*rightly dividing the word of truth*". Yet once you get in a little deeper, and begin to genuinely discern the spirit behind the message, you begin to wonder if these folks are defending the Lord's position or their own. Is Christ being increased or are they? Is it the spirit or the soul doing all the talking? I certainly cannot speak of others, but I know that this was true of myself when I was engaged in this kind of soulish (derived from the soul and not the spirit, which alone can receive the things of God), *proof text religion.*

True biblical discernment, my friends, is the spirit-empowered ability to perceive things from God's perspective, with divine clarity, and it never develops apart from a deepening relationship with Him. Like all heavenly gifts and abilities, it is not something He dispatches to us before heading back to the remoteness of the highest heaven. It grows in us as we grow in Him. If we want His gifts apart from Him, then we will be sorely disappointed, for this is not how it works. The Christian life flows only out of the Living Spirit of Christ that represents our newness of life (Romans 8:9-11). The wonder of the gospel is that the giver and the gift are one and the same. Jesus Christ is both the means and the end of our salvation.

My friends, for many years I belonged to what amounted to a pseudo-christian cult because I fell prey to the arguments of men who could manipulate proof texts better than most followers of Jesus Christ. My response was to learn the Bible so completely that I would never be deceived again; to arm myself with an arsenal of proof texts that might protect me in the future.

For you see my friends, the Bible can indeed become an end and idol unto itself, just like anything else. Does that shock you? It shouldn't. The devil can and will use anything, even good things, to draw us away from an intimate, heart-changing encounter with the Living Word, the Walking Truth, the Light of the World that came down to expose the darkness.

As the Apostle Paul predicted of our present time, many have a *form of godliness* but effectively deny its real power. This, in my view, accurately captures the trend towards cold fundamentalism seen at one extreme of Christendom today. Yet, our Lord promised us so much more than a story about God and holy living; He offered us Himself, and the regenerative power to overcome, to live as children of light in a dark world. He offered us revelation by His Spirit that activates and enlivens the recorded words of Scripture, and turns dry orthodoxy into dynamic and living testimony.

This mystery of godliness, this beautiful process of sanctification whereby we are first unmade by His gracious and loving touch, then built back up again in the image and life of His Son, is the Word lived, and breathed, and spilling out from our lives as a true and powerful testimony. It is so much more than a script, or a topical Bible study. It is Christ Himself. Praise God for that, brethren!

It is one thing to read about love, or to hear choruses sung about love; it is quite another to experience true and selfless love in its purest form and flow. It is one thing to read a history textbook describing one of the epic battles of modern warfare, and it is quite another to have actually been there, to feel the ground shake under the movement of tanks and armaments, to witness the sky explode in a mortar shower.

The Scriptures, and the Lord of the Scriptures, call us to a living and life-changing relationship with Him. The mere ability to perform a word search in an online Bible does not transform a sinner into a saint, or a devil into a disciple. Jesus came into the world to show us by example what this new life looks and feels and sounds like. "*Oh, taste and see that the Lord is good*" cried the psalmist, conveying a relationship that transcends the fleshly mind and penetrates deeper into the very spirit of the redeemed man.

"But wait", come the cries from the back row. "*What about Hebrews 4, what about Hebrews 4?*"

> *For the word of God is living and active and sharper than any two-edged sword, and piercing as far as the division of soul and spirit, of both joints and marrow, and able to judge the thoughts and intentions of the heart. And there is no creature hidden from His sight, but all things are open and laid bare to the eyes of Him with whom we have to do. (Heb. 4:12-13)*

True, my brother. So true. But what you read in your red-letter Bible has no power of and by itself. Behind it all is God, the Living Word, the One that interpenetrates your very being, and refashions you from within. The devil himself can throw Scripture around. He still does so in the church today for those who have ears to hear.

It all begins and ends by us coming to Him, laying our lives down on that heavenly altar, in living sacrifice, completely emptied of ourselves and our intellectual pride. Only then can He build us up again with all of the means at His disposable, including His Word. Certainly He teaches us and corrects us, but never are we to come to the Scriptures alone, then stay there. To the unregenerated spirit of man, it is very much a coded and hidden book. To the children of light, accompanied by the Living Word, it is a light to our path, and that path always and forever leads to Him.

Please don't make the mistake I made and think that the more we know about the Bible – the more we can prove our faith through theological arguments, then the deeper and more intimately we will know Him. This is putting the cart before the horse. What I have discovered is that the more I seek Him and draw near in loving obedience and submission, the more He reveals Himself and His wondrous mysteries within the pages of His Book.

Until this occurs, all they are, and can ever be, are *proof texts.* You may persuade other *proof text* Christians, but at its core, this is not the very best that is available to us as pure and simple Christians.

May the Eternal Father reveal all the riches of His Son in us through His Spirit. May He illuminate our hearts in a new and dynamic way through the living and powerful Word of Life. May we realize our truest potential as we come see to only Him in every passage and page of Scripture. In Jesus' precious name. Amen.

What Is This Love?

In John's gospel, we read that the Jewish authorities of Jesus' day wanted to kill Him for making a man well on the Sabbath day. Unbelievable really, that their religious tradition had so completely blinded them to the love of God. A little while later, our Lord affirms this –

> *"...but I know you, that you do not have the love of God in yourselves." (John 5:42)*

In other passages of Scripture, we are reminded that the very essence of God's nature and personality is love. It is love, more than anything else, that identifies and distinguishes Him as who and what He is. It is love that consolidates and focuses all of His varied and superlative attributes. In the end, brethren, everything in our God operates from the basis of this thing called love.

Here are just a scattering of familiar texts conveying this concept –

> *The one who does not love does not know God, for God is love. (1 John 4:8)*
>
> *We have come to know and have believed the love which God has for us. God is love, and the one who abides in love abides in God, and God abides in him. (1 John 4:16)*
>
> *For God so loved the world, that He gave His only begotten Son, that whoever believes in Him shall not perish, but have eternal life. (John 3:16)*
>
> *Beloved, if God so loved us, we also ought to love one another. (1 John 4:11)*

> *"A new commandment I give to you, that you love one another, even as I have loved you, that you also love one another. By this all men will know that you are My disciples, if you have love for one another." (John 13:34-35)*

> *Now I ask you, lady, not as though I were writing to you a new commandment, but the one which we have had from the beginning, that we love one another. (2 John 5)*

And so we see, brethren, that this thing called love is of the uttermost importance; that it is what both the Father and the Son want us to know about them more than anything; that the very coming down of the Son out of heaven is substantiation of the Father's love for us. And unlike human beings who can only swoon and sing and write empty poetry about love, He demonstrates what it means, how it works, how it is always ready to sacrifice something precious and perfect.

Love is indeed something that God is, and this is true because it represents the very essence of His nature. He is undeniably *loving*, but more than that, dear ones, He is *Love*. The very life and dynamic of God flows out His immeasurable love for all of His creation.

The other night I awoke in the wee small hours of the morning, and the Father reminded me most powerfully how much He loved me. I remember lying there, looking down at my young son beside me, so calm and peaceful. I remember gazing down at him for quite some time, thinking deeply. I reflected on how much I loved him, and how so completely easy and natural it was for me to love him.

But where does this kind of love come from, I wondered? I know for certain I didn't learn it from my own father, as he abandoned the family when I was five years old. It also doesn't have much to do with how lovable, or even likable, my son is. Like most little boys, he is anything but perfect, so it isn't really what he does or doesn't do that makes me love him.

The truth is that I love him, plainly and simply because he is my son, rooted in me, and growing out of me in many ways (both positive and negative). The heavenly Father Himself had planted this love inside of me, and there is no other explanation for it.

As I lay there gazing at my boy, it wasn't long before I started to imagine the Father looking down on me and what He might be thinking at that moment. "*I love you too my son*", came His reply deep down in my spirit. I knew immediately it was Him, and more importantly, I believe I understood in that powerful flash of revelation what all of these Biblical truths were getting at.

I know, my friends, that the Bible has much to say about love; that there are, for example, three Greek words for love in the New Testament, and that the first commandment is to "*Love the Lord thy God*", and all others are summed up in "*Love thy neighbor*". But that is not necessarily how I personally need to understand the Father's love for me.

It is a bond of love, you see, that connects me to Him, and makes me want to serve Him, and follow Him, and manifest the life and glory of His Son through my puny little existence on this fallen earth. If I require some law or commandment pressing down on me to do what should come naturally as a response to God's love, then am I no different that the scribes and pharisees who didn't know God because they didn't want His love.

My friends, the Father's love for us is demonstrated fully and meaningfully by the life of His Son that was breathed into our being at our spiritual birth. It settles once and for all the question of whether God loves us or not.

There is a lot of this sentimental and superficial love floating around lately, not only on the big screen and on the radio, but sadly in our modern churches. Yet this is not the love pouring out from every page of the Holy Scriptures, from the prophets and apostles. This is a worldly and self-gratifying love, which is no love at all. It seeks to get something, not give it up. We know it to be false because it changes no one, and never has. It fails to penetrate the heart and spirit within a man, for it is mere words and empty sentiment.

When God loves us truly, and we come to know that we are loved, wonderful, life-changing things begin to happen. We start to surrender our lives to Him and to love Him in return, albeit imperfectly. We begin to trust Him and include Him, and to lean into Him. Gradually and ever hesitatingly, we begin to loosen our grip on our lives and this fickle world, so that we can reach for Him, and adore Him who has loved us so perfectly.

Our Father's love begins to do what only it can do – change us deep down, improve us top to bottom, and heal us completely of anything that prevents His love from flowing out of our lives into the lives of others.

My brethren and friends, this is the love with which we are loved, and this is the love that must represent the testimony of our lives in this fallen and loveless world. Our singular claim is this: that we have been loved by our Loving Father in Heaven. We can claim nothing else, nor do we need to. If only we can grasp this truth. If only we can see with new eyes the fullest measure of His love for us in Jesus Christ, His Son.

This is my prayer in this hour for all of us. In Jesus' precious name. Amen.

My Statement of Faith

Okay here goes. Are you ready? Have a pencil handy?

> *Immediately the boy's father cried out and said, "I do believe; help my unbelief." (Mark 9:24)*

> *The apostles said to the Lord, "Increase our faith!" (Luke 17:5)*

I believe; help my unbelief! Increase my faith Lord!

Insufficient you say? More detail required? Perhaps you're right. Here's some more then -

> *Now faith is the assurance of things hoped for, the conviction of things not seen. (Heb. 11:1)*

Now faith is the assurance (substance, foundation) of things hoped for, the evidence of things not seen.

What – no mention of the divine inspiration of Scripture, the triune nature of divinity, salvation by grace, baptism, the Lord's Supper, heaven, hell, the afterlife of the saved and the damned?

Strange isn't it, friends, how such things work. At the risk of offending some folks, I dare say that the church in this hour appears, by all accounts, to have elevated doctrine to the same level that the Jews elevated the law.

And when the Holy One, the Son of God, the Divine Man, the Alpha and the Omega, actually stood before them in the flesh, living and breathing, and showing forth the very power and wisdom and love of the Father, they did what?

I can just picture some of them scrambling for their scrolls, fingering chapter and verse in the Torah, trying to make sense of the wonder that stood before them.

"*Could this be the Christ?*" some little ones asked.

Could the law answer that question then my friends? And can doctrine answer it for us now? Perhaps a penetrating word from T. Austin-Sparks –

> *The only knowledge of God which is of spiritual value for ourselves, or for others by our ministry, is that which we have by revelation of the Holy Spirit within our own spirits. God never—in the first instance—explains Himself to man's reason, and man can never know God—in the first instance—by reason. Christianity is a revelation or it is nothing, and it has to be that in the case of every new child of God; otherwise faith will be resting upon a foundation which will not stand in the day of the ordeal.*
>
> *'The Christian Faith' embraced as a religion, a philosophy, or as a system of truth, a moral or ethical doctrine, may carry the temporary stimulus of a great ideal; but this will not result in the regeneration of the life, or the new birth of the spirit. There are multitudes of such 'Christians' in the world today, but their spiritual effectiveness is nil. (from What is Man?)*

Now please don't misunderstand; I am in no way disparaging or negating the sacred truths of the Word of God, and I suppose I do have something of a list of things I believe written in my heart (*there is also perhaps a bigger list of things I used to believe but have since discarded, but that's another matter altogether*). Yet it is not a rigid theological box that defines me, or a set of unbroken lines and limits that prevent me from following the free-flowing, revelation of the Spirit, wherever He leads (Romans 8:13-14). If it were, then I dare say that my precious Lord would be little more than some two-dimensional, cardboard cut-out savior, who moves only 90 degrees on a grid, forward and back, left and right, up and down.

> *You search the Scriptures because you think that in them you have eternal life; it is these that testify about Me; and you are unwilling to come to Me so that you may have life.... "For if you believed Moses, you would believe Me, for he wrote about Me. "But if you do not believe his writings, how will you believe My words?" (John 5:39-47)*

Could it be that doctrine is yet another one of those things we have made an end, when it was always intended to be a means of help to us who believe? Have we raised it beyond the height of God Himself, such as the Pharisees did the law? Or perhaps it would be more accurate to say that maybe we really haven't yet discovered the true position or intent of doctrine in the grand scheme of things, as intended by the God of All Truth and Life!

Something to think about certainly. And no, I do not believe the Holy Spirit would lead us to behave contrary to the very Word He inspired. This wouldn't really make much sense, would it? In fact, the spiritual life represents a law unto itself, as Watchman Nee points out –

> *"The law of the Spirit of life in Christ Jesus has set me free from the law of sin and of death." "But why is this law of the Spirit of life ineffectual in certain people? Again we read: "The righteous requirement of, the law should be fulfilled in us who walk according to Spirit" (Rom. 8:2,4).*
>
> *In other words, the law of the Spirit of life works effectively only for those who are spiritual, i.e., those who mind the things of the Spirit. Who are these? Those who do not mind the things of the flesh. "Mind" can also be translated "to be intent upon, to be attentive to."*

Indeed, by walking most completely in the spirit and abiding in Christ Jesus, we cannot but fulfill all law and all doctrine, for it is the very Life of God being expressed in us. Does this make sense? I know it may seem contrary to much of what is being taught out there, where attention to law and doctrine, to rules and methods, is in the ascendancy. But don't you see that this preoccupation and devotion to ordinances (even though they may be inherently good or innocuous) relies so very much on the outward man – the soul, with all its intelligence and human energy – and they can never fulfill the spiritual purpose for which we were redeemed and enlivened. Again, we turn to Austin-Sparks for insight –

> *Thus, a rich knowledge of the Scriptures, an accurate technical grasp of Christian doctrine, a doing of Christian work by all the resources of men's natural wisdom or ability, a clever manipulation and interesting presentation of Bible content and themes, may get not one whit beyond the natural life of men, and still remain within the realm of spiritual death. Men cannot be argued, reasoned, fascinated, interested, 'emotioned', willed, enthused, impassioned, into the kingdom of the heavens; they can only be born; and that is by spiritual quickening. The new birth brings with it new capacities of every kind; and amongst these, the most vital is a new and different faculty of Divine knowledge, understanding and apprehension. As we have said earlier, the human brain is not ruled out, but is secondary, not primary. The function of the human intellect is to give spiritual things intelligent form for ourselves and for others. (from, What is Man?)*

And here's something else to consider. According to my understanding of the life and word of the Lord Jesus Christ, the two essential ideals to be wrought through abiding in Him fully are –

Love and Wisdom!

Here are the weighty matters of the law indeed! Here is where the rubber meets the road of our walking in Him and deriving every good and precious promise from He who is the Way, the Truth and the Life. Here is the source and flow of all obedience, truth, faithfulness, fruitfulness, and everything pleasing to the Heavenly Father! Here lies the answer to all the weighty questions we should be asking in this hour – the *how*, the *why*, the *when*, the *who*, the *what* – of this newness of life in Christ Jesus. Here is where it all leads in the end, as all things are summed up in He who is the fullness of the Life and Glory and Majesty of the Most High!

Okay, here is your homework for tomorrow then: I would like you to chart or graph all of the places that both love and wisdom intersect with the law and doctrine. Maybe use some of those neat little lines with arrow heads to show all of the correlations and derivations and so forth. Then I would like you to study the lives of all the prophets in the Old Testament, all of the strange things they did, how they lived, what they ate, what they wore, who they married (and divorced), then chart all of this according to how closely it conforms to the Law of Moses and the Deuteronomic Code.

Incidentally, I can almost picture Ahab asking Elijah for his statement of faith, or Zedekiah asking Jeremiah if he believed in sprinkling or immersion. Well, not really, but you get the idea. Is not our God a god of strange and mysterious ways? Is He so limited and confined by our meager understanding of His most perfect Word? I say not.

> *For My thoughts are not your thoughts, Nor are your ways My ways," declares the LORD. For as the heavens are higher than the earth, So are My ways higher than your ways, And My thoughts than your thoughts. (Isa. 55:8-9)*

Wouldn't it be so convenient, brethren, if merely visiting a church's web site and scrolling through their bulleted Statement of Beliefs, would provide some accurate indication that the Lord of all Life was actually present and active there? If only it were so easy. If only there was a way of knowing that these heavenly sentiments were written on the very hearts of the people inside, and especially the man at the front doing all the preaching.

> *"Behold, days are coming," declares the LORD, "when I will make a new covenant with the house of Israel and with the house of Judah, not like the covenant which I made with their fathers in the day I took them by the hand to bring them out of the land of Egypt, My covenant which they broke, although I was a husband*

> *to them," declares the LORD. "But this is the covenant which I will make with the house of Israel after those days," declares the LORD, "I will put My law within them and on their heart I will write it; and I will be their God, and they shall be My people. "They will not teach again, each man his neighbor and each man his brother, saying, 'Know the LORD,' for they will all know Me, from the least of them to the greatest of them," declares the LORD, "for I will forgive their iniquity, and their sin I will remember no more." (Jer. 31:31-34)*

Now lest you think I am a heretic, or worse, I encourage you to deeply and spiritually reflect on this brethren, and pray over what is being conveyed in this passage. Here are the laws of God written on the heart and the mind, not on sheets of paper, stone tablets or a hypertext web page. And the end result is a people (Israel) who henceforth "know the Lord", and He claims them as His own.

> *"I will give them a heart to know Me, for I am the LORD; and they will be My people, and I will be their God, for they will return to Me with their whole heart." (Jer. 24:7)*

Dear brethren, my statement of faith is that I would have such a heart as this; and that I would know the Lord God as He intended from the beginning. My statement of faith is that the often divided and spotted heart currently within me would be made miraculously and supernaturally clean and whole, that I would love Him with all that I am and nothing held back!.

Now I have obviously employed exaggeration in this piece for effect, that we might put things – even good and helpful things – in their proper place, for this too is wisdom. What we believe is important, and the content of our faith, rooted and flowing from the Living and written Word, must certainly have its place.

Yet to have a heart and a hunger to know Him – that is what we should be after, isn't it? Sure you can check the boxes next to the doctrines one subscribes to and somehow think that such a heart and such a hunger exists, but this is not always so. That is the point being made here; and I hope and pray that it has been made. And if not, the fault (as always) lies with me alone and not the Spirit whose work it is to convey the deep and heavenly things of God to our inner man.

If for whatever reason, you find yourself estranged from the One who very much wants you to know Him and to love Him with a pure and whole heart, then I encourage you to return to Him now. For He is faithful and merciful and ever so kind to us who are ever so weak and wandering.

> *If we are faithless, He remains faithful, for He cannot deny Himself. (2 Tim. 2:13)*
>
> *Be strong and courageous, do not be afraid or tremble at them, for the LORD your God is the one who goes with you. He will not fail you or forsake you. (Deut. 31:6)*

No brethren, the One who is abundantly and inherently faithful will not fail us, nor forsake us. He is a Good Shepherd after all, and He is God. May it be that we come to Him and rest in Him most completely, and learn the secret of the vine and the branches, that we are one with Him, and He cannot deny Himself. May we learn that piled up for us, in the vast storehouse of His heart, is a vast and wondrous supply of grace ready to replenish our every need in this dread hour at the close of this age. May we rise up beyond the weakness of our proud flesh in all the power and vitality of His risen and glorious Life! And may we walk only in Him whom we have received. Oh Father, we believe, but help us, dear Lord, to move from faith onward to more faith, only in Your most precious and beloved Son. Amen.

Lord, I believe; help my unbelief. Increase my faith.

Well there you have it – My *Statement of Faith*. I am sorry if it was less than you had hoped for.

Faith Informed and Rewarded

To all His little ones scattered in the wilderness – *grace and peace* to all of you from our Lord and Shepherd Jesus Christ, He in whom we live and move and have our very being. Our sincere prayer for all of you in this hour is that you might continue ever further in His life and light, worthy of all that He is as our truth and wisdom and purpose; that He would be increased and advanced as we learn to live every moment in Him. May our dear Lord preserve us in Himself, that we may be kept from every idol, delusion and distraction that would keep us from looking to His Coming. Amen.

Dear saints, the testimony of Simeon and Anna recorded for us in Luke 2 is profoundly meaningful on so many levels, and I wanted to share some thoughts on this matter as the Lord permits.

Before getting started, here is the text in entirety –

> *On the eighth day, when it was time to circumcise him, he was named Jesus, the name the angel had given him before he had been conceived.*
>
> *When the time of their purification according to the Law of Moses had been completed, Joseph and Mary took him to Jerusalem to present him to the Lord (as it is written in the Law of the Lord, "Every firstborn male is to be consecrated to the Lord"), and to offer a sacrifice in keeping with what is said in the Law of the Lord: "a pair of doves or two young pigeons."*
>
> *Now there was a man in Jerusalem called Simeon, who was righteous and devout. He was waiting for the consolation of Israel, and the Holy Spirit was upon him.*

> *It had been revealed to him by the Holy Spirit that he would not die before he had seen the Lord's Christ. Moved by the Spirit, he went into the temple courts. When the parents brought in the child Jesus to do for him what the custom of the Law required, Simeon took him in his arms and praised God, saying:*
>
> *"Sovereign Lord, as you have promised, you now dismiss your servant in peace. For my eyes have seen your salvation, which you have prepared in the sight of all people, a light for revelation to the Gentiles and for glory to your people Israel."*
>
> *The child's father and mother marveled at what was said about him. Then Simeon blessed them and said to Mary, his mother: "This child is destined to cause the falling and rising of many in Israel, and to be a sign that will be spoken against, so that the thoughts of many hearts will be revealed. And a sword will pierce your own soul too."*
>
> *There was also a prophetess, Anna, the daughter of Phanuel, of the tribe of Asher. She was very old; she had lived with her husband seven years after her marriage, and then was a widow until she was eighty-four. She never left the temple but worshiped night and day, fasting and praying. Coming up to them at that very moment, she gave thanks to God and spoke about the child to all who were looking forward to the redemption of Jerusalem. (Luke 2:21-38)*

Here, in so powerful a narrative, we have a testimony of watchfulness and devotion on the part of these two elderly saints looking longingly for the expected Savior and Redeemer. Both Simeon and Anna arrived at the temple at precisely the time the Firstborn Child was being consecrated to the Lord (see Exodus 13:1).

Now there are many heaven-sent truths to be derived from this account, surrounding the character and circumstances of Simeon and Anna for example, but it appears evident that these two individuals were of only a few who were actively anticipating and seeking the arrival of the Anointed One; the King and Savior of Israel. Where were all the Scribes one wonders, or the Pharisees and Sadducees whose *extensive* understanding of the Scriptures had equipped them to be teachers and guides among the people?

The time of the Messiah's blessed and longed-for arrival was imminent, and yet the majority of Jews were either unaware, unprepared or otherwise distracted by other matters; perhaps the politics of the day, the demands of daily life, the immediate needs of family, or other seemingly ordinary human pursuits. How could this have happened? Why were not the pastors and teachers in Israel, to whom the people were so dependent on for their spiritual life, adequately preparing them for the coming of the Lord?

In contrast we have two insignificant ones, devout and elderly saints led entirely and personally by the Holy Spirit, moved by the urgency of the prophetic moment, "preaching in season and out of season" in the temple, patiently loving the appearing of their King. Though all of the notable elders, teachers and established sects of the day had completely and utterly missed the most important event in the history of the world, a forgotten old man and a lonely old widow were there. It truly makes you wonder, doesn't it, my brethren? Oh how His ways are so much higher and deeper than ours.

Both were prophets in the purest sense of the word. And they knew fully the prophetic Scriptures indicating the imminence of the time in which they were living. Both were empowered and directed by the Spirit to make themselves (and any others who might listen) ready for that day of visitation. For both of them, this was the singular obsession of their lives; nothing came before it in terms of their time, attention or devotion. Theirs was a faith perfected unto endurance by time and testing (James 1:3). With unflinching steadfastness and determination they pressed on, day after day, waiting, hoping, pining for the fulfillment of all that the Word and Spirit had conveyed to them. Rest assured dear saints, that the coming of the King was no peripheral doctrine or teaching, as it was in the synagogues of their day or the churches of ours.

It moved them to watch, to act, to make themselves ready, to purify themselves, and to exhort others in Israel to do the same.

For Simeon (his name means "hearing" in Hebrew), only the vision of the Lord's Christ stood before him and his own mortality, for the Spirit had revealed to him that he would indeed behold the Anointed One before his death. The suggestion here is, I believe, that he must have died shortly after this incident. Imagine if you will, this elderly saint taking the little child in his spindly and wrinkled hands, and the indescribable joy that must have washed over his entire being in that moment. He knew precisely who the little child was. His faith had been rewarded. The Word had been fulfilled. The singular purpose of his life had been realized in that single moment of time.

Unlike Anna, we know very little about Simeon's lineage or personal history. All we know essentially is his name, which he shares with one of the children of Jacob. It may be instructive to highlight here the rather inauspicious history of Simeon, the son of Jacob, as he received no blessing whatsoever when Moses blessed the tribes, and became a scattered and divided people upon entering the land. What we might gather therefore, is that the name *Simeon* in Israel came to be regarded in a derogatory manner. And yet here we have this aged saint being blessed by the grace of God at the arrival of the Comforter of Israel.

And next we learn of Anna (meaning "*grace*" in Hebrew), who over the course of a long and (presumably in the worldly sense) lonely life, fasted and prayed, and spoke out in the temple to all who would hear for many decades (84 years, which is the product of 7 and 12, two numbers rich in Scriptural meaning).

> *Now she who is really a widow, and left alone, trusts in God and continues in supplications and prayers night and day. But she who lives in pleasure is dead while she lives. (1 Tim. 1:5-6)*

Anna, it appears, was not at all caught up in the hopes and affairs of life in the world, or the pursuits or distractions of the day. Hers was not the wholesale religion of the people, for she looked only to God and His salvation, as she was moved and enlivened by His Holy Spirit. She too, as Simeon, was not disappointed, as she arrived at the temple (the Court of Women) at the precise instant the Holy

One was being presented to the Lord. Once again, a faith informed solely by the Spirit, was rewarded. It is interesting to note here how the Scripture records that Anna was the daughter of Phanuel, which means "face of God", of the tribe of Asher, which means "happy". Essentially then, Anna was blessed by the grace of God to experience the measureless joy of beholding the face of God's Anointed. This could not be said for the vast majority in Israel, religious, zealous or otherwise. Truly, our God always preserves for Himself a remnant (Romans 9:27).

Dear brethren, as I meditated on this passage of Scripture, so rich and beautiful in its portrayal of these two devout and steadfast saints, I asked the Lord if there was yet more to its meaning. Was there a message or exhortation for our day perhaps? For myself especially?

In so many ways, the day in which we live is profoundly similar to that of Simeon and Anna, in that the Lord may return at any time now. Just as with them, the singular and defining quality of our lives lies in the hope of His imminent appearing as our Savior and King. What we must learn from the testimony of these two patient and spirit-led prophets is the imperative for patient endurance and faithfulness in all that He asks of us until He comes.

The time is at hand and everything else is secondary. He is coming and there is a prophetic urgency for this generation as never before. Nothing else matters! Not politics! Not the economy! Not our career in this world! Not the unraveling state of the nation! Not our retirement portfolio! Not the amusements and distractions of modern life! Not our big plastic house in the suburbs! Not the desperate and lukewarm condition of the church! No not even, in a relative sense, our own family concerns!

Folks, I have to confess that it absolutely grieved me in my spirit to see the degree of active involvement of the evangelical church here in America during the recent political circus. And by all accounts it would appear that Christians are just as much sold out to the idols of consumerism and covetousness as non-believers. Hopelessly indebted, living beyond their means, addicted to materialism and the culture of more, more, more! *Bigger, bigger, bigger!* How brethren, can this be when our true citizenship is in heaven?

> *Brethren, join in following my example, and observe those who walk according to the pattern you have in us. For many walk, of whom I often told you, and now tell you even weeping, {that they are} enemies of the cross of Christ, whose end is destruction, whose god is {their} appetite, and {whose} glory is in their shame, who set their minds on earthly things. For our citizenship is in heaven, from which also we eagerly wait for a Savior, the Lord Jesus Christ; who will transform the body of our humble state into conformity with the body of His glory, by the exertion of the power that He has even to subject all things to Himself. (Phil. 3:17-21)*

Just like Simeon and Anna, we are to wait patiently for the coming of the Lord –

> *Therefore be patient, brethren, until the coming of the Lord. The farmer waits for the precious produce of the soil, being patient about it, until it gets the early and late rains. You too be patient; strengthen your hearts, for the coming of the Lord is near. (James 5:7-8)*

Patience! What a concept in this *have-it-all-now* generation. Yet our Lord requires so much more of us, those among the Bride who look longingly for the blessed coming of the Bridegroom; He who will make us complete.

Now consider the definition of the word "*steadfast*", brethren, as it so richly conveys what is required of all those awaiting the return of the King from Heaven –

> *Steadfast: 1. fixed in direction; steadily directed: a steadfast gaze. 2. firm in purpose, resolution, faith, attachment, etc., as a person: a steadfast friend. 3. unwavering, as resolution, faith, adherence, etc. 4. firmly established, as an institution or a state of affairs. 5. firmly fixed in place or position. (Dictionary.com)*

And in waiting patiently with unswerving devotion to what lay before them, consider both of these elderly saints who waited their entire lives (Anna was probably over 100 years old when the Spirit directed her to the temple to meet the Lord, and Simeon was at least near the natural age of death) for the coming of the Savior. Their example is recorded forever in the Lord's Book as a testimony, not only to their rock-solid faith and endurance, but as a warning to us today!

No Pharisees, Scribes or Sadducees shared such an honor. There was no established church or denomination, or notable teacher (like Gamaliel, for example) in Israel directing the people to watch and be ready in that hour. This should say something to all those who wish to follow men or groups and not the Living Spirit, who alone can prepare us for the thief-like coming of our Savior. Both Simeon and Anna "*loved his appearing*" (2 Timothy 4:8), not this present world. And this caused them to devote their entire lives and attention to being found ready and available when He came, preaching in season and out of season in the temple to exhort their fellow Jews to watch and prepare, for the Lord's Anointed, the One greater than Moses, was coming!

[Note: Regarding His Coming to Israel, which those who study the Scriptures understand is subsequent to His coming secretly for His church, there will be two faithful witnesses (see Revelation 11) in Jerusalem prior to the coming of the Lord, when He reveals Himself to His own (the nation of Israel, as typified in the story of Joseph revealing Himself to His brothers, and their subsequent repentance), and there were in fact two faithful witnesses (Simeon and Anna) in the temple of Jerusalem at His first coming. Both in the type and the anti-type the message is consistent.]

In Thessalonians, Paul reminds us what the focus of our lives should be in the hour of His appearing –

> *Now as to the times and the epochs, brethren, you have no need of anything to be written to you. For you yourselves know full well that the day of the Lord will come just like a thief in the night. While they are saying, "Peace and safety!" then destruction will come upon them suddenly like labor pains upon a woman with child, and they will not escape. But you, brethren, are not in darkness, that the day would overtake you like*

> *a thief; for you are all sons of light and sons of day. We are not of night nor of darkness; so then let us not sleep as others do, but let us be alert and sober. For those who sleep do their sleeping at night, and those who get drunk get drunk at night.*
>
> *But since we are of the day, let us be sober, having put on the breastplate of faith and love, and as a helmet, the hope of salvation. For God has not destined us for wrath, but for obtaining salvation through our Lord Jesus Christ, who died for us, so that whether we are awake or asleep, we will live together with Him. Therefore encourage one another and build up one another, just as you also are doing. (1 Thess. 5:1-11)*

Notice brethren, in particular, the helmet (protection for the head, which is vital in battle) is the "*hope of salvation*". Now if you are unaware that our salvation is most wonderfully bound up in both the first and second coming of our Lord, you will begin to appreciate what Paul is stating here. Salvation is not solely something that occurred in the past, but it has a past, present and future aspect (pertaining to the *spirit, soul and body)* that is essential to understand. In addition, relative to our current message, consider how this hope of salvation moved both Simeon and Anna to actively prepare and seek the arrival of the Lord.

And in Ephesians, he reminds us how to walk in these evil days prior to our Lord's arrival unto His own –

> *Therefore be careful how you walk, not as unwise men but as wise, making the most of your time, because the days are evil. So then do not be foolish, but understand what the will of the Lord is. And do not get drunk with wine, for that is dissipation, but be filled with the Spirit, speaking to one another in psalms and hymns and spiritual songs, singing and making melody with your heart to the Lord; always giving thanks for all things in the name of our Lord Jesus Christ to God, even the Father; and be subject to one another in the fear of Christ. (Eph. 5:16-21)*

Brethren, this whole question of understanding "*what the will of the Lord is*" requires being actively informed and moved by the Holy Spirit such that you are aware of God's plans and purposes, and what is to be expected and prepared for. Again, consider Simeon and Anna, and the fact that it was no accident or coincidence that they were in the right place at the right time, and in the right spirit. Only the Lord can accomplish this in His servants.

Now as to the many, Peter clearly states that conditions will be much the same as they were in the first century, when all but a few (Simeon and Anna included) were oblivious to the moment –

> *Know this first of all, that in the last days mockers will come with their mocking, following after their own lusts, and saying, "Where is the promise of His coming? For ever since the fathers fell asleep, all continues just as it was from the beginning of creation."*
>
> *For when they maintain this, it escapes their notice that by the word of God the heavens existed long ago and the earth was formed out of water and by water, through which the world at that time was destroyed, being flooded with water. But by His word the present heavens and earth are being reserved for fire, kept for the day of judgment and destruction of ungodly men.*
>
> *But do not let this one fact escape your notice, beloved, that with the Lord one day is like a thousand years, and a thousand years like one day. The Lord is not slow about His promise, as some count slowness, but is patient toward you, not wishing for any to perish but for all to come to repentance. (2 Pet. 3:3-9)*

And in Revelation 3, the Philadelphian church is enjoined to hold fast to what they had, and to overcome, that no one would take their crown, for He is coming quickly! This indeed was the testimony of Simeon and Anna, as revealed to us in the Word of God: That they lived every single day in preparation and anticipation of the coming of the Lord. Their hope was not in the political or even religious rulers of their day, nor in economic independence or fleeting riches, or science or discovery or anything else. Because they "*kept the word of the Lord's patience*" and persevered in watchfulness, faith and purity, their joy was fulfilled, and they alone out of perhaps many thousands in Israel were blessed to behold their King and Savior!

Take heed brethren, for this is indeed a powerful exhortation being offered to us in this hour, through the faithful testimony of these *little ones* at the presentation of Jesus 2,000 years ago.

In conclusion therefore, note that the very last words in the Scriptures read –

> *Behold, I am coming quickly, and My reward is with Me, to render to every man according to what he has done. "I am the Alpha and the Omega, the first and the last, the beginning and the end."*
>
> *Blessed are those who wash their robes, so that they may have the right to the tree of life, and may enter by the gates into the city. Outside are the dogs and the sorcerers and the immoral persons and the murderers and the idolaters, and everyone who loves and practices lying.*
>
> *"I, Jesus, have sent My angel to testify to you these things for the churches. I am the root and the descendant of David, the bright morning star." The Spirit and the bride say, "Come." And let the one who hears say, "Come." And let the one who is thirsty come; let the one who wishes take the water of life without cost.*
>
> *I testify to everyone who hears the words of the prophecy of this book: if anyone adds to them, God will add to him the plagues which are written in this book; and if anyone takes away from the words of the book of this prophecy, God will take away his part from the tree of life and from the holy city, which are written in this book.*
>
> *He who testifies to these things says, "Yes, I am coming quickly." Amen. Come, Lord Jesus.*

The grace of the Lord Jesus be with all. Amen. (Rev. 22:12-21)

Both Simeon and Anna responded to the Holy Spirit, and as a result they were found ready and worthy at the Lord's first coming to His own. They studied the Scriptures and faithfully responded to the prophetic urgency of the time in which they lived. Nothing deterred or distracted them from the singular occupation of their hearts and lives; not the noise and commotion of the Roman Empire subsuming everything around them (as the American empire is doing in our day); not the lifeless religion and mindless man-following being perpetrated in the synagogues every Sabbath, not the scoffers who must have certainly plagued them constantly in the temple.

No, they loved their Lord! They believed their God! They listened to the Holy Spirit, not religious experts!

And they alone were ready. They alone were there to meet the Child who was the Savior of the World, and the King of Israel, and the Hope of the Gentiles!

Will you? Will I?

Dear Father in Heaven, Lord of All Life, please help us to take this message to heart and to put off all things that lead us away from what is truly essential in this hour – being found ready and watching at the Coming of Your Son! When He comes the second time to the earth, out of heaven, He will not be a babe, nor a lamb, but the Lion of the Tribe of Judah, the King and Judge over all the heavens and the earth, He who wields the sword from out of His mouth to slay all of His enemies and establish His Righteous Kingdom forever and ever!

In the name of our Lord and King, Jesus Christ. Amen.

The Wind, the Water and the Faithful One

Recently, while out walking and sharing with Father, two Scriptures came together in my spirit, *Matthew 14* (Jesus walking on the water) and *Hebrews 12:2*. Here are the texts –

> *Immediately He made the disciples get into the boat and go ahead of Him to the other side, while He sent the crowds away. After He had sent the crowds away, He went up on the mountain by Himself to pray; and when it was evening, He was there alone. But the boat was already a long distance from the land, battered by the waves; for the wind was contrary. And in the fourth watch of the night He came to them, walking on the sea. When the disciples saw Him walking on the sea, they were terrified, and said, "It is a ghost!" And they cried out in fear. But immediately Jesus spoke to them, saying, "Take courage, it is I; do not be afraid."*
>
> *Peter said to Him, "Lord, if it is You, command me to come to You on the water." And He said, "Come!" And Peter got out of the boat, and walked on the water and came toward Jesus. But seeing the wind, he became frightened, and beginning to sink, he cried out, "Lord, save me!" Immediately Jesus stretched out His hand and took hold of him, and said to him, "You of little faith, why did you doubt?" When they got into the boat, the wind stopped. And those who were in the boat worshiped Him, saying, "You are certainly God's Son!" (Matt. 14:22-33)*

> *...fixing our eyes on Jesus, the author and perfecter of faith, who for the joy set before Him endured the cross, despising the shame, and has sat down at the right hand of the throne of God. (Heb. 12:2)*

Here we see that Peter, leaving the security of the boat in the midst of the storm, did in fact walk on the water a ways. We are not told how far or how many steps he took, before giving way to the elements around him. What we are told is that he saw that the wind was "*contrary*" (or boisterous) and this led to fear and in turn his starting to sink.

We can assume then, that while successfully walking atop the waves Peter was concentrating on something other than the "*boisterous*" waves, the wind, and the storm. And there can only be one object of his fixed attention and this could only be the Lord. "*Looking unto Jesus –*" we are told in Hebrews, "*the author and finisher of our faith*".

So Peter (*I am one of those who strongly feels Peter is treated far too unkindly by commentators and Christians in general*) started well (*no other disciples asked the Lord to command them to come to Him*). And he even entered into the faith of the Lord by doing what was naturally impossible to do – he, a full grown man, did indeed stride atop the waves that he knew all too well as a seasoned fisherman. He did so because, for a short time anyway, he fixed his gaze on the only One who could perform His word; one sovereign over the natural elements.

And so, I started to reconsider all my concepts of faith – what it was, how it grew, what it means to our Heavenly Father and our Lord Himself. Clearly then, many of our religious notions regarding faith may in fact be confounding or distorting what is really a simple matter – *fixing our spiritual eyes on the Faithful One*!

> *Now faith is the assurance (or substance) of things hoped for, the conviction of things not seen. (Heb. 11:1)*

How does our faith grow and mature then? Not by striving after more faith. Not by fixing our attention on faith itself even. Not even solely by studying great exploits in faith by so-called champions of faith (although this can certainly be most encouraging).

He is the beginning, the source, and the fulfillment of faith, yet He is also the object of it; what faith looks to. Peter knew the waves and the sea all to well. He had been tossed and turned by its swells and moods all of his life. He had no doubt looked long at the heaving tides that surrounded that little boat. He knew all too intimately the wind and storm too no doubt; the often fierce and unpredictable tyranny of the elements on the Sea of Galilee. We too, my friends, know this world all too well, how it moves and turns and tosses us about, and we have all, over the course of our lives, devised soulish ways of responding to it – *instincts, habits, patterns, routines* – based on all that we are and have become in this life.

Faith, as I am slowly coming to learn, is simply turning our attention; fixing our eyes on Jesus – the *Way, the Truth and the Life*, the *Author and Perfecter of Faith*, the *Beginning and the End* of all the plans and purposes of the Most High God. Then faith is *release*; releasing all of our cares and concerns and well-being (both spiritually and physically) into the hands of He alone who is faithful and steadfast. Oh brethren, that we would learn the wonderful secret of letting go, of releasing all that we are to the Captain of our Souls!

Pray that the Lord God would help you to release everything unto Him – *thoughts, notions, arguments, weaknesses, ideas, assumptions, strongholds, habits, experience, history, hurt, pain, earthly wisdom* – everything in fact that confounds and limits His divine purpose in us. We must leave the boat – everything that represents security and safety and familiarity in this world and in ourselves – in order that His life would be released and enlarged in us. And it is faith that moves us to ask Him to come to Him, to stand up, to step out, when everything in us screams that we will go under; that it is absurd for a man to think he can walk on the water.

Let us consider what T. Austin-Sparks offers in this regard –

> *Then comes the establishment in faith. This means the removal of all false ground - any ground of confidence or trust which is other than God Himself. In this cat-*

> *egory of false ground come our feelings, theories, traditions, and all external supports. All these will prove false and incapable of bearing the strain of true faith's testing. In order to keep to reality and true life God shatters all false positions, shakes all false ground, and strips off all vain confidence. (from, Faith Unto Enlargement Through Adversity)*

It is vital to recognize that the Lord cannot hope to establish His Son in us until He alone becomes our *true ground*. This requires the continual testing of our faith and the stepping out into Him upon whom we must stand and walk. There is in this a constant leaving behind of all that represents "*false ground*"; the boat in other words, or anything else that we trust in to keep us safe and secure in this world. Where there is faith, there will always be a proving of that faith, to enlarge the Lord Jesus as our confidence and life. Do you see this dear saints? Oh Lord, bring this home to your little ones in this hour.

Now saints, we cannot work to attain greater faith – we must come to rest solely and intimately in the only One who is faithful. Praying for increased faith is fine, but we must understand how the Father might respond to this prayer – by removing all else that we trust in to hold us together in this world; like Peter's fishing boat for example. It is the Father's will that all be lost that we would gain His most precious gift – His Son. For what can a man hold onto while walking on the boisterous sea? For what will secure his footing atop the waves? He can reach out, but truly there is nothing there; nothing that is but the Lord Himself. This is precisely how the Father increases our faith through His Spirit, as He draws us out of our safe and familiar surroundings in our lives and places us in situations where all we have is His Son.

Are we then being tested and tried? Are the waves of hardship, loss, reduction and persecution spilling over into our little boat? Is our first temptation and response to fix our attention on the storm and the swell, the noise and the uncertainty all around us, and even how small and insignificant we are in the midst of it? These are certainly fearful and uncertain times dear brethren, times of wind and storm, and I certainly do not wish to negate how difficult daily life is becoming for many of the Lord's people. And if my sense of the prophetic moment is anywhere near to being correct, then things are poised to get a whole lot worse before they get better.

The disciples, having set out ahead of the Lord (it was He who sent them on ahead without Him, indicating that this whole ordeal was a God-ordained training exercise), had to learn a lesson that we too must learn, and it is that He will never leave us nor forsake us. Though He was not physically with them in the boat, they were not left alone to their own doom, destiny and devices. For He was there with them in the midst, and even above the storm; there almost in view, "*like a ghost*", but certainly no mere apparition or shadow, but the "*substance of things hoped for*".

For our Lord was with them indeed, and as real and even more real than the water, the wind, the waves and even the boat that stood between them and the deep. As Hudson Taylor has shared, having discovered this secret long before us, brethren –

> *Faith, I now see, is "the substance of things hoped for," and not mere shadow. It is not less than sight, but more. Sight only shows the outward form of things; faith gives the substance. You can rest on substance, feed on substance. Christ dwelling in the heart by faith (i.e., His Word of Promise credited) is power indeed, is life indeed. And Christ and sins will not dwell together; nor can we have His presence with love of the world, or carefulness about "many things."*

Interesting, brethren, that faith and substance (or assurance) are here associated together, for it would appear on the surface, that faith would be opposed or contradictory to substance (or the possession in hand of the thing in view). I personally have always assumed that to touch and see is superior to belief; that faith was less than sight. Yet apparently, the Lord wants us to see that this is in fact not the case, and that our faith in His Word (both the Scriptures and the Living Word made flesh) is something He takes very personally.

Dear brethren, children of the day, please pray for one another in these fearful times, that we would show forth our Lord in all

His fullness and love to one another, as He cares for His Body, and brings us all to that state of readiness and maturity in faith that we know must be His will. Encourage and uplift each other, dear brethren, in the Spirit and in the Faith, whenever and wherever you have opportunity, for the days are short, and His Kingdom will soon be upon us. Exhort and admonish one another in the faith, to true steadfastness and endurance, looking to the prize of our upward calling that is out ahead of us, and not to the storm and swell that encompasses us in this hour.

Gracious and Wondrous Father, Lord of all life and strength and victory, please help us, Lord, to fix our attention on He who is the Substantial One, the Faithful One, who loved us and gave Himself for us, and who has promised us so great a future in His Kingdom. Though the wind and the storm swells all around us in this dark hour, and though each of us is being tried and tested in each our own way, help us not to suffer the natural temptation to fixate and focus on circumstance, environment or any other consideration that takes our eyes off of Him. Thank you, Lord. In Jesus glorious name, we pray. Amen.

Seeing the World Through Heavenly Eyes

> *"The eye is the lamp of your body; when your eye is clear, your whole body also is full of light; but when it is bad, your body also is full of darkness." (Luke 11:34)*

> *Do not love the world nor the things in the world. If anyone loves the world, the love of the Father is not in him. For all that is in the world, the lust of the flesh and the lust of the eyes and the boastful pride of life, is not from the Father, but is from the world. The world is passing away, and also its lusts; but the one who does the will of God lives forever. (1 John 2:15-17)*

My friends, to see clearly, with eyes wide open in the spirit, is everything. Nothing really happens in this living walk until you come to see things through God's eyes. To see the world, and all that it represents; to see what is behind and beneath it all, where it leads, its scope and sphere, is absolutely essential for the student and servant of Jesus Christ. Now this may sound simplistic, but everything must be reduced down to a crystal clear contrast between light and darkness, between life and death. In so many ways, this is where the process of forsaking and overcoming the world begins and ends.

> *"Blessed are the eyes which see the things you see..." (Luke 10:23)*

Oh that our Lord would open and enlighten our spiritual eyes to see clearly what the world is and what He sees. Not only the overtly evil and unholy things, but all things conceived by the god of this world to undermine the work of the Holy Spirit and the purpose of the Lord our God.

The Scriptures are clear that all of the world wrought in Adam is under the dominion and influence of the evil one. It is also under a sentence of death, waiting to be carried out at our Lord's return. It is a settled matter and there is no future for it. The world and all who represent it, fuel it and feed it, have already been judged and found guilty. The judgment, although delayed, is certain. Seeing this is key, my brethren.

When you were saved, what was it you were saved from? Was it not the world and its most certain destruction? Yes, we go on living in the world, touching the things of the world, but our life and hope is not in them. This is no more our home than the desert is the habitat of fish. We are *sojourners and pilgrims* here, looking forward, like Abraham, to a *better country*; a heavenly kingdom where the glory and will of God will be preeminent. We are sustained in this hostile and alien environment by His heavenly life in us, breathing in His Spirit, assuming His character, life and light.

Oh but we know how this world appeals to the flesh in us, don't we? We are acutely aware of how it teases and tempts it. This is why our Lord minced no words, when He declared that the *flesh* (the life of Adam) *profits nothing*. It is very much at home in this world. It speaks its language and understands its ways perfectly. It quite naturally pursues its wealth and prominence. It's life and destiny is linked to the world, and its roots run deep into it. The way of the flesh is the way of the world, for they are one and the same, nurturing one another unto death and destruction.

Those born from above in the spirit know such things. They recognize and appreciate that every time they touch the world (and how can we not) there is the danger that the flesh in them will rear up and reach for a bite. They understand perfectly that only the world can appease the lusts and appetites of the flesh, and they are forever watching and praying that their Lord would keep them safe from the evil one. In touching the world, they are careful not to let it touch them or get inside them. They have given their heart to another, and their loyalty and allegiance to another kingdom.

All that is the world; all that engenders and defines it – *its economics, politics, religion, culture, science and technology, etc.* – is at enmity with the Maker of the Universe. It is nothing less than the collective expression of the pride and lust of every individual in and of the world. Behind its very institutions and systems, its *'isms* and *'ologies*, and wisdom and ways are ancient and powerful spiritual forces, principalities and powers, all doing the will of their wicked taskmaster; the one who was a murderer and a thief from the beginning. Although his days are numbered, and all that remains is for judgment to fall, he still actively rules this world with an iron fist.

Dear brethren, to behold the world clearly with spiritual eyes, to perceive it as our Lord did when He walked this earth, and as He does now, is to negate its power and influence. It is by seeing that light infuses the entire body. Yes, our Lord, in His munificent glory and grace, has chosen to sanctify us in the world, not to immediately remove us from it. But make no mistake, we are not of this world, and we are not to be associated with it. We are a heavenly people, called into the household and kingdom of our God. Our treasure and pearl of great price is not to be found in this world, but above. For our treasure is the Lord Himself, and to desire Him above all else is to shun the world and all of its empty promises.

To truly see with heavenly eyes is to reject all that the world offers and represents. Satan may tempt us with gold or pleasure, but we see only rust and death. Temporal things no longer have any appeal for those with eternity in their hearts. They see through the veiled promises, pain and lies of the devil and His world. All has lost its shine. It is revealed only for what it genuinely is – hollow, empty and short-lived.

To forsake the world while still in it, and to effectively expose it for what it is by manifesting the light of truth that is Jesus Christ; this is the power and wonder of our God in this age of grace and gathering. Wouldn't it be so much easier to extricate us from it all and make us holy in heaven or somewhere else beyond Satan's sphere of influence?

No, His light and life would emanate through His called out children in the very midst of the darkness, delusion and death that is the world. The very Kingdom of God, the antithesis of all that the world represents, would meet it head on, just as when the man

Jesus Christ was born into it, and stepped out in it, and exposed it for what it is.

Let us ask the Lord, my brethren, that He would grant us the heavenly vision to see the world only as He does, and that we would forsake it and come out of it in our hearts. Not to be physically removed from it, for this is not His will at all, but to be released from its grip in authentic spiritual separation. To have our hearts purged of all desire for the world and its painted treasure.

I really like the way A.W. Tozer suggested this when he wrote of the Christian's "*smiling indifference to the world's attractions and their steady resistance to its temptations.*" He continued –

> *the true saint – cares little for passing values; he looks forward eagerly to the day when eternal things shall come into their own and godliness will be found in all that matters.*

Amen to that. Yet this separation is of the heart and spirit, not some form of physical asceticism. Those who seek hermetic isolation from the world have not truly seen it for what it is. In fact, this tendency to isolate oneself from the life of the world is more an expression of the world's religious spirit than the will of God. You can't hide or remove yourself from it, and that is not our Lord's intent for us here and now anyway. We are to be like Daniel in the midst of Babylon, who kept himself pure by unceasingly abiding in the grace of His god. We are to expose the world by walking as heavenly lights in the darkness. We either believe that He who is in us is greater than he who is in the world and that we are complete in Him or we don't.

> *If you have died with Christ to the elementary principles of the world, why, as if you were living in the world, do you submit yourself to decrees, such as, "Do not handle, do not taste, do not touch!" (which all refer to things destined to perish with use)—in accordance with the commandments and teachings of men? These are matters which have, to be sure, the appearance of wisdom in self-made religion and self-abasement*

> *and severe treatment of the body, but are of no value against fleshly indulgence. (Col. 2:20-23)*

See, dear brethren, how even such religious sounding prohibitions against contact with the world are very much part of what it represents; and they have no place for the Christian who holds all things loosely. Many think that they do, in fact, have value against the indulgence of the flesh, but Paul says the opposite here; that they are actually just as much a part of the world and the flesh as the things we are not to touch, taste or handle.

And neither is the world like some modern city, with good neighborhoods and bad, some safe and some deadly. The world is not found in its location or activity, but in its universal and antagonistic spirit that pervades all life under heaven. And it is all under the dominion and influence of the devil, and the judgment of God, enacted at the cross of Christ. We, as children of the family of God are either crucified to it, and it to us, or we're not. It either still exercises power and control over us, or it doesn't.

We either *abide in Christ*, or we *abide in the world*. And the measure in which we are living in Him, is directly proportionate to the measure in which we are living in the world. To come *out of the world*, in other words, is to abide further *in Christ Jesus*. Do you see this dear saints? I pray that you might. The life that we previously had in this world, sustained by the fruit of *the tree of knowledge of good and evil*, is gradually being replaced by newness of life in Christ Jesus, sustained by the fruit of the *Tree of Life*.

> *You are from God, little children, and have overcome them; because greater is He who is in you than he who is in the world. They are from the world; therefore they speak as from the world, and the world listens to them. We are from God; he who knows God listens to us; he who is not from God does not listen to us. By this we know the spirit of truth and the spirit of error. (1 John 4:4-6)*

Again, we cannot emphasize enough this capacity for seeing clearly, for even the devil can make death and darkness appear as life and light. Indeed, although many do not have the eyes to see it, the vast majority of our churches are under his immediate control, and much of what we consider organized Christianity ("*speckled birds*" as Watchman Nee so aptly called them) has aligned itself with the world and its ways. That the *wheat and the tares* would grow up together (Matthew 13) and be virtually indistinguishable to the natural eye indicates the enemy's mastery of subterfuge and deception. For those of the world, even darkness appears as light. Yet this is not so for the children of God, whose eyes have been enlightened with true heavenly light. To really see, with eyes wide open in the spirit, is a profound a heavenly gift that accompanies our salvation and newness of life.

Yes, dear friends, we do indeed go on living in the world, employing the things of the world – its money, government and institutions, for example – but they and the spirit behind them are not ours at all, and our hope and confidence is not in them. The way of get, greed and godlessness that characterizes life in this world is no longer our way. All that is in the world, and employed by the adversary to undermine the plans and character of the Eternal God, actively working to draw souls away from Him, down into the pit of despair, delusion and death – this no longer has any claim on us.

We must surrender our hearts to the Living God who will soon pour out His righteous fury and wrath on this world and its own. No longer should the cares of this world define and manipulate us. No more should we befriend the world as it stands in enmity and opposition against all that is holy and true. The gospel of Jesus Christ, the gospel of the kingdom – was preached as a witness against this present world, and there is no future for it! All that chokes the life of Jesus Christ in us; the *cares of the world, the deceitfulness of riches, and the desire for other things*; all of this will soon meet a violent end! We who are called sons of light, who anticipate God's mercy and deliverance, stand in stark contrast to those who are the sons of this world, who stand blindly in the path of eternal judgment.

Dear brethren, the time has come to stop trying to patronize and appease this world, as so many pretenders are doing in this hour. Our Lord never promised us such affinity with this world, only its rejection and scorn. Yet just as He overcame the world, we too must overcome it in Him. Here is the glory and power and wonder of our Heavenly Father, that He would claim us as His own in the world and redeem us to its face, in blatant opposition to it.

> *You adulteresses, do you not know that friendship with the world is hostility toward God? Therefore whoever wishes to be a friend of the world makes himself an enemy of God. Or do you think that the Scripture speaks to no purpose: "He jealously desires the Spirit which He has made to dwell in us"? (James 4:4-5)*

How glorious that we can be in the world, touching it daily, and yet not be conformed to it, or corrupted by it. No longer does its wisdom wield any influence with us, for we see the foolishness and death that it represents. No longer do we desire the world's spirit, its greedy desire for more, its delusion and obsession with earthly things and painted treasures. Better to be despised by the world and accepted by God, to live by His grace and not the world's carnal pursuit of life apart from the Creator.

> *And you were dead in your trespasses and sins, in which you formerly walked according to the course of this world, according to the prince of the power of the air, of the spirit that is now working in the sons of disobedience. Among them we too all formerly lived in the lusts of our flesh, indulging the desires of the flesh and of the mind, and were by nature children of wrath, even as the rest. (Eph. 2:1-3)*

Here we see that origin is everything; and that everything runs its own course. What matters, in this context, is not good or evil per say, but who and where you are from. If we are of Adam, then our future is earthly and short-lived. If we are of Christ Jesus, then we have received the gift of eternal life; the very life of God. Our destiny is bound up with Him. The life of heaven has been extended to us.

It is this foundation and beginning in Christ Jesus, and our newfound nature in God, that determines the course of our lives now. He is our way and path and life. A fundamental part of this is the widening of our eyes in real heaven-sent revelation, that we might see the world as it really is, with all its glitter and paint stripped away. It is in truly beholding it, and comprehending what it represents in its opposition to our Holy Father and His Beloved Son, that we forsake and overcome it. In the Scriptures things are less defined by what they do but rather where they are from. And every man's life and existence is either rooted in God or rooted in the adversary and the world. It is that simple. For –

- You either have a *fleshly* mind or a *spiritual* mind.

- You are either inspired and led by the *spirit of the world* or *God's Holy Spirit.*

- You either serve the *Lord Jesus Christ* or *Satan* the thief and pretender.

- You either walk according to the *basic principles of the world,* leading to condemnation and death or by the *life of Jesus Christ* leading to heavenly blessing and life.

- You are either a child in the household of God or a son of disobedience and the world.

- You are either a friend of the world and at enmity with God, or you are friend of the Lord Jesus Christ, at peace with the Father in Heaven.

- You either love the world and the things in the world (prominence, property, power, etc.) or you love the Father in Heaven.

- You are either compelled by the *spirit of the world* and antichrist or you have the *Holy Spirit* within you transforming your heart and mind into the very image of God.

- You are either led by the human *soul* (intelligence, reason, emotion, sentiment, and self-will), or the human *spirit* as animated and directed by the Holy Spirit of God.

Dear friends, there is nothing to fear or be intimated by, for *He who is in us is greater than he who is in the world.* And again, the world is everything constituted by man's philosophies and politics and principles, whispered into his soul over thousands of years by the liar himself. Its reach is universal and complete. Will you hide from it, dear ones, or shrink back from it? Will you be intimidated by it when the Lord Himself placed you right in the center of it for His glory alone, as a demonstration of His ascendant power and wisdom?

Consider the following wisdom from Watchman Nee –

> *Religious people – attempt to overcome the world by getting out of it. As Christians, this is not our attitude at all. Right here is the place where we are called to overcome. Created distinct from the world, we accept with joy the fact that God has placed us in it. That distinctiveness, our gift from God in Christ – is all the safeguard we need!*

Again, we must emphasize that the world, and all that it represents as a spiritual order and system, is under the judgment of death, enacted by God's holy law. It has been condemned, and all that remains is the penalty phase to be applied. In no place in the Scriptures do we read anything of God reforming or improving this present world or its principalities and powers. Rather, He demonstrates His love for the world by supplanting it with His order and system – *the Kingdom of God and His Christ.*

> *Then the seventh angel sounded; and there were loud voices in heaven, saying,*
>
> *"The kingdom of the world has become the kingdom of our Lord and of His Christ; and He will reign forever and ever." (Rev. 11:15)*

In proclaiming and advancing the Kingdom of God, Jesus offered a spiritual alternative to this world's reality lived out in the power of the flesh, according to carnal pursuits. To enter His kingdom is to escape the world as we know it. Herein lies our full salvation wrought in Christ Jesus, for no longer are we subject to the world and aligned with its impending judgment and death.

Truly, my brethren, to see rightly is everything. If the lamp of the body is full of God's heavenly light, then the world no longer holds any power over us. Its bond of deception is broken, and we are truly free indeed. No longer are we to worry about our temporal condition as the world does – *what we will eat and what we will wear;* what men think of us; what lies out ahead in our earthly lives. No longer is survival and material comfort and security all that drives us in life. Our focus and devotion will turn to our Heavenly Father who provides everything we need in His Only Begotten and Beloved Son through His Holy Spirit. Here is our peace and provision in the world, and to see this is to be truly free indeed!

Oh Most High and Holy Father – Oh Lord, Mighty and Loving God – By Your grace we abide here in this world, the domain of devils and every vile and abominable thing. Grant, Oh Lord, that Your might and power and wisdom would be revealed as You claim us and sanctify us as Your own! Grant that we would have eyes wide open in the spirit to see, and that the lamp of the body would shine brightly on all darkness and delusion. Oh Father in Heaven, please keep us unto Yourself in Your Beloved Son and Spirit. In His Name, we pray always. Amen.

The Scab of Unbelief

> *Only a soul fed with pure truth accepts each new phase of it, and thereby grows in intelligence and confidence towards God. The soul that refuses truth is hindered in its course, stunted in its spiritual growth, and moves farther toward the flesh and the world with each rejection. (Robert Govett)*

Dear friends, precious to our Lord and Shepherd and King –

To walk by ever-increasing faith is everything, and yet it is that which is least amenable to this old man who lives persistently by his will, desires and worldly wisdom (all entering his being through the eyes primarily). Notice here what Robert Govett has written about this –

> *"There are many wrong motives and states of the heart, but there is only one right motive. Whatsoever is not of faith – is sin."*

As the Lord, through His Spirit in the Word, reveals His treasures to us (especially those related to our heavenly inheritance as adopted sons and co-heirs in His Kingdom), He expects us to be perfectly obedient to that truth, wherever that obedience might lead. As the Lord forewarned all those contemplating allegiance to Him –

"Count the Cost!"

– for the costs are high – rejection, hardship, false accusations, sacrifice, loneliness, the forsaking of all that people of the world take for granted, the waiting indefinitely for a home and a place where you truly belong.

For Robert Govett, it meant the abandonment of all the security, honor, worldly esteem, and privilege bound up in a clerical career with the Church of England. And yet our Lord blessed this faithful servant mightily in the priceless revelation of His Word, perhaps unrivaled since the time of Paul the Apostle (and I choose this comparison most carefully).

If however, we are disobedient to that which our Lord and teacher reveals to us, a *scab of unbelief* will develop and fester upon our hearts. He will no doubt persist with us for a time, as He is ever gracious and longsuffering with His little ones. But if this pattern of unfaithfulness and disobedience persists, this *dullness of hearing and hardness of heart* will develop into what well may be an irreversible condition of blindness and unprofitableness, such that He no longer reveals His treasures to us at all. This happened to the children of Israel, and it can happen to spirit-begotten followers of the Lord's Anointed as well.

How pitiful and tragic!

At that point, although birthed spiritually from above, at a most precious cost (in the blood of His Beloved Son) to Himself, we are (or become over time) good for nothing. Our salvation (the regeneration to life of the spirit within us making it possible to receive spiritual food) has thereby become cheapened and wasted. We have become what the Scriptures refer to as a *vessel of dishonor*, and vomit for the spittle –

> *"So because you are lukewarm, and neither hot nor cold, I will spit you out of My mouth." (Rev. 3:16)*

Dear ones, please let the enormity of all of this settle deep into your spirit for as long as it takes. These are His own He is referring to here, so please do not be deceived into thinking that these are the lost in the world or any such thing. Here the Prince of Peace is actually spewing from His mouth those to whom He gave His precious and perfect blood to redeem. Astounding and terrifying indeed!

> *"Therefore, knowing the fear of the Lord, we persuade men..." (2 Cor. 5:11)*

Now it was said of the children of Israel after being brought out of Egypt with a mighty hand, that they failed to understand the Lord's wonders wrought on their behalf –

> *Our fathers in Egypt did not understand Your wonders; They did not remember Your abundant kindnesses, But rebelled by the sea, at the Red Sea. (Psa. 106:7)*

After this it is revealed that they actually forgot these very wonders, but before this they failed to comprehend what the Lord was doing in saving and redeeming them. I considered this prayerfully for some time and I believe the Lord was impressing on me how vitally important it is that I comprehend what my spiritual birth means in the larger context of His glorious purpose in Christ and His Kingdom.

To be saved, or born again (as a spiritual life), is indeed a marvelous and splendid thing, dear saints, no less a miracle than when the Creator brought forth Adam from the dust and breathed life into him, or the Lord delivered Israel mightily out of the land of death, through the sea. Yet, we also, as His elect in this age, can fail to understand the Lord's ultimate and age-lasting intent in showing forth His life-giving power on our behalf.

For Adam, it was that he would exercise dominion over that which the Lord God had restored, in consort with the queen that was to come from his very body.

For the nation of Israel, it was that they, as His first-born son, would fellowship with Him in the wilderness, become a holy and enlightened people, then subsequently inherit the earthly and heavenly promises given to Abraham, and ultimately be a light of salvation and blessing to the gentiles.

And for us, it is precisely the same, that we might rule and reign from the heavenly places (in place of the current angelic hosts; see Hebrews 2:5), over the dominions of the earth, with our King on His eternal throne, in all holiness, justice and wisdom, for a thousand years and beyond.

And so to first understand what is involved and at stake is everything, isn't it? Then to trust Him and obey Him and follow Him as He leads us the long way home to the promised inheritance by One greater than Moses is essential. The lessons preserved for us are more than clear for those with eyes to see them, and a heart to receive them.

Oh that we would learn such lessons from former times and people; that there is in fact no good (none whatsoever) in ourselves; that, quite apart from how enlightened or fit to rule we think we are, there is no light in our eyes, and that to think we can attain the prize without first being trained and tested and brought to brokenness, holiness and wisdom, is a delusion straight from the serpent. Indeed, this is the first lie isn't it – that we can exercise the intended dominion without the requisite wisdom of God (fruit of the tree of life) to do so. To reign over God's domain, apart from Himself – His blessing and provision, such that He receives no glory whatsoever? This is preposterous! For we were born anew solely that we might display His preeminent glory among those who have no knowledge of Him and His ways –

> *"And I will set My glory among the nations; and all the nations will see My judgment which I have executed and My hand which I have laid on them." (Ezek.39:21)*

Fellow saints and brethren in the Lord, I must follow Him and be faithful to Him wherever that leads, and to be perfectly honest at this point, I am not sure where or what this is. Yet He who authored my faith (when I was born in Him) will also finish (or perfect) it at His coming. I believe this with all my heart and mind and spirit. It is truly all I have to hold on to. And yet it is enough to be sure.

[Though on far too many days, more than I care to admit, I do not live up to these high sounding ideals, and become fearful, self-willed and small, distracted and hesitant to accept the full cost of obedience – forgive me and cleanse me, dear Lord, for my heart so often dreams that which I cannot live up to].

But oh that He would enlighten my eyes, and help my unbelief, and bring me further into the wisdom of His Kingdom, into the mature knowledge of His Word, into a more perfect and complete understanding of the riches of His grace in Christ Jesus. Oh that I would enter deeper into His fullness, that will one day fill all things; that I would trust Him completely and absolutely and without equivocation. For it is not He or His Word that is untrustworthy, inconstant and faithless, but I. I have failed Him many times, but it is impossible for Him to fail me.

Impossible, dear ones –

> *Faithful is He who calls you, and He also will bring it to pass. (1 Thess. 5:24)*
>
> *But the Lord is faithful, and He will strengthen and protect you from the evil one. (2 Thess. 3:3)*
>
> *God is faithful, through whom you were called into fellowship with His Son, Jesus Christ our Lord. (1 Cor. 1:9)*
>
> *"Know therefore that the LORD your God, He is God, the faithful God, who keeps His covenant and His lovingkindness to a thousandth generation with those who love Him and keep His commandments" (Deut. 7:9)*

Please pray for me my friends, and all of His little ones who hear His voice from outside the door of this Laodicean age, that we would hear Him and follow Him, whatever the cost; that we would be found faithful at His coming to gather His first-ripe wheat into His barn; that we would follow Him alone as the Way and Truth and Life, through this wilderness onward to perfection, maturity and glory.

All is by faith! All we have and need is to be found faithful to His Word (Read all of Psalm 119 – on your knees preferably). Though everything seen and all evidences known may contradict His Word and His promises, we must grip tightly to all that He has *breathed* into the world, lest this scab of unbelief lead us away from Him and we die in this wilderness, not having received the promised inheritance. The threat is real and tangible, and the many in this generation will (tragically) fall away. But let it not be said of us, that we did not endure to the end, that we did not keep the word of His patience with steadfastness, that we failed to overcome, that we did not trust the good report of the land out ahead of us, and the Lord's ability to establish us therein.

> *"He who has an ear, let him hear what the Spirit says to the churches." (Rev. 3:22)*

Oh Gracious and Loving Father, Lord of all Life and Glory –

Please complete that mighty work which You began in us, and lead us to the ultimate purpose for our being created anew in Your Beloved Son – to reign with Him in His Kingdom such that You alone might receive all the glory, Father. Help us, Lord, to walk by faith alone, and to abide by every word that You have breathed into this world. Teach us and feed us with Your glorious and precious Word, Lord, and lead us in all things by Your most Holy Spirit. In patience correct us, and help us to lay down all and anything that is revealed to be false or incomplete, regardless of the price to be paid – the approval of men, church membership, security in this world, job and salary, even family and friends – whatever the cost, however high, Oh Lord, help us to be willing to pay it in faith and love to everything You have commanded us. Thank You, Father, that all of Your promises are AMEN, and that Your Word will not and cannot ever fall to the ground; that everything that we have set our hopes on will be fulfilled. Lead us home to the place You have prepared for us, dear Lord, such that we might serve You and love You forever.

In Jesus' Precious Name. Amen.

The Lord's Wilderness

"Beware that you do not forget the LORD your God by not keeping His commandments and His ordinances and His statutes which I am commanding you today; otherwise, when you have eaten and are satisfied, and have built good houses and lived in them, and when your herds and your flocks multiply, and your silver and gold multiply, and all that you have multiplies, then your heart will become proud and you will forget the LORD your God who brought you out from the land of Egypt, out of the house of slavery. "He led you through the great and terrible wilderness, with its fiery serpents and scorpions and thirsty ground where there was no water; He brought water for you out of the rock of flint. "In the wilderness He fed you manna which your fathers did not know, that He might humble you and that He might test you, to do good for you in the end. "Otherwise, you may say in your heart, 'My power and the strength of my hand made me this wealth."' (Deut. 8:11-17)

For careful students of the Bible, the concept of the wilderness should be most familiar. Abraham left his homeland and family to venture forth into an unknown land of promise. Moses left the palatial comforts of Egypt to dwell among the rocks and wild beasts. The tribes of Israel wandered 40 years in the wilderness prior to occupying the land of Canaan. Job lost everything that He might glimpse the Eternal One at the edge of the valley of death. David fled from Saul and spent years eluding him in the pathless wilderness. Most, if not all of the Lord's holy and faithful prophets abandoned all they knew and loved to live alone with the Lord in His company and care. John the Baptist conducted his prophetic ministry as one *"crying in the wilderness"*. Jesus was led by the Holy Spirit into the wilderness forty days and forty nights, tempted of the devil and ministered to by angels. The Apostle Paul spent much of His life and ministry imprisoned, isolated, imperiled and alone. And the woman of Revelation 12 is sheltered and nourished in the wilderness immediately prior to our Lord's return to this earth.

My friends, this wilderness theme runs all through the Scriptures, and through the varied lives and experiences of God's children. It has always been an essential concept to be grasped, yet I believe this may be even more true today. It is vital that we understand what it teaches us about how our Heavenly Father, the Son and the Holy Spirit bring us to true faithfulness and blessing.

Now the concept of the wilderness as it affects others is one thing – yet the actual experience of the wilderness as it impacts our own life and faith is quite another. It is a very intimate matter you see, challenging everything we think we know about God and the Christian life, the actual and the superficial. It is wrought with difficult questions and seemingly few answers. It is typically invested with profound emotion, loneliness and even confusion. And it is more of a valley than a mountain-top, with again, seemingly little evidence that heaven is still there, and that Our Lord is still caring for His sheep.

To understand the wilderness we must go deeper and further into the very heart and mind of our Heavenly Father, as He loves and nurtures His children. We must look beyond our teachers and books, for they, by and large, don't really understand it. We must divest ourselves of any fluffy religious notions that really don't get to the heart of a man or what really happened in that garden. We must also resist the theological urge to generalize or systematize, as God's wilderness is as varied as His people, and as unlimited as His vast, creative mind.

We are addressing this topic generally, in order that we might understand it better. We are also more specifically hoping to edify and encourage those, who like ourselves, find themselves outside and apart from the traditional church organization, having left it behind in order to more perfectly hear and follow the Lord in the spirit.

The Exodus from the Organized Church

Today, we are witnessing an interesting phenomenon where many – God knows the numbers – are leaving the relative structure and security of organized churches, denominations and memberships, to follow hard after their God, to a wilderness of sorts, a strange and unfamiliar place little understood by establishment Christianity. Perhaps the Lord is calling His remnant to Himself in simplicity and purity at the end of this age. Perhaps the prophetic ministry from outside the walls has begun, or at the very least is being perpetuated at this time. Perhaps a time of final testing for the church and Israel is poised to begin. Whatever the ultimate reason, many are coming out, and almost immediately they will need to adapt to this new and strange environment where the Lord alone is all that they have.

It is quite common to hear the following sentiments today from God's people –

"The glory of God has left my church."

"Jesus is no longer at the center of our fellowship! All we seem to do is talk about Jesus. Yet why do we never seem to actually meet Him?"

"My church has aligned itself with the ways of man and the world."

"My church functions more like a club than an expression of the life of Jesus Christ!"

"The Holy Spirit has gone out of the church."

"The church is of the world and the world is in the church."

Indeed, the world has infiltrated the church to such a degree, and corruption has become so rampant and pervasive, that it is practically impossible to keep abreast of all of the apostasy and defilement within.

By much spiritual evidence and observation, the *church on the corner* is either dying or already dead. This is apparent to any with eyes wide open in the spirit, to those with true spiritual insight. Only those with a vested and carnal interest in perpetuating the corpse, and holding it up with strings will deny this. True spiritual discernment speaks otherwise however. A.W. Tozer and Leonard Ravenhill, for example, twenty to forty years back can still be heard on creaky recordings woefully proclaiming the life of God pouring out of contemporary Christianity. Theirs were the prophetic fore-warnings from within, all decrying the forces marshaled against the historic church – materialism, humanism, pragmatism, psychology, modern marketing, etc. Then, such corruptive forces were pressing at the edges; today, they are rooted into the very fiber of institutional Christianity, across all lines, divisions and denominations. Those who would weep the tears of our Lord are indeed weeping, with great heaviness of spirit and heart.

"*Come out of her my people*!" is the message of the hour! "*Come out of her, lest you share in her sins and her judgment!*" But to where and to what? – this is the question of the hour. Quite often when the Lord draws us out of something and back to Himself, we are led by way of the wilderness. It is this wilderness that concerns us here, and by His grace we will endeavor to more completely comprehend it.

What it is and Why

In this brief message, we would like to touch on some key elements in this wilderness experience, including what it is, and why our Lord, in His infinite and loving wisdom might draw His children into such a condition. Perhaps you reading this now are in what you might consider a wilderness, alone with God, cut off in large measure from all you have ever trusted or known. Nothing now seems to make sense, even your religion or relationship with God. Everything appears dark and the way forward seems unfamiliar. Your faith is challenged like never before. The ground beneath your feet is shifting like loose sand. You turn to fellow saints for help and encouragement, but they just don't seem to understand. All they seem to have is an argument or proof text trying to convince you that you are either in sin or rebellion.

My brothers and sisters, we know that you are out there, and that you may be at this moment feeling isolated and alone. It is our hope and prayer that you will be encouraged and edified by the fact that you are not in any manner abandoned by our Good Shepherd, and that you are still very much in His capable and loving care. This wilderness you are in is not a denial of Christ's blessing on your life by any means, but living proof that He loves you more than you can ever know. Indeed, the wilderness – however it is applied to the servants of the Living God – is first and foremost God's idea. It is His wilderness. It is His way back to Himself. He needs to know that there are no circumstances, nor people that will cause you to deny Him. He needs to know that He alone is your first love. He needs to know that, stripped of all religion and corporate piety and spiritual machination, you will seek Him alone, for Himself and His glory. He needs to know that you love Him for Him and not just His gifts, and all of the many things church may have restored to you.

All of the biblical examples given above can provide us with valuable insight into what the wilderness is, what it looks like (in general terms, as we are also acutely aware that the wilderness experience is manifest differently for each of us as God's children) and what we can expect to find there.

To begin, it is a new and strange place – a circumstance or condition that is foreign to all we know. Consider Abraham and Moses leaving the familiarity and security of their home and family and all they have ever known to venture out into a new and strange land. For the most part they are alone in the wilderness. They often don't know exactly where they are being led. There is little to no explanation. God Himself has called them out, drawing them to Himself that they might follow Him in simple faith and trust. He is their way, and they must look to Him in perfect confidence that His guidance and provision will lead only to blessing.

The Lord, in drawing us to Himself, often brings us through the wilderness. Here we learn not to trust in ourselves, but in Him alone. He draws us out of wherever we are that we might learn to lean on Him for everything. He is now our way and our provision. It is a time of total and absolute dependence on Him. He draws us away from all of the props and dependencies, our friends and family, our everyday structures and support mechanisms, that He might be the All that holds us up, and maintains our lives. We must learn to trust God rather than circumstances or people. We must look for the bread that comes from heaven and the water that comes from the rock. We must turn our backs on all we know, even those we love, so that He might know that we love Him first and most, that He is enough, even if everything and everyone else is stripped from us.

I have been considering something that A.W. Tozer once said in a sermon, and it was this – "*What if all we Christians had was God?*" Not His things, nor blessings per say, but only Him. Not a hundred fired up preachers or prophets telling us about Him, but only Him. Alone with Christ, and He asking us "*Do you love Me more than these?*" as He did to Peter. "*Am I enough for you, or are there other things you desire?*" My friends, this is essentially what the wilderness is for – to provide our Lord with the answer to this most essential question.

[Have you ever pondered the idea that the modern church – with all of its structure and activity and paraphernalia – is endeavoring to answer questions that God has probably never even asked? Something to think about.]

All of my *religious* life I kept looking for Him in other things – people, groups, movements, teachings, systems – you name it. Yet in the end He has brought me to Himself, quite part from anything else that may claim to represent Him. This is the wonderful thing about the wilderness – it reduces everything down to bare-boned, spirit-touching-bone reality. It clears away all the haze and noise that may be preventing you from seeing and hearing God. There He is right out in front of you, and you are finally able to apprehend Him in all of His fullness and reality.

If you have become a Christian, for example, to gain friends and community – if this is what you seek primarily – then the wilderness will isolate you so that He is your only friend and fellowship. Then our Lord will ask you bluntly – *Am I enough for you? Do you Love me more than these?*

If this Christian thing and church membership is mostly about a healthy environment for yourself and your kids, for activities and programs, then here again the wilderness will reveal this for the idol it is. The Lord must know, you see. And we must know also. Many will admit that so much of what we do as *church* today keeps us from coming into direct and personal contact with essential things; with the Lord Himself in His living reality.

The wilderness is a wonderful instrument for stripping away all of our dependencies on things and shadows, isn't it? It is about survival and spiritual reality, life and death, hunger and thirst, breathing in and breathing out. Is He your All, my brother? Does living for Him alone define you, my sister? We are religious by nature, but only His nature in us, refined and perfected by His Holy Breath and Spirit will satisfy the burning ache in your spirit. We must have Him, and know Him, and want Him, and trust Him, before He will grant to us all of the many blessings pouring out of Him.

Is the wilderness a pleasant place? Not really, not how the world measures things anyway; for only here it seems do we come to recognize what we are actually made of, that we are carnal and earthbound, that our faith is largely theoretical, not tried and tested in the fiery furnace of experience. Like earthbound Jacob, wrestling with the Lord, we come to the end of ourselves that He might begin in us anew.

Yet we also come to see our God for what He is, in all of His transcendent power, wisdom and glory; in all of His grace and truth, and love and light. In seeing Him as He truly is, everything else is seen as it really is. Every created thing, including ourselves, can be seen in its true light, the light of the Bright and Morning Star, the Day Star that scatters all darkness. As there are so few distractions, everything in the wilderness is reduced to the most basic of questions, such as –

> *"…do you love Me more than these?" (John 21:15)*

and –

> *"Who is this that darkens counsel, By words without knowledge? (Job 38:2)*

My brethren, I am sorry if this seems so different from what you have been taught to expect. Yet it is the truth and it is the Lord's way. It is not the church's way, and so for the most part those affiliated with it will spurn it and judge it as illegitimate. Those who seek to save us from all that such a wilderness will present, will obviously fight against it with all they have. It represents no small threat to all organizations and mediated leadership; to the self-exalted priest-class that has come to rule so much of the body of Christ in our day.

Though He slay me, I will hope in Him. (Job 13:15)

Read Job's account and affirm what some of us have already discovered in our wilderness walk – that even God's peace and presence is seemingly withdrawn, causing us to question how much we really trust Him. Even when He withholds the manifest evidence of His presence, when He appears to have turned His back to us and stopped His ears, will we continue to bless Him and to love Him? Despite an often prolonged and overwhelming sense of bewilderment, discouragement, isolation and even guilt, will He remain our only hope, our Heavenly Father and loving Shepherd? Will we hold fast to Him with enduring faith and trust or let Him go? Trust is often forged in darkness and silence, when our experience and expectation of what this new life means appears to be in contradiction. My friends – this reveals yet another aspect of God's wilderness.

All of the so-called experts tell us how human beings innately require a community; yet what happens when the Lord is our only community, when all we have is Him, when even the ones we love abandon and forsake us? When all of their words make us feel only guilt and even more bewilderment, when they cannot seem to comprehend the legitimacy of what is happening to us. So much easier to pray down God and all His angels to extricate us from our isolation and hardship. And it is inconceivable to so many believers, not knowing the Lord or His wilderness, that this very thing could be sanctioned and even enabled by God Himself, out of His love and mercy for His beloved children.

"I will build my church", proclaimed the Lord Jesus Christ. Yet this is apparently not good enough for the many man-sized church-

builders among us, who seek to separate us from God with all their various methods and mediators. By directing all of their soulish resources at maintaining and perpetuating their precious institutions, they fail to recognize that the God they serve doesn't care one bit for their institutions. He cares for His children and will spare no effort – even resorting to the wilderness if necessary – in building them up to perfection in His Beloved Son!

Hear this please, all those who have ears to hear. I believe the Lord may be trying to get the attention of His people.

The Wilderness Part of God's Larger Plan

We like to be busy, don't we? We almost have an inborn, driving need to advance, to move forward, to produce great things for the Lord. Results and numbers and growth are the painted idols of our day, and they have penetrated the church of Jesus Christ.

My friends, if the Lord Himself was so concerned about tangible results and numerical growth, then why did He choose to sideline the greatest evangelist who ever lived? Why indeed did the Apostle Paul spend so much of his ministry shipwrecked on remote islands, and in prison when the entire world awaited? Have you ever wondered about this? I have. Perhaps the Lord was ministering unto Paul during this wilderness time. Perhaps He didn't want Paul to get too heady about all of the wonderful things (the results) God was doing through Him. Perhaps our Lord was communicating intimately with Paul some of the awesome concepts and revelations found today in His epistles to the churches. Perhaps there were people and connections that could only be cultivated there in the wilderness, off the beaten path, there in the shadows. Perhaps the sufficiency of the Lord's grace can only truly be realized and appreciated in conditions of extreme and enduring isolation and dependence. And on another level, perhaps the Master, in His ultimate wisdom, didn't want these new disciples to become too dependent on His servant Paul. The milk might flow readily in familiar and comfortable surroundings, yet the meat can only be given in the wilderness.

My brethren – there really is so much the Lord does not allow us to see, in terms of His larger plan, isn't there? To our carnal nature, to the human soul, and to all that we are as men, this wilderness makes absolutely no sense at all. We want to get into the game desperately, and yet the Lord wants us on the sidelines, or maybe even outside the arena and cut off entirely from all the action. He wants us to Himself. He wants to know if He is enough all by Himself, independent of His gifts and blessings, and all of the noise and trappings of religion and community. He wants to get at the place within us where spirit touches bone; deep beyond the body and the soul, and the expression of such in this world.

But for how long, you say? Certainly not for years and years. My dear brethren – it is up to Him entirely as our wise and loving Father. Consider that David, running for his life from King Saul in the wilderness, could have ended his isolation on more than one occasion. Yet he trusted in the Lord, that at His appointed time, he would be restored to the fellowship of Israel and his family. Keep this in mind when you are tempted to forsake the wilderness on your own terms. There are spiritual things that we can only learn inside the darkness of a cave, on the run with no soft place to lay your head, where your only protection, provision and security lies with your God.

Consider Job's friends who sought to convince him of his sin and to curse God and die. Heaven is silent while the church is having a party down the block. What will you do? You look for sense when nothing, not God, nor the situation itself, makes any sense at all. Your soul screams for answers, yet they are few, if any. You can either come to hate the wilderness and seek a way out, or you can trust He who loves you enough to allow such things. His plan is so much larger and wider and deeper than our loneliness and disillusionment. As God, He is under no obligation to reveal all or even any aspect of it to us. He wants us to know Him and trust Him for absolutely everything.

> *"Therefore, listen to me, you men of understanding. Far be it from God to do wickedness, And from the Almighty to do wrong." (Job 34:10)*

Is the devil in the wilderness? Likely he is. Yet the Lord and His angels are there too, ministering to us, teaching us, tearing us down and binding us up, comforting and communing with us, revealing His glory to us in quiet revelation and intimate miracles. It is the place where a still small voice can always be heard, where the grandest and god-sized things are reduced down that we might grasp them and go with them. It is the barren and rugged terrain of the prophet not the priest; where created things are laid naked before the great "*I Am*" – that awesome, uncreated One who broods over all the earth, seeking merely one who will prove faithful.

The Wilderness and His Remnant

My friends, I don't pretend to see it all clearly yet, but I believe that in the last days of this present age the remnant of the Lord (the few out of the many) will commune with Him in the wilderness in preparation for His coming. Always between the gardens is a wilderness, it seems, where saints have long hungered and thirsted after God. Perhaps it is in the wilderness where the Church and Israel are ultimately reconciled in the heart of God. The Book of Revelation hints at this. Perhaps in these last tumultuous days, there is spiritual and even physical protection to be found here for the Lord's own. Perhaps the true church of Jesus Christ has always been a wilderness people, largely unreported, off the radar, disenfranchised, delegitimized by establishment and institutional Christianity. Quietly and faithfully and simply, they go on serving the Lord in the back alleys of life, away from the rush and clamor of church bells and choirs.

Is your faith rugged enough, my brother? Has it been tested by wind and storm? Can you still follow Him without a scripted program, a schedule, a holy day, a church bulletin? Can you worship Him without a music director, without a big band and choir, without the oft-rehearsed lyric of the song sheet?

He is coming! And He will first come to His own. If this be true, and it is – then where will they be found in these final hours of Adam's reign? What will be sustaining them as they wait patiently for Him? Will it be the bread from heaven and the water from the rock? Or will it be the delicacies of Egypt – meat and wine that turns foul in their bellies? When all mediators between them and God are removed, and He stands before them, will they be able to recognize Him, and love Him, and hear Him? Will His sheep follow Him at this time when their very lives will depend on it?

Precious Father, blessed are Your purposes for us in this wilderness oh Lord, and blessed is Your wonderful Son! We need You Lord! We just plain need You. It is that simple and that profound Lord. Oh how mysterious are Your ways within a man, as You remove him to the pathless wilderness to turn him from a Jacob to an Israel, from a Saul to a Paul, from a child to a first-born son in Your household. Father, I pray that Your grace would minister to Your children here and there as needed; and that Christ Jesus would be formed and increased in us. Increase our faith in Jesus' name, dear Father; please increase our faith.

Oh Lord Jesus, we turn to Thee as our first love – please cleanse Your bride by the washing of water with the word, that You might present Your church to the Father in all her glory, having no spot or wrinkle or any such thing; but that she would be holy and blameless. We thank You Lord for Your imputed righteousness that we have received as a gift by faith; and yet we also pray for the fine linen of the saints; which is the earned righteousness we need to enter in Your Kingdom as Your Bride; the righteousness of good works; of keeping Your Law of Love for another.

We ask all of this for Your Glory. Come quickly Lord; please come quickly for us. Amen.

And the People Love it So!

As always, my brethren, I am not really sure where this message will go, so please forgive me if it jumps around somewhat. Also know that my heart and spirit is with all of you *out there* in this pathless wilderness, where only the sound of His voice and His Word leads us from moment to moment, and place to place. Our time will come, dear saints. The sands of the hourglass marking the end of this present age are falling little by little now, and His coming is imminent; I can almost feel it in my bones, if you know what I mean.

I pray that this message finds you strong and patient, dear brethren, and that you are redeeming the time with much prayer and petition and seeking Him with all thirstiness in this barren wilderness. Oh that He might refine and prepare His own, as did David his mighty men in the dark caves of mystery leading up to his manifestation to all Israel as their rightful king. Let us not be tempted to expedite the arrival of the glorious reign before the time of readiness, as did those who would have readily dispatched Saul into Sheol; for the times and seasons, my friends, lie with the Lord –

> *"It is He who changes the times and the epochs; He removes kings and establishes kings; He gives wisdom to wise men, And knowledge to men of understanding." (Dan. 2:21)*

Our place is not with this world and its kings; with its wisdom and ways; with its lofty words and hollow rhetoric. For the illegitimate reign of Saul (Satan) will soon be at an end, by the Lord's hand and not ours. Our hope must not be bound up in the empty promises of those who know not that this present world has already been judged, and that the sword has already been drawn from its sheath, ready to strike at His word. There is no future for the nations as we know them, nor for anything wrought in this day of Adam, this day of man –

> *"Now judgment is upon this world; now the ruler of this world will be cast out. "And I, if I am lifted up from the earth, will draw all men to Myself." (John 12:31-32)*

Yet now is the time for those loyal to the future King to do great exploits in the spirit; to prepare for battle against the world, the flesh and the devil with all provision and preparation, for the days are evil, and all that is presently veiled in mystery and hidden from men (including most believers, sadly), will soon be made manifest –

> *For the mystery of lawlessness is already at work; only He who now restrains will do so until He is taken out of the way. And then the lawless one will be revealed, whom the Lord will consume with the breath of His mouth and destroy with the brightness of His coming. The coming of the lawless one is according to the working of Satan, with all power, signs, and lying wonders, and with all unrighteous deception among those who perish, because they did not receive the love of the truth, that they might be saved. And for this reason God will send them strong delusion, that they should believe the lie, that they all may be condemned who did not believe the truth but had pleasure in unrighteousness. (2 Thess. 2:7-12)*

My prayer for you in this dark and final hour is that of the Apostle Paul, who knew intimately that we are the "mighty men" of this age, and that the enemy before us is great; not only the Canaanite in the land, but all those among the redeemed who follow Saul, and seek the scraps from his table –

> *Finally, be strong in the Lord and in the strength of His might. Put on the full armor of God, so that you will be able to stand firm against the schemes of the devil. For*

> *our struggle is not against flesh and blood, but against the rulers, against the powers, against the world forces of this darkness, against the spiritual forces of wickedness in the heavenly places.*
>
> *Therefore, take up the full armor of God, so that you will be able to resist in the evil day, and having done everything, to stand firm. Stand firm therefore, HAVING GIRDED YOUR LOINS WITH TRUTH, and HAVING PUT ON THE BREASTPLATE OF RIGHTEOUSNESS, and having shod YOUR FEET WITH THE PREPARATION OF THE GOSPEL OF PEACE; in addition to all, taking up the shield of faith with which you will be able to extinguish all the flaming arrows of the evil one. And take THE HELMET OF SALVATION, and the sword of the Spirit, which is the word of God.*
>
> *With all prayer and petition pray at all times in the Spirit, and with this in view, be on the alert with all perseverance and petition for all the saints, and pray on my behalf, that utterance may be given to me in the opening of my mouth, to make known with boldness the mystery of the gospel, for which I am an ambassador in chains; that in proclaiming it I may speak boldly, as I ought to speak. (Eph. 6:10-20)*

The hour is close is my friends, and our hearts must be set on His soon coming, and being prepared in all readiness in the Spirit. The fig tree (Israel) is in bud (Luke 21:29-33), as are the other nations (those nations around her and especially mentioned in the prophecies related to the closing of this age), and this generation will by no means pass away until all things are fulfilled according to His Word. Dear friends and saints – His Word cannot and will not fail us! Yet we can most certainly fail Him! Let that not be so among those who love Him and love His appearing; those who seek a place at His table in His Kingdom; those who are running the race so as to win that crown of righteousness for all those found worthy at His seat of judgment.

> *Then He spoke to them a parable: "Look at the fig tree, and all the trees. When they are already budding, you see and know for yourselves that summer is now near. So you also, when you see these things happening, know that the kingdom of God is near. Assuredly, I say to you, this generation will by no means pass away till all things take place. Heaven and earth will pass away, but My words will by no means pass away." (Luke 21:29-33)*

If this be so brethren, that His words will by no means pass away, why is it that so many of us so readily, so casually it seems, set His words aside and trust rather in the empty claims of men – men of science, politics, religion, philosophy, etc. – who have no power whatsoever to bring it to pass? It is as though Christians today (the majority anyway) want so much to believe that there is a future for their particular nation, or the world at large, when such an investment of hope is foolish and contrary to everything recorded in the prophetic word of Scripture.

A WORD OF EXHORTATION, FOR THOSE WHO WILL RECEIVE IT –

I want to exhort all of you who name the name of Christ Jesus, in the Spirit and the love of Christ, to hearken to the Word of the Lord. For if we refuse to acknowledge and take to heart what became of His people Israel, and fail to understand the message to our generation – then we may very well suffer the same loss and rejection at His Coming (please read that again and ask the Lord, by His Spirit to impress this truth upon your heart).

Consider the word given to Jeremiah, for example,

> *An appalling and horrible thing Has happened in the land: The prophets prophesy falsely, And the priests rule on their own authority; And My people love it so! But what will you do at the end of it? (Jer. 5:30-31)*

Here we have a most deplorable condition among those blessed as the very apple of Jehovah's eye (Zech. 2:8), and yet the very worst part of this is not so much that the priests and prophets (spiritual leaders in the land) had abandoned the Lord and His truth (this is sad enough to be sure), but that –

THE PEOPLE LOVE IT SO!

Folks, as I drive around my community here in the mid-west U.S.A., and behold these colossal (christian) "mega" churches springing up in so many former corn fields, with false teachers "*teaching falsely*" and "*ruling on their own authority*", it mystifies me that so many of our Heavenly Father's blood-washed children actually join themselves in spirit to these worldly bodies.

Now we know, of course (or should know), at the end of this age that the tares must proliferate among the wheat, and the leaven must permeate the lump, just as our Lord assured us. Yet the degree to which His own, those precious sheep for whom He gave His very life, would so readily, so casually, and so willfully forsake His Word for the scraps at Saul's table is positively alarming to this observer.

> *To whom shall I speak and give warning That they may hear? Behold, their ears are closed And they cannot listen. Behold, the word of the LORD has become a reproach to them; They have no delight in it. (Jer. 6:10)*

Astounding! Incredible! Rather than tremble at the Word of God, and come to see it as the path to all blessing and life, the people of Judah utterly rejected it. It became, as the Scripture says, a "reproach to them". They took no delight in it, and for that reason they failed to understand the work of the Lord in their lives, and the path to glory. Now there were many false prophets in Jeremiah's day as there are in our own, and just as Judah was quick to receive these smooth and easy words, so the many in the church today seek those who will flatter and tickle their ears.

BEWARE, MY BRETHREN!

Do not be deceived when you feel that light and wispy sensation tickling your ears and puffing up your heart and mind. For such words are not from the Lord at all but from somewhere else. This is not the time for the easy way, but to be tested in the harsh wilderness and caves, such that we might be found worthy at the inauguration of the TRUE and RIGHTEOUS KING! If we, like David's mighty men, are to reign with the King, we must also suffer His rejection and testing. The Kingdom of God and of His Christ has been won most certainly; yet it lies in mystery for an appointed time (and this time is close, my brethren, very close). And during this time the King is training, testing and hardening all those who will rule with Him in His Kingdom as His officers. He must not only prove their love in this hour, but also their loyalty and steadfastness. He must know as a certainty that they will never leave Him nor forsake Him, nor discount His Word, regardless of what happens around them. They must be found faithful, not living by bread alone, but by every word breathed into the world by their Heavenly Father and His Son –

> *But He answered and said, "It is written, 'Man shall not live by bread alone, but by every word that proceeds from the mouth of God.'" (Matt. 4:4)*

> *It is the Spirit who gives life; the flesh profits nothing. The words that I speak to you are spirit, and they are life. (John 6:63)*

Oh how I pray you will receive this, dear ones, for it is not this writer's opinion but the truth of the Living God to be sure. His Word is food and it is life.

And to reject His Word is to rebel against Him, and rebellion is not something the Judge of all the earth sniffs at or takes lightly. It makes Him angry! Yes, angry at His own people! It is as reprehensible to Him as witchcraft, and a rebel will never hold a place at the Master's table.

Indeed, had Judah, remaining in the land of promise, hearkened to the Word of the Lord and considered His judgments, they would have been severely admonished by what happened to their brothers in the north a short while earlier. For the house of Israel became wholly given over to idolatry and willful disobedience. They had effectively closed their ears and hearts to all that the Lord wanted to give them, and they would not receive correction, but chose rather to stiffen their necks and reject the Lord who bought them at such a price. This is important, brethren, so I am inserting here the whole sad conclusion of the matter as provided in 2 Kings 17 –

> *Yet the LORD warned Israel and Judah through all His prophets and every seer, saying, "Turn from your evil ways and keep My commandments, My statutes according to all the law which I commanded your fathers, and which I sent to you through My servants the prophets." However, they did not listen, but stiffened their neck like their fathers, who did not believe in the LORD their God. They rejected His statutes and His covenant which He made with their fathers and His warnings with which He warned them. And they followed vanity and became vain, and went after the nations which surrounded them, concerning which the LORD had commanded them not to do like them. They forsook all the commandments of the LORD their God and made for themselves molten images, even two calves, and made an Asherah and worshiped all the host of heaven and served Baal. Then they made their sons and their daughters pass through the fire, and practiced divination and enchantments, and sold themselves to do evil in the sight of the LORD, provoking Him. So the LORD was very angry with Israel and removed them from His sight; none was left except the tribe of Judah.*
>
> *Also Judah did not keep the commandments of the LORD their God, but walked in the customs which Israel had introduced. The LORD rejected all the descendants of Israel and afflicted them and gave them into the hand of plunderers, until He had cast them out of His sight.*
>
> *When He had torn Israel from the house of David, they made Jeroboam the son of Nebat king. Then Jeroboam drove Israel away from following the LORD and made them commit a great sin. The sons of Israel walked in all the sins of Jeroboam which he did; they did not depart from them until the LORD removed*

Israel from His sight, as He spoke through all His servants the prophets. So Israel was carried away into exile from their own land to Assyria until this day. (2 Kings 17:13-23)

Now brethren, I would strongly encourage you to read all of the chapters leading up to this one in 2 Kings, and again ask the Lord to make it real and alive to you, in terms of its message and application. I was practically trembling as I made my way through this sordid history of rejection, abandonment and scornful rebellion shown by those who had been so blessed at the Lord's hand.

So, despite the mournful pleading of the prophet Jeremiah, who came to them crying, "Hear the Word of the Lord", Judah scoffed at the Word and hardened their necks to anything the Lord had to say. In fact, by this time their spiritual condition had become terminal, as evidenced by Jeremiah's prophecy –

"I brought you into the fruitful land, To eat its fruit and its good things. But you came and defiled My land,

And My inheritance you made an abomination. "The priests did not say, 'Where is the LORD?'

And those who handle the law did not know Me; The rulers also transgressed against Me, And the prophets prophesied by Baal And walked after things that did not profit." (Jer. 2:7-8)

And lest you think that this was describing but a few in the land; a minority perhaps, think again –

"For from the least of them even to the greatest of them, Everyone is greedy for gain, And from the prophet even to the priest, Everyone deals falsely.

"They have healed the brokenness of My people superficially, Saying, 'Peace, peace,' But there is no peace.

"Were they ashamed because of the abomination they have done? They were not even ashamed at all;

> *They did not even know how to blush. Therefore they shall fall among those who fall; At the time that I punish them, They shall be cast down," says the LORD. (Jer. 6:13-15)*

Everyone, from the least to the greatest, my friends, and to make matters worse, they were most especially confident and content in their condition. After all were they not God's chosen people; His elect? Had He not brought them out with a high hand from bondage in Egypt, and did He not dwell among them in the house they had built for Him?

> *Thus says the LORD of hosts, the God of Israel, "Amend your ways and your deeds, and I will let you dwell in this place. "Do not trust in deceptive words, saying, 'This is the temple of the LORD, the temple of the LORD, the temple of the LORD.' "For if you truly amend your ways and your deeds, if you truly practice justice between a man and his neighbor, if you do not oppress the alien, the orphan, or the widow, and do not shed innocent blood in this place, nor walk after other gods to your own ruin, then I will let you dwell in this place, in the land that I gave to your fathers forever and ever. (Jer. 7:3-7)*

Such things mean nothing to He who searches the heart and knows our true condition. And just to draw this cord a little tighter if I may, perhaps it would be helpful to translate this verse for our own days; something like this perhaps –

> *Thus says the LORD Jesus Christ, King of King and Lord of Lords: "Amend your ways and your doings, and I will cause you to sit on my throne with Me in My kingdom. Do not trust in these lying words, saying, 'The church of Jesus Christ, the church of Jesus Christ, the church of Jesus Christ are these.'*

Now the house of Israel (the ten northern tribes), removed from the land over 2,700 years ago, have never returned, and will not until the Shepherd of Israel draws them home. They were accounted unworthy to retain the promises in that day. And although there is a Jewish population in the land of Israel today, they reside there in unbelief, before the time, and their current spiritual condition and response to the Word of the Lord has not changed from what it was in the time of Jeremiah.

Consider therefore, my brethren the "*kindness and severity*" of the Lord, and that these things are so; and that for whom much is given much more will be expected –

> *Behold then the kindness and severity of God; to those who fell, severity, but to you, God's kindness, if you continue in His kindness; otherwise you also will be cut off. (Rom. 11:22)*
>
> *– but the one who did not know it, and committed deeds worthy of a flogging, will receive but few. From everyone who has been given much, much will be required; and to whom they entrusted much, of him they will ask all the more. (Luke 12:48)*

Followers in Christ Jesus in this age of grace (while the kingdom is held in abeyance, and the King, although anointed, suffers rejection by the many) have the tragic example of the children of Israel fleshed out before them, and, although many feel that the Lord expects less of us than He did the people of the land, the very opposite is true. And further, although there are many who believe that there is nothing we can do to forfeit our inheritance in His Kingdom, saying effectively "peace, peace", the very character of God stands against this heresy, as does the entire counsel of His Word. Be not deceived dear ones, for the gift of salvation by faith in the shed blood of the Righteous Lamb is merely preliminary to the prize or reward of entering His Kingdom once He assumes the throne of heaven and earth.

[Note: if the concept of being accounted worthy to enter into the Kingdom is a new concept to you, I would suggest becoming acquainted with the writings of *Robert Govett, G.H. Pember, Watchman Nee, G.H. Lang, and T. Austin-Sparks*, for a good beginning.]

And so I put this to you dear reader – How do you presently receive the Word of the Lord when it is brought to you? Do you receive it gladly, with delight, or do you scoff at it, privately despising it in your heart for the many ways you feel it constrains and binds you?

If the Word of the Lord demanded hard things, or in some way challenges you, or exacts a cost from you, how do you handle this? If the Word of the Lord was to open your eyes to error or idolatry within your heart or even your local church (or denomination), would you immediately dismiss it? Or would you follow it wherever it leads; whatever the price? If the Lord was to ask you to give up all that you possess in this life; all that defines and clothes you - home, family, security, king, country, etc. – how might you respond to this? If like Jeremiah, all that the Lord permitted you to possess in this life was Himself and His Word, would that be enough? Or is your life yours alone to define and determine?

What, in the end, is your attitude towards obedience to every Word the Lord has breathed into the world? Do you see His Word, in fact, as the animating principle of all life; even your own? Do you understand what the Scripture means when it says - "*In the beginning was the Word, and the Word was with God, and the Word was God*"?

Can you say with the psalmist –

> *I have inherited Your testimonies forever, For they are the joy of my heart. I have inclined my heart to perform Your statutes Forever, even to the end. (Psa. 119:111-112)*

and –

> *Consider how I love Your precepts; Revive me, O LORD, according to Your lovingkindness. The sum of Your word is truth, And every one of Your righteous ordinances is everlasting. (Psa. 119:159-160)*

Is the Word of the Lord something you hold in your hand or in your heart?

When His Word offers the way of direction, do you obey it readily, and when it offers the promise of things unseen, do you believe heartily?

Have your eyes been opened in the spirit, beloved of the Lord, to behold the many wonders and precious treasures contained in His Word; or is it mere orthodoxy, scholarship, moral injunction, dusty history?

And if proving faithful and obedient to His Word will invariably lead to persecution, affliction and rejection by the many, how will this affect your response to it? Will you therefore lay it down, or maybe in some sophisticated way convince yourself that it wasn't really for you anyway?

Interesting questions to ponder, most certainly, and I leave them with you, as the Lord has laid them before me. We must all decide, dear saints, what we do, and how far we will go on behalf of He who awaits His Kingdom and Glory. And as I have perhaps said far too much here, I will end with something else for you to consider, and it is this –

Why in 2 Samuel 23, is not Joab, David's trusted general and confidant for many years, not listed among his mighty men?

Hmm.

What is the lesson for you and me, that in 1 Kings 2:34 it is told that Joab died "*in the wilderness*"?

I will leave this message there for now and pray that the Lord will bring it home to your hearts in His grace and mercy. In Jesus' mighty name. Amen.

If You Love Me

Most of us modern Christians will confidently profess our exclusive and uncompromising love for our Lord and Savior. Most will have no difficulty mouthing the lyrics of the many Christian songs and hymns that echo such sentiment in strident and sentimental terms. Many still, perhaps, have practically memorized 1 Corinthians 13 on the varied characteristics of love.

Yet, the potential stumbling block appears at the point where the Lord, in John 14 affirms –

> *"If you love Me, you will keep My commandments." (John 14:15)*

Here is the place where song and sentiment ends, and where real hard and fast definition begins. For these are the dagger-sharp words that pierce through any supposed love of good intentions and worldly affection, and effectively separate any who would merely assume that they are represented in the Bride of Christ, and those who actually are.

Here brethren, without compromise or condition is the love of the Bride for her Bridegroom. Here is that first love for Himself that He requires and deserves –

> *"But I have this against you, that you have left your first love." (Rev. 2:4)*

Indeed, no less than five times (John 14:15, 14:21, 14:23, 15:10 and 15:14) does the Lord Jesus Christ affirm the fundamental reality that only a life of obedience can ever be the signature expression of love and friendship for Him. Quite apart from what we think or believe or pretend, dear saints; quite apart from our carnal and emotional opinions of what love is, and how casually we throw this word around in the modern church, only those who do what He commands actually love Him.

> *"If you love Me, you will keep My commandments." (John 14:15)*

> *"He who has My commandments and keeps them is the one who loves Me..." (John 14:21)*

> *"If anyone loves Me, he will keep My word; and My Father will love him, and We will come to him and make Our abode with him. He who does not love Me does not keep My words; and the word which you hear is not Mine, but the Father's who sent Me." (John 14:23-24)*

> *"If you keep My commandments, you will abide in My love; just as I have kept My Father's commandments and abide in His love." (John 15:10)*

> *"You are My friends if you do what I command you." (John 15:23)*

What the Lord requires of us and thereby deems as our love for Him, is complete faithfulness to all that He has commanded us as His friends. And this is no different from what was required of Him and deemed as love for His Father –

> *"...but so that the world may know that I love the Father, I do exactly as the Father commanded Me." (John 14:31)*

Now to hold faithfully to all that the Lord commanded us includes it all, does it not? All of His moral injunctions in Matthew 5 and 6; all the prohibitions against lust and pride and covetousness and feigned religiosity; the forgiving of all who wrong us, the seeking first His kingdom and His righteousness, the banishment of all anxiety over temporal cares.

Yet here in John's gospel, Jesus draws out one aspect of this love that we would like to focus on here, the Spirit permitting –

> *"This is My commandment, that you love one another, just as I have loved you. "Greater love has no one than this, that one lay down his life for his friends. "You are My friends if you do what I command you. "No longer do I call you slaves, for the slave does not know what his master is doing; but I have called you friends, for all things that I have heard from My Father I have made known to you. "You did not choose Me but I chose you, and appointed you that you would go and bear fruit, and that your fruit would remain, so that whatever you ask of the Father in My name He may give to you. "This I command you, that you love one another. (John 15:12-17)*

Here we see that the Bride abides in her Beloved's love by expressing His very self-sacrificing love for others in His body, just as He did. She fulfills what He has commanded, and this alone expresses genuine love for Him. She receives this love by abiding faith and continued prayer, asking the Father for it in the name of His Beloved Son, Jesus Christ.

Dear saints, the days are so dark in this hour, are they not? So many hard and long trials and challenges buffeting the people of God. So many suffering great needs of the body and the spirit it seems, at least as far as this observer is aware. Oh how we need each other brethren; oh how we need to be actively obeying the command of our Lord to love another as He has loved us; to allow ourselves to be poured out for one another; to give as He has given to us all.

Many saints in these days are suffering the loss or reduction of income. Others are suffering from sickness and chronic health concerns. Still others are losing property, familial ties and liberty for their testimony of the Lord Jesus. Oh praise the Lord that we would be so blessed as to partake of His rejection and suffering in this world!

Yet it is so hard at times, isn't it? We would be lying to ourselves if we thought otherwise. The temptation is very real because the burden is very real, and often so prolonged and persistent. This is why, after all, it is called suffering and loss and reduction and discipline.

Yet our Gracious Lord knows what we can handle, and He also provides His grace, doesn't He, and it is ever so sweet and precious when it comes to us in so many strange forms and expressions.

I would like to offer my perspective on this grace, if I may, and it is this – we Christians often think His grace is like some form of magic pixie dust that He sprinkles down on us from heaven to keep us from falling or surrendering to our circumstances. I think more often than not, it is not as fantastic as this, brethren, but it comes in the form of others in the body, whom the Lord has inspired and empowered to encourage us, to meet some momentary need, to exhort and edify us as the Lord knows we need. It comes in a word, or a single touch, or some relief in the way of goods or resources when we have arrived at the end of our ability to cope or continue.

We remember Paul, and how he suffered, how he was buffeted always by forces outside of Him. And we think of the thorn in His flesh, and that the Lord assured Him that His grace would be enough. Well, how did this grace fall into Paul's life? Was he empowered from within by the Spirit of power? Certainly! Was he spurred on by the Word of God and its promises of the reward out ahead for those who endure? Absolutely! Yet equally so, he was ministered to by those whom the Lord raised up to bear his burdens.

> *And He has said to me, "My grace is sufficient for you, for power is perfected in weakness." Most gladly, therefore, I will rather boast about my weaknesses, so that the power of Christ may dwell in me. (2 Cor. 12:9)*

The Father's grace is so often ministered to us by other servants who are simply and merely obeying their Lord's command to love each other. Consider all of the names, preserved for eternity in the Scriptures, of those who ministered to Paul in his moments of severe testing and deprivation, imprisonment, physical hurt and pain.

> *Bear one another's burdens, and thereby fulfill the law of Christ. (Gal. 6:2)*

Oh that we would see this, and serve one another in the Love of our Lord, and keep His Law of Love, and thereby abide in His love!

It is interesting to me that one of the initial outward manifestations of the pouring out of the Holy Spirit (in the Book of Acts) resulted in the saints all dispensing of what they had to contribute to the needs of the body at large.

> *Everyone kept feeling a sense of awe; and many wonders and signs were taking place through the apostles. And all those who had believed were together and had all things in common; and they began selling their property and possessions and were sharing them with all, as anyone might have need. Day by day continuing with one mind in the temple, and breaking bread from house to house, they were taking their meals together with gladness and sincerity of heart, praising God and having favor with all the people. And the Lord was adding to their number day by day those who were being saved. (Acts 2:44-47)*

This fellow saints, is nothing short of the free-flowing, magnanimous love of the Lord being manifest in those in the spirit who knew what their Lord commanded. This was the obedience of the Bride; those who will hear the "*well done good and faithful servant*"; those who will enter into His Kingdom and Glory, as His Help Meet and Queen.

Brethren, my sense is that conditions in this country and around the world are poised to get much, much worse, despite what you might be reading in the press by worldly pundits who know not the Lord and His plans. This talk of recovery is strange to me – recover to what I ask – to the excessive consumerism and greed and corruption that brought us here in the first place? No, my sense in the Spirit is quite the opposite; that we are going to need each other increasingly as the dark days advance; as widespread loss grows and conditions become more severe.

A final word of encouragement for all those granted the spiritual gift of teaching, prophecy or exhortation (see 1 Corinthians. 12; 14:1). We will need you to be faithful to our Lord more than ever dear saints. If you truly love the Lord, then you will indeed allow the expression of this gift in you for the building up and feeding of the body in this hour. Consider the following –

So when they had finished breakfast, Jesus said to Simon Peter, "Simon, son of John, do you love Me more than these?" He said to Him, "Yes, Lord; You know that I love You." He said to him, "Tend My lambs." He said to him again a second time, "Simon, son of John, do you love Me?" He said to Him, "Yes, Lord; You know that I love You." He said to him, "Shepherd My sheep." He said to him the third time, "Simon, son of John, do you love Me?" Peter was grieved because He said to him the third time, "Do you love Me?" And he said to Him, "Lord, You know all things; You know that I love You." Jesus said to him, "Tend My sheep." (John 21:15-17)

"Therefore be on the alert, for you do not know which day your Lord is coming. "But be sure of this, that if the head of the house had known at what time of the night the thief was coming, he would have been on the alert and would not have allowed his house to be broken into. "For this reason you also must be ready; for the Son of Man is coming at an hour when you do not think He will.

"Who then is the faithful and sensible slave whom his master put in charge of his household to give them their food at the proper time? "Blessed is that slave whom his master finds so doing when he comes. "Truly I say to you that he will put him in charge of all his possessions. "But if that evil slave says in his heart, 'My master is not coming for a long time,' and begins to beat his fellow slaves and eat and drink with drunkards; the master of that slave will come on a day when he does not expect him and at an hour which he does not know, and will cut him in pieces and assign him a place with the hypocrites; in that place there will be weeping and gnashing of teeth. (Matt. 24:42-51)

"A disciple is not above his teacher, nor a slave above his master. "It is enough for the disciple that he become like his teacher, and the slave like his master. If they

> *have called the head of the house Beelzebul, how much more will they malign the members of his household!*
>
> *"Therefore do not fear them, for there is nothing concealed that will not be revealed, or hidden that will not be known. "What I tell you in the darkness, speak in the light; and what you hear whispered in your ear, proclaim upon the housetops. "Do not fear those who kill the body but are unable to kill the soul; but rather fear Him who is able to destroy both soul and body in hell. (Matt. 10:24-28)*

Oh dear saints, do we love Him then? I mean really and genuinely, as He Himself has defined this love? Is ours the love of a bride for her beloved groom, to enter into all of His suffering and purposes? Or is it a worldly, sentimental love; one that is quick to swoon and sing but slow to serve and sacrifice?

The days are short brethren, perhaps much shorter than we think; and you can be absolutely certain that the Master will indeed test our love for Him, such that He might know that we would be willing to release everything as necessary. For He must know that our love for Him preempts and precedes all other loves; that it is indeed a first love.

> *"He who loves father or mother more than Me is not worthy of Me; and he who loves son or daughter more than Me is not worthy of Me. "And he who does not take his cross and follow after Me is not worthy of Me. "He who has found his life will lose it, and he who has lost his life for My sake will find it. (Matt. 10:38-39)*

And brethren, lest we be misunderstood regarding how this obedience is made possible; this law of love, and all that He commands us is not something outside of us that He expects us to go off and keep apart from Himself. Yes, He has given us His requirements, but He has also given us His abiding presence within; His very life and love, that we might attain the mystery of godliness, and the hope of glory. Apart from Him we can do nothing! And He has promised that we might thereby abide in His love as He abides in His Father's love.

> *Beloved, let us love one another, for love is from God; and everyone who loves is born of God and knows God. The one who does not love does not know God, for God is love. By this the love of God was manifested in us, that God has sent His only begotten Son into the world so that we might live through Him. In this is love, not that we loved God, but that He loved us and sent His Son to be the propitiation for our sins. Beloved, if God so loved us, we also ought to love one another. (1 John 4:7-11)*

> *We have come to know and have believed the love which God has for us. God is love, and the one who abides in love abides in God, and God abides in him. By this, love is perfected with us, so that we may have confidence in the day of judgment; because as He is, so also are we in this world. There is no fear in love; but perfect love casts out fear, because fear involves punishment, and the one who fears is not perfected in love. We love, because He first loved us. If someone says, "I love God," and hates his brother, he is a liar; for the one who does not love his brother whom he has seen, cannot love God whom he has not seen. And this commandment we have from Him, that the one who loves God should love his brother also. (1 John 4:16-21)*

This love requires that we will fulfill all that He has given us to do, not as slaves but as friends; not begrudgingly, but willingly and joyfully, knowing that it is the Father's joy to sum all things up in His Son, and that only by abiding in Him and His love will we gain entrance into His soon-coming Kingdom.

Heavenly Father, we know that every good thing comes in and through Your Most-Perfect Son, Jesus Christ. Dear Lord, please let His love for His Body flow through Your people in this dark hour. We also know that only He can truly fulfill all that He has commanded of us, and that only in Him can we prove faithful in this and anything else. Oh Father, we pray all of this, in Jesus' Name. Amen.

Closing

In closing, brethren, it is our sincerest hope and prayer that this series of messages has proven to be a blessing to you in the way of spiritual edification and exhortation. Oh that our Gracious Lord would anoint these words, from one so weak, that even some small, heavenly blessing might be derived for His people.

The *Real Thing*, in the end, is, and can only ever be, the Lord, Jesus Christ. He is the *Real Thing*, because He is the *only thing*! And we pray for all of you that He alone would be the *sum of all things*, and the *center of everything* in your life.

To live as a Christian in this world, at the end of this age, is to live *in Christ*. To abide most fully in Him is the single, great imperative for this, and any generation of twice-born believers. The only fruit that will bring glory to our Heavenly Father is the fruit of the True Vine, and only the life of the Vine will bring forth life through the branches.

Additional Copies: Additional copies of this book can be ordered from the following –

Web: *www.livingwalk.com*

Email: *orders@livingwalk.com*

Please direct orders for 10 or more copies to our email address: *orders@livingwalk.com*. Please be sure to visit our website (*www.livingwalk.com)* to provide feedback, or for messages similiar to those contained in this book.

4764409R0

Made in the USA
Charleston, SC
12 March 2010